EARLY CAREER ENGLISH TEACHERS IN ACTION

"This is a gem of a book. It will stay on teachers' shelves long after they have emerged through their teacher preparation programs and first years of teaching as an invaluable resource for thinking about their lives as teachers, their teaching, and the students and issues that confront them."
Melanie Sperling, University of California, Riverside, USA

The first few years of teaching are critical to the professional development of effective English teachers. In these crucial years, new teachers establish their identities, learn the ins and outs of the curriculum, acclimate to unfamiliar communities, and cope with student behaviors that they never expected. All of this can be daunting for novice teachers. This book can help. The stories within are written by English teachers in the early stages of their careers. In their carefully crafted narratives, teachers offer practical strategies, professional insights, and a wealth of tips for surviving the first years in the classroom. The narratives are grouped into thematic chapters with brief introductions of key terms, helpful learning activities, and provocative discussion questions, all intended to foster critical conversation about beginning a career teaching English.

In a time when many teachers leave the profession too soon, *Early Career English Teachers in Action* gives voice to those who have decided to stay. More importantly, this book validates teacher narratives as a powerful way of understanding what happens inside of the classroom—a way that provides more authentic evidence of learning than standardized test scores will ever supply.

Robert Rozema is Associate Professor of English (Secondary Education), Grand Valley State University, USA. Before coming to Grand Valley, he taught high school English for eight years.

Lindsay Ellis is Associate Professor of English, Grand Valley State University, USA. She directs the Lake Michigan Writing Project.

EARLY CAREER ENGLISH TEACHERS IN ACTION

Learning From Experience, Developing Expertise

Edited by
Robert Rozema
and
Lindsay Ellis

Routledge
Taylor & Francis Group

NEW YORK AND LONDON

First published 2015
by Routledge
711 Third Avenue, New York, NY 10017

and by Routledge
2 Park Square, Milton Park, Abingdon, Oxon OX14 4RN

Routledge is an imprint of the Taylor & Francis Group, an informa business

Library of Congress Cataloging-in-Publication Data
Early career English teachers in action : learning from experience, developing
  expertise / edited by Robert Rozema, Lindsay Ellis.
    pages cm
  Includes bibliographical references and index.
  1. English language—Study and teaching.   2. English teachers—Training of.
3. English teachers—In-service training.   4. Language arts.   I. Rozema,
Robert.   II. Ellis, Lindsay.
  LB1576.E17 2014
  428.0071—dc23
  2014010961

ISBN: 978-0-415-74341-9 (hbk)
ISBN: 978-0-415-74342-6 (pbk)
ISBN: 978-1-315-81364-6 (ebk)

Typeset in Bembo
by Apex CoVantage, LLC

Printed and bound in the United States of America by Publishers Graphics,
LLC on sustainably sourced paper.

To Dad
—Robert Rozema

To my tenacious National Writing Project colleagues
—Lindsay Ellis

CONTENTS

FOREWORD

I know from eleven years of teaching pre-service teachers that stories matter; they contextualize and focus complex issues, large and small, that practicing teachers confront every day. I, like my colleagues in teacher education everywhere, build programs and design courses to include as many practical experiences in classrooms and with practicing teachers as possible. Still, it's difficult to orchestrate enough immersive experiences to ensure that pre-service students have sufficient "real world" knowledge to begin developing and refining a teaching identity. Robert Rozema and Lindsay Ellis, both experienced teacher educators par excellence, have created this book to offer an additional option for creating immersive experiences in pre-service teacher education classes. This collection of beginning teacher stories provides authentic narrative voices that share the positive, neutral, and negative realities of teaching. The vicarious experience serves as a means to help pre-service teachers envision their roles and the many choices, from overall career choices to the miniscule daily decisions they will make as teachers.

The narratives in this collection also address the problem of "apprenticeship of observation"; pre-service teachers often overly rely on their prior experiences in the classroom *as students* to provide narrative context for pedagogical discussion. They don't yet have the practical teaching experiences to contextualize theoretical concepts, making it difficult to bridge the practice/theory gap in the classroom. Each chapter of the book offers a well-balanced combination of research, theory, and analysis with engaging, enlightening narratives, providing practical context for including theory and research in ways that will make sense to pre-service teachers. In this way, theory contextualizes the narratives without overpowering them.

As told through the eyes of new teachers, these authentic stories address practical issues facing teachers: student and teacher assessment, IEP meetings, understanding student identity and dealing with oppositionality, basic essentials of classroom management, school safety; the narratives represent school communities ranging from an inner-city alternative high school to a rural hunting community. These experiences are even more powerful in that they are the memoirs of master teachers reflecting on their first years with the added wisdom of hindsight and experience. The combined depth and breadth of experience, details of the joys and challenges of teaching, and voices of teachers who tell it like it is provide a unique and powerful resource for discussion and further research. Rozema and Ellis have assembled a panel of master teachers to share their stories of being a new teacher—a unique and valuable opportunity for all pre-service teachers and the teacher educators.

For example, Adam Kennedy's powerfully honest discussion of his evolving methods of classroom management clearly narrates his growth as a teacher dealing with the challenges of troubled students (see Chapter 6). The author's narrative provides excellent material for discussion of theory and practice in assessment, classroom management, flexibility, and instructional planning relevant, particularly, to English language arts and literacy education. Another teacher, Tami Teshima, shares an important question she was asked during her first year teaching a difficult group of students, "What are you doing for yourself?" (see Chapter 3). Her answer is one that every new teacher should hear.

I also serve as a university supervisor for student teachers and appreciate Rozema and Ellis's vast experience with and knowledge of student teaching and supervision. I often find myself vacillating between enthusiastic supporter and critical evaluator of student teachers: how do I strike the delicate balance between encouraging the important and difficult learning that takes place during the student teaching experience and still rigorously evaluate specific pedagogical requirements necessary to prepare the student teacher to step into the professional role of teacher upon completion? Rozema and Ellis provide specific talking points and access to further resources to open up productive dialogue *before* the student teaching experience—in methods courses. They address the issues that are foremost on students' minds in the weeks and months before student teaching and, without trivializing, provide a consistent analysis and calm voice to put it all into perspective—and set up analysis of the beginning teachers narratives that follow each section.

The precise and accessible discussions of school climate and culture, for example, provide the context for having difficult discussions about student teaching in the relative safety of the methods course; I'm inspired to conduct a deep and reflective revisions to my methods course syllabus to include new material for discussion and analysis. I look forward to using this text in the semester before student teaching to better prepare my students, and myself, for the realities of student teaching that are so difficult to adequately address with either concrete but removed from reality lesson/unit plans or theoretical analysis of current educational policy and data. Such exercises are necessary, but the teacher stories in this collection provide "real world" situations to puzzle through and analyze.

At a time when too many new teachers arrive in their classrooms unprepared for the realities of teaching, in part because of the political emphasis on "fast track" teacher certification programs that inadequately prepare teachers to become long-term professional educators, I appreciate and applaud Rozema and Ellis for bringing these teacher voices together, scaffolding productive, generative discussion in pre-service classes. Indeed, it is the responsibility of teacher educators to prepare teacher candidates to understand that they, too, can grow into a master teacher: developing a career experiencing the joys of learning compassionately with their students, not leaving the profession out of confusion and frustration. Rozema and Ellis offer theoretically sound, research-based, experiential and rigorous teacher education that is necessary for continuing to prepare teachers to meet contemporary and future challenges as public intellectuals, advocates for their students and communities, and pedagogical leaders who can usher in a new progressive era of education. I look forward to adding this text to my repertoire of course materials for pre-service methods courses.

Lisa Schade Eckert

PREFACE

"If there is a book you really want to read but it hasn't been written yet, then you must write it," Toni Morrison counsels. We wrote this book with Morrison's advice in mind. As we developed our concept, recruited our contributors, and worked through drafts together, we focused on creating a book that we would want to *read*. But we also took Morrison's suggestion in a new direction: we hoped to write a book that we would want to *teach*. Lindsay and I teach methods courses in a secondary English education program, and we have long wished for a book featuring writing by early career English teachers, teachers whose newness to the profession would resonate with our students and with pre-service teachers in similar programs across the country.

And so, we envision *Early Career English Teachers in Action* as a teaching resource. We hope its contributors, all early career English teachers writing from firsthand experiences, provide helpful, real-world instruction on a range of issues that new teachers encounter. But knowledge transfer is not the most important goal of this book. Times are changing too fast. Digital technologies, economic reconfigurations, and politically charged reforms of education are changing the landscape of teaching. So, our book goes beyond methods and strategies, as its contributors, like good teachers everywhere, reveal their humanity in the stories they share. The narratives in this collection are full of wisdom, good humor, and heartbreak, and they are meant to foster empathy in our students and others who read this book.

We trust that every reader identify with at least one teacher in these pages. Our contributors teach in urban middle schools, rural high schools, alternative high schools, and K–12 schools overseas. Their buildings are brand new. Their buildings are crumbling. They have supportive administrators and hostile administrators. They teach AP classes and remedial reading. They work in large English departments, and they are the only language arts teacher in town. The variety of their positions reflects the growing diversity of our population and the ever-expanding nature of teaching English.

Each of our writers has contributed a single or multiple narratives to the following chapters. Working with them over the past three years, Lindsay and I identified five recurrent themes in their narratives: school culture, school climate, curriculum, teacher identity, and that old worry of new teachers, student behavior. These five themes do not encompass all of the passions, frustrations, and successes of our first-year English teachers, but they do represent essential questions that all new English teachers ask before taking roll on opening day: *What is this school like? What am I supposed to teach? Who am I as a teacher? Who are my students?*

Each chapter in this book addresses one of the major themes we have identified, providing narrative answers to the fundamental questions posed above. To make this book as useful as possible to you, we provide short introductions to each chapter, defining terminology associated with the chapter theme, reviewing significant scholarship, and focusing the reading with guiding activities. Each chapter then offers several narratives written by early career English teachers, stories we hope will help you anticipate your future career.

To teach a book, of course, means to read it over and over again. It means to ponder and to discuss it, letting the text spark the construction of new understandings with each new reading. To foster discussion of the narratives, we include questions at the conclusion of each chapter.

Finally, we encourage readers of this book to write their own narratives about their teaching lives, perhaps using the stories here as models. We believe in their power, as we hope this book attests.

Robert Rozema
Lindsay Ellis

ACKNOWLEDGMENTS

The authors would like to thank all of the contributors to this volume, who had the tough job of being teachers *and* writers over the past two years. We are also grateful to Naomi Silverman at Routledge, for sharing our vision for this book.

We appreciate all of our friends and colleagues who made this book possible. Robert Rozema is grateful to Brian White, for reading drafts and providing encouragement; to Lisa Schade Eckert, for believing in teacher narratives; and to Robert Rozema, Sr., for his discerning editing and moral support. Lindsay Ellis would like to thank Deans Fred Antczak and Anne Hiskes for granting her sabbatical; her neighbors on Eligenstraat, Utrecht, NL, for offering such a warm welcome; and Brian Staggs for establishing our good work ethic in the Utrecht University library. We also can't thank our families enough for the joy that they bring us at the end of each day.

Lisa Schade Eckert

1

INTRODUCTION

Why Early Career English Teachers?
Robert Rozema

I left high school teaching over a decade ago, just a few months after terrorists struck the Twin Towers on September 11. That singular day was my most memorable as a teacher. Though I cannot recall the names or faces of the students in my class, I do recollect that the poetry of Wilfred Owen was on the agenda for the day, but discarded when the South, then the North Tower shuddered and collapsed. Another unforgettable moment of that day was an exchange that I shared with my principal in the dim hallway outside my room. Only minutes after the attacks began, he was walking from room to room, checking on his teachers and their students. When he came to my door, he said, "Robert, the world will never be the same." He was right, of course, and his judgment bears testimony to his years teaching history and to his wisdom in recognizing the importance of geopolitical events. Well over a decade later, long after the death of Osama Bin Laden, American soldiers grind on in Afghanistan, and I know that he was right.

My stay as a high school English teacher was just eight years—a brief candle amid the long, illuminating careers of many of my colleagues. But despite their brevity, my teaching days gave me many stories, and while none, thankfully, are as harrowing as September 11, they are nevertheless reminders of my teaching life. A ninth grader runs me down in the hallway, jumps on my back, and demands a piggyback ride. A clueless but enthusiastic sophomore volunteers "Pronoun" as the theme of "The Road Not Taken." A pregnant senior has her water break during class.

All teachers—and perhaps English teachers especially—traffic in these kinds of narratives. As entertainment, these stories can make the trip to the lounge worthwhile. As therapy, they can keep teachers from burning out or blowing up. But they do more: stories help us think through our practices and make changes for the better. As we listen to stories and narrate our own, we take a step toward *reflective practice*, the cycle of action, reflection, and adjustment that is at the heart of effective teaching. We know that reflective practice occurs during teaching (reflection-in-action), when we respond to unexpected situations, and before and after teaching (reflection-on-action), when we anticipate or look back at our teaching (Schön, 1983). Storytelling is a natural form of reflection-on-action and plays an important role in our professional practice. Schön notes:

> Storytelling represents and substitutes for firsthand experience. Once a story has been told, it can be held as datum, considered at leisure for its meanings and its relationships with other stories. . . . By attending to a few features which he considers central, the [professional] can isolate the main thread of a story from the surrounding factors which he chooses to consider as noise.
>
> (p. 160)

For new teachers in particular, the stories told by colleagues can offer a rich data source to help shape their own practices (Elbaz, 2005). And yet, we know that too few teachers are staying in our profession long enough to learn from these stories and their own. The attrition of new teachers is itself a story that we can and must learn from: recent research finds that about ten percent of beginning teachers leave after their first year (Kaiser, 2011). More troubling, the most academically gifted teachers are also the most likely to quit, as are teachers working in schools with high poverty populations (DeAngelis & Presley, 2011). New English teachers are not immune to this trend, though they are slightly less likely to leave after their first year than their colleagues in other content areas (Hahs-Vaughn & Scherff, 2008).

New English teachers face significant challenges that are unique to our field: heavy grading loads, challenging content, and high-stakes testing in reading and writing. All of these put extraordinary pressure on early career English teachers. The novice teacher today also begins her career in the era of corporate reform—a time when giant publishing-testing companies such as Pearson and McGraw-Hill have unprecedented influence on standards, curricula, and assessment. Supported by powerful lobbies, wealthy foundations, and politicians on both sides the aisle, educational corporations have crafted and profited from No Child Left Behind and Race to the Top. One signature element of Race to the Top is the requirement that teachers be evaluated based on the test scores of their students, another crushing pressure for new teachers. As Diane Ravitch (2013) notes:

> Certainly teachers should be evaluated, but evaluating them by the rise or fall of their students' test scores is fraught with perverse consequences. It encourages teaching to multiple-choice tests; narrowing the curriculum only to the tested subjects; gaming the system by states and districts to inflate their scores; and cheating by desperate educators who don't want to lose their jobs or who hope to earn a bonus.
>
> (p. 111)

A perverse consequence of test-based teacher evaluation, of course, is that our profession becomes far less inviting for newcomers. Indeed, teaching can seem a world away from *Dead Poet's Society*, with far too little poetry and far too many test booklets. This fundamental mismatch between what new English teachers expect and what they actually experience can contribute to their decision to quit (McCann, Johannessen, & Ricca, 2005).

Despite these challenges from within and without, the vast majority of new English teachers do stay in their classrooms beyond their first year. They stick it out for many reasons, but one of the most significant predictors of teacher retention is the presence of a mentor teacher. Mentors offer novice teachers a combination of personal support and professional guidance. Mentorship varies from school to school and is often bundled within larger induction programs that provide professional seminars for new teachers, time for planning with colleagues, regular communication with administrators, and guidance from an experienced teacher in the same field. Such induction programs have grown in popularity over the past two decades, with proven results: new teachers who participate in formal induction programs are about half as likely to leave teaching than those without such programs (Smith & Ingersoll, 2004).

New English teachers also stay when they like the way the school works and feels. In a healthy school, teachers are engaged, friendly with one another, and willing to collaborate; administrators are supportive and communicative; and there is a collective sense that the school is a positive learning environment. In these kinds of schools, the rituals and routines that accompany education—issuing report cards, disciplining students—are carried out with a clear purpose and with the consensus of the faculty. In contrast, an unhealthy school has little teacher collegiality, festering distrust between administrators and faculty, and an overwhelming sense that the school is failing. Lindsay and I believe that school health is comprised by both school culture and school climate, and we discuss both of these ideas in the upcoming pages. Unfortunately, many new teachers begin their careers in unhealthy schools, and these teachers are more likely to leave the profession (Hancock & Scherff, 2010).

Whether the school is unhealthy or healthy, starting any job can be an isolating experience, and this is particularly true of teaching. Novice English teachers may be afraid to ask for help from their colleagues, fearing to be judged incompetent. Or they may be buried under papers and prep work, with little time to talk to their colleagues down the hall. New teachers are often asked to teach outside of their expertise area, further distancing them from colleagues. Whatever the cause of isolation, it is clear that when new teachers feel disconnected from their colleagues, their chance of leaving increases (Rogers & Babinski, 2002).

In short, it is tough business being a new English teacher. This book cannot change that fact, at least not in a conventional way. You will not find ready-to-use lesson plans, fail-proof classroom management strategies, or the secret formula to first-year success. What the book does contain is stories, compelling accounts of first-year teaching, told by early career English teachers just like you. We believe these stories are vital to surviving what can be a brutal initiation into our profession. Reading them, we know we are not alone, even as we see situations well outside of our own experiences.

Lindsay Ellis is Associate Professor of English, Grand Valley State University, USA. She directs the Lake Michigan Writing Project.

Why Teacher Narratives?
Lindsay Ellis
Grand Valley State University, USA

The stories that follow may seem like ones that you would hear if you shared a cup of coffee with these teachers. We wanted it to be that way, yet this familiarity is partially deceptive. Stories can be enjoyable reading because they provide familiar structures: readers meet characters, experience their dilemmas, and long for resolution. Such structure, however, is something that our contributors constructed over multiple drafts.

Turning life into a written story is difficult. Every hour, every day, we receive complex information through our five senses. Days within school are particularly complex, where hundreds of lives are lived out in close proximity. Conversations overlap. Bodies collide. Learning takes place in multimodal and individually particular ways. Teachers hear students' voices and read their faces. They think about curricular content.

Out of the jumble of visual, auditory, physical, and emotional memories of days in school, our contributors have drafted narratives. These narratives are constructions of reality that emerged as our contributors sifted, selected, and ordered their memories from their first years in the classroom. This act of creation was itself a learning process. Not only have our contributors created stories from which others can learn, they have created understandings for themselves in the act of storytelling. These constructions exemplify what is called narrative learning (Goodson *et al.*, 2010).

In their study of narrative learning, Goodson and his colleagues observe that while all humans understand their lives through storytelling, some narrativize more than others. Of the ones who live an "examined life," some are able to mine their narratives for wisdom about how to live with skill and happiness. On the other hand, some of us live with such "high narrative intensity and elaborate analysis" that reflection "can be a 'narrative maze' imprisoning the individual in learning without empowerment" (Goodson *et al.*, 2010, p. 125). Writing, we have found, helps us to use narrativizing to our advantage—to avoid the maze. Writing stories down helps us to escape endlessly rehashing "How could I have done that better?" because it forces us to move through a beginning, middle, and end of the swirl of our thoughts. Writing also gets the events out of our brains and onto paper. We can then revisit and reconsider them later with specific questions in mind. In this book, then, we privilege a particular kind of narrative—the kind that leads to well-informed action.

To assist new teachers with this construction of meaning, Rob and I held several writing retreats for our group. We shared what we knew about composing written narratives out of remembered experience. Together, our group reviewed the Guided Reflection Protocol recommended by Simon Hole and Grace Hall McEntee (2003) in their book *At the Heart of Teaching: A Guide to Reflective Practice*. After taking the time to write brief stories about "what happened" during one significant memory, teachers shared their stories and discussed "why did it happen?" and "what might it mean?"—questions provided by the Protocol. These questions helped the writers not only to develop narratives, but also to begin to analyze and evaluate the meaning of their stories.

During another Saturday writing retreat, we studied a text rich with both narrative detail and analysis. Todd DeStigter's (2001) ethnography, *Reflections of a Citizen Teacher: Literacy, Democracy, and the Forgotten Students of Addison High*, alternates between plot and commentary. For our writing group, DeStigter's work served as what Katie Wood Ray calls a *mentor text* (Ray, 2006). By studying and discussing his graceful step from dialogue to exposition, we began to understand the thinking that gave birth to that form. This led to informed discussion of the differences between narrative and expository modes. While we were not asking the teachers in our writing group to write ethnographies, if they wanted to communicate some of what they were learning as they composed, then they, too, would have to craft smooth transitions between modes in their work.

It is our hope that these chapters may, in turn, become mentors for others. We believe that this can happen on several levels. As DeStigter did for us, we hope to model thinking and writing processes that you may follow as you make meaning of your memories of teaching. We also believe that reading these narratives can foster a wisdom that comes from reflection. While these early career teachers would not claim to be wise beyond their years, their stories offer readers vicarious experiences that can be discussed critically. This offers two benefits. First, by describing years of work in a variety of settings, this collection is a supplement to firsthand experience. Second, by prompting and facilitating critical reflection and discussion, this collection offers a hold on the pace of teaching, which in life is so fast-paced and multilayered that reflection is difficult (Dolk & den Hertog, 2008).

As we wrote, we considered the possible critiques of a collection of personal narratives. We know that the national education pendulum has swung toward the analysis of data to inform best practices. I have experienced this firsthand. For many of the last six years, I annually visited Washington, DC, to talk about the future of the National Writing Project with policy and lawmakers. Teachers who had completed a National Writing Project Summer Institute often came with me to testify to the power of the program and to describe the positive changes that resulted from the federally funded scholarships that they had received. Many of the representatives with whom we met were eager to discuss teachers' stories of transformation.

Then, it seemed, the winds shifted.

On my last visit to Washington, representatives from the Department of Education clearly articulated their growing commitment to experimental research and quantifiable data. As we discussed the thirty-year history of "teachers teaching teachers" during NWP summer institutes, the Department of Education employees told us something like this: we know that teachers love the National Writing Project institutes, but we need more than satisfaction surveys. We need solid research that proves that the work of the National Writing Project improves student learning. That sounded reasonable. Indeed, the National Writing Project has conducted not only rigorous research on participants' program evaluation (Stokes, 2011), but also such research on the effects of its programs ("Research Brief," 2010; Swain, Graves, & Morse 2007; Blau, Cabe, & Whitney 2007). But for my own work, while a golden inch of verifiable statistics would result from an experimental, double-blind research study, a mile of human detail would be lost about the effectiveness of my teaching of teachers as an NWP director. What variables would I try to isolate and to measure? Each of the teachers with whom I work is so unique, and each designs an independent research project to answer a specific question that has arisen in the context of his or her teaching. Their writing tasks are designed to help them hone their strengths and shore up the weak places in their own writing lives. Each teacher has a singular story.

This collection, then, is not a replacement for experimental research. We know that experimental research is vital for understanding the relationships among isolated variables in controlled conditions, yet we think that it cannot predict what will foster learning in classroom conditions where hundreds of variables are at play. Experimental science gives us information about "what works" for the highest number of humans across a spectrum (i.e., the center of the bell curve). As Donald Polkinghorne (2010) puts it, "in the social sciences, theories are not about concrete individuals, but about the average of an aggregate of people . . . [They] are about] what works on average rather than what will work for each individual" (p. 393). In this, positivist experimental research does not instruct teachers about how to respond in particular situations with unique children, for it only gives us information about how isolated practices affect isolated variables for an average person in a controlled situation.

Like this collection, the detailed stories of transformation that my NWP colleagues and I were telling on Capitol Hill are examples of what Jerome Bruner has called *narrative thinking*, and the request for statistical analysis of program effectiveness is an example of *paradigmatic thinking* (Bruner, 1990). *Paradigmatic thinking* makes sense of the world by placing particular events into categories and then determining the relationships among those categories. In education, paradigmatic thinking seems to be on the rise, especially when we look at the ubiquity of big category words like Annual Yearly Progress, success or failure, and little category words for behaviors like hyperactivity or phonemic awareness.

In contrast to paradigmatic thinking, narrative thinking tells stories of human actions across time. Reading narratives helps us to understand the complexities of living through vicarious experience and reflection. As is common knowledge in the field of literary studies, we can read texts in multiple ways. One way is to suspend disbelief and fully enter the story world, vicariously experiencing what the characters are experiencing. As readers, we move with these teachers through their days, learning as we recreate the scenes evoked by their words. This imaginative work is highly valuable. Research on learning suggests that imaginatively rehearsing even a singular skill leads to improved performance (Suinn, 1972; Leahy & Sweller, 2004; Sanders et al., 2004).

Reading these narratives empathetically, then, will allow you to rehearse future choices and actions. Alongside our contributors, you can learn about what you might encounter in the future: what authority principals might wield, what curiosity or apathy students might display, what closeness or emotional distance other teachers might expect. As you imagine yourself in the shoes of each of these teachers, you can ask yourself, "What would I do in a similar situation?" The benefits of this kind of reading are manifold: broadening experience, enlarging our capacity for empathy, and even improving our ability to make good decisions. With other scholars in education and the social sciences, we are not alone in our faith in the effects of reading narratives, and we hope that this book will broaden your own experience and foster reflection as you talk about them with others (Polkinghorne, 2004; Hatton & Smith, 1995).

Critics of this collection might say that we are promoting teaching strategies that are not proven. They might argue that it's irresponsible to teach by anecdote, to draw conclusions from a sample size of one. But we want to make it clear that this is not a research study. This is a collection of non-fiction stories. We hope that these stories pulled from the web of school interactions enable your imagination to focus on moments of choice. When faced with teaching dilemmas, our contributors may have made different choices than you think that you would. This is, after all, not a research study reporting on statistically reliable strategies to reach measurable learning outcomes. It's a book of human perspectives. And yet, by compiling many narratives into a single volume, we hope to clarify what the view is "from the ground." We believe that these stories will point readers back to the research on the issues that they raise, both qualitative and quantitative, and each chapter provides go-to lists for additional reading.

Our experience, as teachers of teachers, is that research studies are only interesting to those who have asked for themselves the questions that the research is addressing. We wanted to write this book to generate urgency to study and to fix problems and to help our students avoid the mistakes made in the past by learning more. We hope these stories will create that urgency.

In addition to broadening your experiences, fostering reflection, and sparking an interest in further research, we also hope that you study these narratives as texts. To reflect on the ways that the stories function, you might consider how time is represented, how the writers assert their agency, what story arcs are present, and how the formal features of the narrative (like verb tenses) signal their genre. In other words, in order to learn as much as possible from *narrative thinking*, we need to think carefully about what makes narratives work (Bruner, 1991).

The first textual aspect of the narratives in this collection to consider is that, as with all narratives, these texts are *temporal*. They make readers aware of the passage of time, even when they flash forward or backward. Time in written narratives is different than time on a clock. It signals the significance of events—expanding or contracting to serve the meaning of the text (Ricour, 1992; Bruner, 1991).

The writers of the narratives in this collection, as early career English teachers, have a unique relationship to time as it is structured in schools. Having finished one or two years of teaching, our contributors have just begun to experience the rhythms of teaching. Rhythm, if you think about it, is experienced not in any single moment but only over time, when events (like a beat) repeat themselves in patterns. The teaching life, over time, is particularly rhythmic. Teachers experience hourly rhythms (each class period includes greeting, settling down, teaching, wrapping up); daily rhythms (prepping, teaching, grading, planning for tomorrow, packing up, recovering); curricular rhythms (introducing a unit, doing activities, giving an assessment); holiday rhythms (anticipating a new season, celebrating the holiday, disrupting the regular schedule and recovering equilibrium); and yearly rhythms (beginning school in autumn and working toward summer vacation). What we see in these early career narratives are some first encounters with these rhythms. Our contributors are witnesses, too, to the effect of these rhythms on their veteran colleagues, without having themselves felt the pattern repeat itself (Clandinin & Connelly, 1986).

Another quality of these narratives to consider is that in contrast to paradigmatic texts that categorize teaching practices, the stories in this book are told by and about people making choices. Characters exert agency. They have intentions and they try to carry them out. Indeed, plots often turn on the fulfillment or the frustration of these intentions. Our contributors often testify to the choices that they were making. Writing these narratives down helped them to reflect, and part of their reflection includes interpreting the reasons behind their actions (Bruner, 1991).

As you read, then, try to be aware of your own interpretations of their choices, as well as your own ideas about what choices were not available. Without losing the benefits of entering the story world, also try to reflect critically, analyzing the writers' actions within their historical, political, social, and cultural contexts. We hope that thinking about their choices will help to deepen your own capacity for reflection-on-action and even reflection-in-action (Schön, 1983; Hatton & Smith, 1995).

After agency, we want to encourage you to think about whether the narratives you are reading have a recognizable plot structure. Of course, these are personal narratives, not pulp fiction. They are first-person slices of what might be called our contributors' *identity stories*—the stories each of us might tell to explain who we are and what we are like. Our contributors worked hard to turn their inchoate impressions and experiences of their first years as teachers into linear words on the page. This was an act of translation. Each one has taken a part of their inchoate *identity story* and translated it into a written story subject to the grammar and generic features of narratives (Polkinghorne, 1991, 1996). While these narratives are as true and as unique as the writers could tell them, they use conventional tropes to structure their experience. Can you identify any ways that an author is one of the "thousand faces" of a hero figure (Campbell, 1972)? Can you find any other conventional characters: virtue misunderstood, the benevolent gift-giver, a youth coming-of-age and losing innocence? As writers ourselves, we know that we are not completely in control of the tropes and metaphors upon which we draw. The language that we wield is given to us, as are the ways that we understand our experiences as unique manifestations of conventional plots. The language through which we think constructs us and our minds as much as we use it as a tool of construction. So, as writers and readers, we study stories to understand the limits and possibilities of our language(s) and our narrative tropes and structures (Bruner, 1991).

Some of the qualities of the language in these narratives was shaped by us, the editors. Not only did we ask all of the contributors the same questions to prompt their writing, but we also collected and copy edited drafts, sometimes helping to keep verb tenses consistent, other times suggesting revisions to the organization of sections. I noticed, as I worked on the drafts, that writers usually began in the past tense, but sometimes they moved into the present tense. So immersed were they in the memory of their experience, that their minds recreated it in the present. As readers, you might consider how the formal features of the language define the genre you are reading.

Finally, we think that these stories are not only good reading to understand vicariously what a new teacher might encounter during his or her first years, but they are also good reading to think about what identity stories are meaningful to teachers right now. This is, after all, a time of great flux in education. Digital technologies are changing the face of schooling daily as we wrestle to make the best of their potential. Just consider the trends in the last decade: video lectures, individualized modules, social networks, and logarithmic assessment of test scores and other big data. Global economics has also affected local public school budgets, which in turn have shaped teacher hiring, pink-slipping, and pensions. In addition, the growth of the number of charter schools and home schooling networks that now have free access to vast online content like the Kahn Academy have made citizens view education through the lens of the concept of choice. In combination, these trends influence how each teacher understands his or her story: its scene, its actors, their actions, their agency, and their purposes (Burke, 1945). As schooling changes, our stories will have to change as well. We hope that this collection will foster reflection to help you write your own story as an effective educator in this exciting field.

References

Blau, S., Cabe, R., & Whitney, A. (2007) *Evaluating IIMPaC: Teacher and student outcomes through a professional development program in the teaching of writing.* Berkeley, CA: National Writing Project.

Bruner, J. (1990). *Acts of meaning.* Cambridge, MA: Harvard University Press.

Bruner, J. (1991). The narrative construction of reality. *Critical Inquiry, 18*(1), 1–21.

Burke, K. (1945). *A grammar of motives.* Berkeley: University of California Press.

Campbell, J. (1972). *The hero with a thousand faces.* Princeton, NJ: Princeton University Press.

Clandinin, D. J., & Connelly, F. M. (1986). Rhythms in teaching: The narrative study of teachers' practical knowledge of classrooms. *Teacher and Teacher Education, 2*(4), 377–387.

DeAngelis, K. J., & Presley, J. B. (2011). Toward a more nuanced understanding of new teacher attrition. *Education and Urban Society, 43*(5), 598–626.

DeStigter, T. (2001). *Reflections of a citizen teacher: Literacy, democracy, and the forgotten students of Addison High.* Washington, DC: National Council of Teachers of English.

Dolk, M., & den Hertog, J. (2008). Narratives in teacher education. *Interactive Learning Environments, 16*(3), 215–229.

Elbaz, F. (Ed.). (2005). *Teachers' voices: Storytelling and possibility.* Charlotte, NC: Information Age Publishing.

Goodson, I. F., Biesta, G., Tedder, M., & Adair, N. (2010). *Narrative learning.* New York: Routledge.

Hahs-Vaughn, D. L., & Scherff, L. (2008). Beginning English teacher attrition, mobility, and retention. *The Journal of Experimental Education, 77*(1), 21–53.

Hancock, C. B., & Scherff, L. (2010). Who will stay and who will leave? Predicting secondary English teacher attrition risk. *Journal of Teacher Education, 61*(4), 328–338.

Hatton, N., & Smith, D. (1995). Reflection in teacher education: Towards definition and implementation. *Teaching and Teacher Education. 11*(1), 33–49.

Hole, S., & McEntee, G. H. (2003). *At the heart of teaching: A guide to reflective practice.* New York, NY: Teachers College Press.

Kaiser, A. (2011). *Beginning teacher attrition and mobility: Results from the first through third waves of the 2007–08 beginning teacher longitudinal study. First look.* NCES 2011318. Washington, DC: National Center for Education Statistics.

Leahy, W., & Sweller, J. (2004). Cognitive load and the imagination effect. *Applied Cognitive Psychology, 18*(7), 857–875.

McCann, T. M., Johannessen, L. R., & Ricca, B. (2005). Responding to new teachers' concerns. *Educational Leadership, 62*(8), 30–34.

Polkinghorne, D. E. (1991). Narrative and self-concept. *Journal of Narrative and Life History, 1,* 135–153.

Polkinghorne, D. E. (1996). Explorations of narrative identity. *Psychological Inquiry, 7*(4), 363–367.

Polkinghorne, D. E. (2004). *Practice and the human sciences: The case for a judgment-based practice of care.* Albany: State University of New York Press.

Polkinghorne, D. E. (2010). The practice of narrative. *Narrative Inquiry, 20*(2), 392–396.

Ravitch, D. (2013). *Reign of error: The hoax of the privatization movement and the danger to America's public schools.* New York, NY: Random House.

Ray, K. W. (2006). *Study driven: A framework for planning units of study in the writing workshop.* Portsmouth, NH: Heinemann.

Research brief: Writing project professional development continues to yield gains in student writing achievement. (2010). Berkeley, CA: National Writing Project. Retrieved from www.

nwp.org/cs/public/download/nwp_file/14004/FINAL_2010_Research_Brief. pdf?x-r=pcfile_d

Ricour, P. (1992). *Oneself as another* (K. Blarney, Trans.). Chicago, IL: University of Chicago Press.

Rogers, D. L., & Babinski, L. M. (2002). *From isolation to conversation: Supporting new teachers' development.* New York, NY: SUNY Press.

Sanders, C. W., Sadoski, M., Bramson, R., Wiprud, R., & Van Walsum, K. (2004). Comparing the effects of physical practice and mental imagery rehearsal on learning basic surgical skills by medical students. *American Journal of Obstetrics and Gynecology, 191*(5), 1811–1814.

Schön, D. (1983). *The reflective practitioner: How professionals think in action.* New York, NY: Basic Books.

Smith, T. M., & Ingersoll, R. M. (2004). What are the effects of induction and mentoring on beginning teacher turnover? *American Educational Research Journal, 41*(3), 681–714.

Stokes, L. (2011). *The enduring quality and value of the National Writing Project's teacher development institutes: Teachers' assessments of NWP contributions to their classroom practice and development as leaders.* Inverness, CA: Inverness Research. Retrieved from www.inverness -research.org/reports/2011–11-Rpt-NWP-NWP-Survey-TeacherInst-Final.pdf

Suinn, R. M. (1972). Behavior rehearsal training for ski racers. *Behavior Therapy, 3*(3), 519–520.

Swain, S., Graves, R., & Morse, D. (2007). *Effects of NWP teaching strategies on elementary students' writing.* Berkeley, CA: National Writing Project.

2

SCHOOL CULTURE

Introduction
Robert Rozema

As the television show *Friday Night Lights* remind us, high school athletics can play an enormous role in the community life of a school. For the fictional town of Dillon, Texas, where the show is set, and for actual towns across America, Friday night football games are more than just sporting contests. They are expressions of what the town believes—a sort of religion, with their own rituals, values, and social expectations. The cheerleaders, the marching band, the coach, the players themselves, and their friends and family watching the game all participate in the event, reinforcing their common values week after week until the season ends.

I attended a high school that loved football, but I taught for eight years at a school ruled by another sport: basketball. Here, all of the attendant social values that many school communities ascribe to football seemed to find expression on the hardwood. Our team played in a tough league and lost most of its games, despite the ardent support of the students and the community, who packed the stands, even on Tuesday evening games. Like students everywhere, ours sometimes misbehaved, but during one particular losing streak, their behavior got ugly.

We were playing a rival team from a rural school six or seven miles out of town. Our students were mostly suburban kids from affluent homes. Many wore Abercrombie and Polo and drove Volkswagens or Hondas. After graduation, the vast majority attended four-year universities. Our rivals were from working- and middle-class families. They wore cowboy boots and flannel shirts and drove pickup trucks. Some went to college, but many went straight into manual labor jobs in construction or agriculture. Our students saw them as hicks, and during one twenty-point drubbing, they found a cheer to voice their bigotry: *It's all right! It's okay! You'll all work for us someday!*

The misbehavior of our students could be considered an isolated event, a moment when they lost control and let loose with the most harmful invective they could muster. Our students did not invent the snob cheer, as we came to call it. But as I reflect on that day, I wonder how much my high school had sanctioned their misbehavior—not explicitly, of course, but in the assumptions and beliefs that lay beneath the surface. What conditions within our school and our community had contributed, even indirectly, to the snob cheer? Did our emphasis on academic achievement, honors societies, and college admission somehow foster their prejudice against the working class? What degree of responsibility should be borne by their parents, nearly all white-collar professionals with college degrees? And finally, what steps could our school take to combat these tendencies?

In asking these questions, I am focusing on *school culture,* an idea that is difficult to define but well worth examining, especially if you are just starting to teach. In fact, we hope this chapter will help you recognize and understand the cultural underpinnings of the school where you are teacher assisting, student teaching, or beginning your career. And while my example describes a unattractive element that surfaced within my school, school culture is never monolithic; never uniformly good or bad. Many of the teachers, administrators, and parents in my school and community, for example, may have deplored the classism that I witnessed at the basketball game against our rivals.

So, what exactly is school culture? One way to begin understanding your school culture is to assume the role of an anthropologist. From an anthropological perspective, the culture of a school can be defined, broadly, as the language, knowledge, values, beliefs, symbols, rituals, and social norms that characterize a given school. Put more simply, school culture is the "way we do things around here" (Deal & Kennedy, 1983), a set of written and unwritten rules that guide everyday living, defining the reality of those who live within its boundaries (D. Hargreaves, 1995).

In my brief example, we can see the *value* placed on academic and athletic success, the *symbols* of wealth in name-brand clothing and expensive cars, the *ritual* of attending basketball games, and perhaps a set of *social norms* functioning tacitly within an affluent school community. In such an environment, for example, discriminating against the less well-off may have been socially acceptable among students. Not all students held to this norm, of course. Many were likely embarrassed by the snob cheer. Further inquiry might uncover embedded *beliefs* about socioeconomic diversity, perpetuated sometimes unconsciously by the curriculum, teachers, and parents in the community. More positively, if my school had identified the problem and tried to address it, we might see *language* about tolerance in the school mission statement or on hallway posters. Teachers, students, and administrators alike would be able to articulate their *knowledge* about the problem, its solution, and their responsibilities to promote class awareness among the student body and surrounding community.

Even from an anthropological viewpoint, however, identifying school culture can be challenging. Cultural insiders can be blind to the rules governing their community, and you, as an outsider trying to analyze them, might not know where to start. You will likely discover that school culture is hard to measure in exact terms, and that it is used interchangeably with another closely related term, *school climate*, which we will discuss later in the book. We suggest breaking this large subject into more manageable pieces. Though school culture is never dissectible into neat parts, you might start by examining three overlapping areas that contribute to school culture: organizational culture, teacher culture, and student culture (D. Hargreaves, 1995).

Organizational culture, a term borrowed from business, can refer to the culture generated by the power structure of a given institution (Schoen & Teddlie, 2008). This structure distributes power and relegates tasks, enabling the school or organization to function. Your school, for instance, likely has a hierarchical power structure, with the school superintendent at the top, followed by the school principal, assistant principal, athletic director, and the teachers, who themselves are ranked according to experience and positions, such as department chair. There may also be official committees with varying degrees of influence and prestige. Your school shares this generic power structure with schools across the country. What may be unique to your school, however, are the informal groups of teachers and administrators that form to share resources, to talk about methods and materials, or to address a perceived problem. The way in which these groups and individuals share power and accomplish goals is a function of organizational culture. If your state passed Right to Work legislation recently, for example, the organizational culture of your school may be shifting, as the teachers' union loses members and, consequently, political power.

Teacher culture is rooted in the professional lives of the educators within a school building. Organizational culture can contribute to teacher culture; likewise, teacher culture influences organizational culture. The best way to identify teacher culture in your school is to observe how faculty members collaborate. The English teacher just down the hall might be isolated from you, despite his proximity, as he designs his own lessons and bears responsibility for their success or failure. In this kind of isolationist environment, one teacher may not know what another colleague is teaching, which gives him a great deal of autonomy but can lead to territorial disputes with other teachers—*You taught* The Giver *last year? I always teach this novel in eighth grade!*—and an incoherent curriculum (A. Hargreaves, 1994).

A collaborative teacher culture, in contrast, is one in which faculty members interact frequently, sharing materials, exchanging ideas, and evaluating their own practices, all without being told to do so. If you have shared planning time built into your daily schedule, talk with colleagues between classes, converse with other teachers about your successes or frustrations during your lunch period, find a new resource or friendly note in your mailbox, or ask a trusted mentor to observe your class, then you are likely part of a collaborative culture. Most teachers in this kind of environment enjoy working with their colleagues, but some may resent the frequent intrusions on their teaching lives. If such resentment becomes widespread, teachers may collaborate only when they are forced to do so during professional development days or team meetings. This kind of contrived collaboration often does more harm than good. When your math colleague spends his planning hour airing grievances about his colleagues instead of contributing to the interdisciplinary project, or when English department meetings turn into gossip sessions about students, your teacher culture might be collaborative in name alone (A. Hargreaves, 1994).

New teachers may also find themselves in a culture that is neither isolationist nor collaborative, but characterized by small enclaves of teachers working in unofficial alliances. In its most innocuous form, this kind of culture might yield teacher cliques that can be perfectly healthy: you might notice that the math and science teachers always occupy one corner of the lounge during break, or that the history teachers always attend basketball games together. In a more corrosive form of this balkanized culture (A. Hargreaves 1994), however, small groups of teachers dismiss or exclude colleagues, causing divisions within the faculty. *Stay away from that bunch! Everyone knows they are burned out.*

The final component of school culture is student culture. Like organizational and teacher culture, student culture is a dynamic and complex phenomenon. If you wish to investigate the student culture of your school, you should begin by asking how the organizational structure and teacher culture serve the student population. Are students tracked into high- and low-ability classes, a stratification system proven to be harmful to student achievement (Oakes, 2005)? Do teachers employ student-centered pedagogies that value student autonomy (Schoen & Teddlie, 2008)? How much power do students have to affect school procedures and policies? These and similar questions explore how students are situated in the school power structure—as citizens of a democracy, or less positively, as serfs in a feudalist system.

Your examination of student culture should also focus on student social groups. Popular books and movies portray adolescents as members of distinct social subcultures, stereotypically labeled as jocks, nerds, Goths, or burnouts, to name a few. These depictions are exaggerated, but schools do seem to have recognizable crowds, or subcultures of students who are grouped by their reputation, who share language, adhere to specific social norms, practice rituals, and express themselves with symbols. The cross-country team, for instance, might constitute a crowd: its runners use a specific terminology, such as *PR* (personal record), its norms tacitly forbid alcohol use, it meets every Monday morning for a donut ritual, and team members symbolize their solidarity by wearing road-race T-shirts. Adolescents are distinctly aware of the prestige rankings of social groups, with the most popular crowds tending to embody what the school values, perhaps athletics or academic accomplishment. Moreover, students in popular crowds have higher self-esteem than those in low-ranking crowds (Kinney, 1993).

Of greater influence on adolescent identity than the crowd, however, is the peer network, or clique, the group of three or four friends who spend extensive time socializing during the school day. Most adolescents report belonging to a clique, and this small group exerts a considerable effect on its members, influencing school behavior for good or for ill (Ellis & Zarbatany, 2007). Your school, then, might have observable social subcultures—crowds of football athletes, drama students, or quiz-bowl members—as well as countless microcultures of three to four students apiece (Schein, 2010).

Beyond the cultures generated within the school itself, students also belong to macrocultures, or wider ethnic, religious, sexual, socioeconomic, and national cultures that do not disappear when first hour begins (Schein, 2010; Prosser, 1999). In the high school where I taught, the relatively affluent socioeconomic status of the school constituency shaped the social norms that governed the student body: without the daily reality of poor and working-class students, my more privileged students were not forced to confront their assumptions about success and status. Similarly, a white teacher in a low-income, predominantly African-American school might mistakenly equate the multiparty talking occurring in her classes with disrespect, when in fact this kind of communication characterizes African-American discourse and may signify deep engagement with the material (Lee, 2007). It is both overwhelming and exciting to conceptualize culture in such broad terms. In all likelihood, your classroom will be home to wide range of macrocultures. Refugees, exchange students, English language learners, third culture kids, gay and lesbian students, sons and daughters of the working poor and the highly affluent, Muslims, and Christians may all occupy your desks someday. Of course, teachers, administrators, and parents also belong to macrocultures of their own.

School culture, then, is a complex combination of organizational, teacher, and student cultures, a web of meaning that informs and responds to everything that happens in and around a school community. With no disrespect intended, school culture is much like the Force of the *Star Wars* films: it surrounds us; it penetrates us; it binds the galaxy—or school—together. To follow the analogy, a new teacher must learn the ways of the Force, working toward *cultural competence*. This widely used term denotes a combination of attitude and ability: to be culturally competent, a teacher must be aware of her own cultural biases and assumptions, must respect cultural differences, and must choose content and pedagogy that respond to the cultural conditions on the ground.

But how can new English teachers gain cultural competence? We hope the narratives that follow provide some answers. Each of our writers—Jeremy, Adam, David, and Blaine—begins teaching in a new, unfamiliar culture, and each initially struggles to learn how things work. Before reading their narratives, however, consider completing the following exercise. The survey shown in Figure 2.1 is not comprehensive, but it does get at most components of school culture. If you are already in a school as a teacher assistant, a student teacher, or a new teacher, try answering the items below about your school. If not, base your answers on your middle school, high school, or university. Your responses, when taken together, should give you a better sense of your school culture.

References

Deal, T. E., & Kennedy, A. A. (1983). Culture and school performance. *Educational Leadership, 40*(5), 14–15.

Ellis, W., & Zarbatany, L. (2007). Peer group status as a moderator of group influence on children's deviant, aggressive, and prosocial behavior. *Child Development, 78*(4), 1240–1254.

Hargreaves, A. (1994). *Changing teachers, changing times: Teachers' work and culture in a postmodern age.* London: Cassell.

Hargreaves, D. H. (1995). School culture, school effectiveness and school improvement. *School Effectiveness and School Improvement, 6*(1), 23–46.

Kinney, D. A. (1993). From nerds to normals: The recovery of identity among adolescents from middle school to high school. *Sociology of Education, 66*(1), 21–40.

Lee, C. D. (2007). *Culture, literacy, & learning: Taking bloom in the midst of the whirlwind.* New York, NY: Teachers College Press.

Oakes, J. (2005). *Keeping track: How schools structure inequality.* New Haven, CT: Yale University Press.

Prosser, J. (Ed.). (1999). *School culture.* London: Sage.

Schein, E. H. (2010). *Organizational culture and leadership.* San Francisco, CA: Jossey-Bass.

Schoen, L. T., & Teddlie, C. (2008). A new model of school culture: A response to a call for conceptual clarity. *School Effectiveness and School Improvement, 19*(2), 129–153.

Figure 2.1 School Culture Survey

Rate each statement on the following scale
1 = Strongly Disagree   2 = Disagree   3 = Neutral   4 = Agree   5 = Strongly Agree

1. Administrators seek teacher input on important issues such as school policy, curriculum, hiring practices, and professional development.	(1) SD	(2) D	(3) N	(4) A	(5) SA
2. Without the consent of teachers, administrators cannot make significant changes to school policy, curriculum, hiring practices, and professional development.	(1) SD	(2) D	(3) N	(4) A	(5) SA
3. Administrators trust the professional judgment of teachers.	(1) SD	(2) D	(3) N	(4) A	(5) SA
4. Administrators support teachers during conflicts with students, parents, or community members.	(1) SD	(2) D	(3) N	(4) A	(5) SA
5. Administrators facilitate teacher collaboration by providing time and resources for teachers to work together and encouraging teachers to share ideas.	(1) SD	(2) D	(3) N	(4) A	(5) SA
6. Administrators provide meaningful professional development opportunities for teachers.	(1) SD	(2) D	(3) N	(4) A	(5) SA
7. Administrators evaluate teachers fairly and consistently.	(1) SD	(2) D	(3) N	(4) A	(5) SA
8. Administrators understand and promote the mission of the school.	(1) SD	(2) D	(3) N	(4) A	(5) SA
9. Teachers have opportunities for dialogue and planning across grades and subjects.	(1) SD	(2) D	(3) N	(4) A	(5) SA
10. Teachers spend significant time planning together.	(1) SD	(2) D	(3) N	(4) A	(5) SA

11. Teachers are involved in decisions concerning school policy, curriculum, hiring practices, and other important issues.	(1) SD	(2) D	(3) N	(4) A	(5) SA
12. Teachers understand and promote the mission of the school.	(1) SD	(2) D	(3) N	(4) A	(5) SA
13. Teachers value professional development opportunities such as in-services and conferences.	(1) SD	(2) D	(3) N	(4) A	(5) SA
14. Teachers are current in their content areas and their pedagogical methods.	(1) SD	(2) D	(3) N	(4) A	(5) SA
15. Teachers cannot make significant changes to course materials or curricula without consulting colleagues within the department and school.	(1) SD	(2) D	(3) N	(4) A	(5) SA
16. Teachers frequently evaluate the effectiveness of the curriculum.	(1) SD	(2) D	(3) N	(4) A	(5) SA
17. Teachers understand the broader purposes of the curriculum.	(1) SD	(2) D	(3) N	(4) A	(5) SA
18. Teachers are kept informed about important issues within the school.	(1) SD	(2) D	(3) N	(4) A	(5) SA
19. Teachers spend time observing colleagues teach.	(1) SD	(2) D	(3) N	(4) A	(5) SA
20. Students are able to articulate the mission of the school.	(1) SD	(2) D	(3) N	(4) A	(5) SA
21. Students have prominent roles in the governance of the school.	(1) SD	(2) D	(3) N	(4) A	(5) SA

(Continued)

Figure 2.1 (Continued)

Rate each statement on the following scale
1 = Strongly Disagree   2 = Disagree   3 = Neutral   4 = Agree   5 = Strongly Agree

	(1) SD	(2) D	(3) N	(4) A	(5) SA
22. Students have channels to make suggestions and raise concerns about school issues.	(1) SD	(2) D	(3) N	(4) A	(5) SA
23. Students understand the purpose of the curriculum in any given course.	(1) SD	(2) D	(3) N	(4) A	(5) SA
24. Students generally accept responsibility for their education by completing homework and engaging in class.	(1) SD	(2) D	(3) N	(4) A	(5) SA
25. Students have ample opportunities to demonstrate their learning to their teachers, their classmates, and community members.	(1) SD	(2) D	(3) N	(4) A	(5) SA
26. When students are disciplined, the process is fair and consistent.	(1) SD	(2) D	(3) N	(4) A	(5) SA
27. No single student crowd (e.g. football athletes) is given preferential treatment by teachers or administrators.	(1) SD	(2) D	(3) N	(4) A	(5) SA
28. Bullying is not a problem at the school.	(1) SD	(2) D	(3) N	(4) A	(5) SA
29. Racial diversity is not a source of conflict in the school.	(1) SD	(2) D	(3) N	(4) A	(5) SA
30. Religious or cultural diversity is not a source of conflict in the school.	(1) SD	(2) D	(3) N	(4) A	(5) SA

	(1) SD	(2) D	(3) N	(4) A	(5) SA
31. Differences in sexual orientation and gender are not a source of conflict in the school.	(1) SD	(2) D	(3) N	(4) A	(5) SA
32. Socioeconomic diversity is not a source of conflict in the school.	(1) SD	(2) D	(3) N	(4) A	(5) SA
33. Students see differences in race, class, gender, and culture as assets to the school.	(1) SD	(2) D	(3) N	(4) A	(5) SA
34. Students in minority groups—race, culture, gender, or class—feel safe in the school.	(1) SD	(2) D	(3) N	(4) A	(5) SA
35. School has a set of values that are promoted by administrators, teachers, and students.	(1) SD	(2) D	(3) N	(4) A	(5) SA
36. School has rituals and traditions that express and reinforce its values.	(1) SD	(2) D	(3) N	(4) A	(5) SA
37. Community members believe the school shares their values.	(1) SD	(2) D	(3) N	(4) A	(5) SA
38. Community members trust the judgment of teachers.	(1) SD	(2) D	(3) N	(4) A	(5) SA
39. Teachers recognize and make use of community resources in their teaching.	(1) SD	(2) D	(3) N	(4) A	(5) SA
40. Teachers recognize and respond to community issues, needs, and problems.	(1) SD	(2) D	(3) N	(4) A	(5) SA

Select survey questions based on *School Culture Survey Form 4–98*, developed by Steve Gruenert & Jerry Valentine, Middle Level Leadership Center, University of Missouri.

Jeremy Battaglia teaches high school English in the Midwest. He recently completed an MA in Secondary Education and now leads professional development for lesson planning and formative assessment in his school. He has two daughters, and at the time of this writing, his wife, Melissa, is expecting. In his spare time, Jeremy builds forts in the living room, holds extensive tea parties, and reads a new story every night.

Lessons From the Scrap Yard
Jeremy Battaglia
Bradly Middle and High School

Both of my parents were teachers. It was common to see books and papers strewn about the dinner table. My parents spent weeknights prepping for the next day and weekends grading papers. So, I never doubted the value of education. Education was the answer. It improved life. It is one thing to preach its importance, but it really sinks in when it is just the way things are. In my home, education was a part of life. Not surprisingly, I became a teacher.

My first teaching job led me two hours south from my parents' home to Bradly Middle and High School. Along with my books and classroom materials, I carried my conception of education with me. It was not so much of a perception of the way things should be. I just believed, naively, that my upbringing was typical. As I drove toward my new rural district, however, I slowly left that world behind. The town was located roughly twenty miles off the highway. Turn after turn took me through woods, across streams, and around open fields. To the south of the town was nothing but mile after mile of agriculture: cornfields and nurseries full of flowers. In every other direction, there seemed to be nothing but wilderness.

The town itself literally had one stoplight. There was a McDonald's, a bowling alley, two dollar stores, and a supermarket. It was the type of district that routinely gave two-hour fog delays because so many students relied on the bus. When winter came, these delays turned to cancellations as the plows could not make it far enough down the gravel roads to plow the snow. While I did wonder what my Friday nights might look like, I never really thought about my students and their families. What did they do with their time on the weekends? What was the source of their income? How did they put food on the table? I knew that the place where a person lives has so much to do with who the person becomes, but even as I passed the dilapidated homes, abandoned buildings, and scrap yard after scrap yard, these questions never really entered my mind.

I soon settled into the rhythm of teaching middle school. I remember a day shortly after the first round of reading proficiency tests. The teachers were given the scores. Our scores were below state average. The administration emphasized, heavily, that our seventh and eighth graders needed to show significant growth. This was not the last time those words—*significant growth*—would ring in my ears. My district, like many in my state, was beginning to use merit pay, an evaluation system that based part of teacher salary on student test scores. Ineffective teachers were in danger of losing their jobs. Even as a first-year teacher, I knew this was an absurd way to do things. I saw merit pay breed unhealthy competition, foster unethical practices, and create far more gaps than bridges in student learning. Still, the administration continued to remind us of the *importance* of such data. In fact, data were so forcibly stressed that I soon forgot I had people in front of me, and freshmen at that. At times, I saw only raw numbers, scores, growth charts, and proficiency ratings.

The tests were done three times a year, officially. However, this did not stop teachers from testing more often. By doing so, these teachers could handpick the set of scores they submitted at the end of the year. The name of the game was growth. So, if a particular student did not show growth from the first test to the next, the teacher would continue to test until the student got an improved score, even if the improvement was incremental. Not only that, I suspected something more sinister was occurring: to me, it looked like the first round of the test was rigged to guarantee low scores. No one was standing at the back of the room banging pots and pans together, but the first day of testing was not designed for optimal results. This could be achieved in very subtle ways. Allowing the students to pick their testing seat, interrupting to give sudden *useful* announcements, not stopping students from chatting, rushing them to finish certain portions, and skipping the directions. These were just some of the ingenious ways teachers devised to ensure low performance. One way of securing growth is to have a low score to begin with. Everyone wins right? The administration would see a clear increase from this woeful beginning, and the teacher would seem to have done a remarkable, even miraculous job. I often wondered if the students were onto this, and if so, what they were learning from the way we did things.

You might think that teachers under pressure to raise test scores would recognize how much pressure their students are under, not only from frequent high-stakes tests but also from their peers and their families. Although we once sat in the desks, we often fail to see things from the perspective of our students. When I looked around the room during that first semester, I did not see adolescents with confidence issues. Nor did I recognize students who were trying hard to fit in, worrying about the weekend party, or wondering if their girlfriends or boyfriends were being faithful. Unfortunately, we often overlook these concerns. They are not factored into any growth report I have come across, but they are infinitely more valuable.

During the second round of tests, I too was feeling the pressure. My focus was on a small segment of my students who needed to bring up their scores, and I was oblivious to their adolescent concerns, their personal histories, or their cultural values. And without fail, every test period developed into a pattern. Although the test was supposed to take forty-five minutes, a handful of students miraculously finished in a matter of minutes. Didn't they know these results would be factored into an equation that would reveal my effectiveness as a teacher? After all, 3.14 times the number proficient, divided by those who showed significant growth is the best way to determine if a teacher is effective! I write with levity now, but during my early days as an English teacher, I was terrified. I wanted my students to do well. I was going over all of the things I could have done, but didn't do. I was a nervous wreck. Through my conversations with other teachers, veterans and novices alike, I know that I was not alone.

Some of you may know the way it feels to see students fly recklessly through a test, as though they were being graded on how fast they completed it. Like clockwork, every hour produced one or two students who finished just shortly after my parting words of instruction, "Take your time." They would click their final answer and then proceed to put their heads down, draw, or worst of all, begin to distract others. So, it was with irritation that I would inevitably ask these students into the hall. My hallway talks, though stern, were designed to give them confidence, to show support, and above all, to convince them to go back over their answers. I did want my students to do their best, even though I didn't believe in the test or in the merit system it created.

Bill was one student who received many of my hallway pep talks. Bill was repeating the ninth grade. He was tall, dark haired, and popular with the girls. He was the student who was asked to take his hat off four or five times during a day: abiding by the rules was just not as important as his outward appearance. He was something of a class clown. To Bill, it seemed far more socially acceptable to laugh off an assignment than to struggle with it. Bill came from a family without one high school graduate. In fact, if given the chance, he would tell anyone listening a story about his dad. His dad once saw a former teacher at a restaurant. Apparently, the teacher, like me, stressed the importance of education, probably with a prepared speech proclaiming how a diploma was essential for financial success. Well, Bill's dad sauntered over and paid for that teacher's meal in an effort to show what a success he was, even without a diploma. Bill told this story often and with certainty: education and financial independence had no correlation whatsoever.

"Bill?" I asked during one of our hallway conversations, "Just out of curiosity, are you planning to graduate?"

"Yeah, I guess. Haven't really thought about it much, Mr. B."

I coached Bill in football earlier that autumn. He was the type of kid that did well as long as things were going smoothly. However, if he dropped a pass, he would mentally check out of the next series because he was so preoccupied with his mistake. If one little thing went wrong, he pouted and worried, even as his performance continued to get worse. Once that started, it was a vicious cycle: a second dropped pass, a missed tackle, a fumble.

"Well, have you thought about what you want to do after high school?" I tried to carry on an easygoing tone.

"Oh, yeah, I'm going to work at the scrap yard my dad owns," he said confidently. The largest scrap yard in town was run by his family. It sat on a huge lot right off of the main drag. Bill spent his weekends riding his four-wheeler across the grounds, salvaging this and that for his father, whom he idolized. Dad, on the other hand, seemed very aloof and unconcerned with the business of his son, let alone school. I never met him at a conference. There was the rare football game or two that he would attend. Bill was especially worked up and worried on these days.

"Well, what if you don't like working at the scrap yard?"

"Oh, I will! I already work there part time."

"Well, Bill, if you just bomb these tests, you won't graduate." Even as I said this, I knew what his response would be.

"That's fine. You don't need a diploma. My dad doesn't have one, and look at him."

"But, Bill, what if you want a loan from the bank? What if you want to expand? What if you marry someone who wants to live in Florida? What if the competition picks up? Bill, what if you just decide you want to do something else? I want you to have options, and if you don't get a diploma, those options may not be there for you."

I had a flash of this young man in ten years, still no diploma, paying child support, escaping his bleak reality to go to the woods, the one place that could still give him worth. In my most extreme version of his future, Bill would become an alcoholic and accumulate a mountain of debt, the linoleum counter of his office/kitchen behind the scrap yard piling up with empty bottles and unpaid bills. Unlikely, I knew, but I wanted Bill to see some of the disadvantages of life without a high school diploma.

Bill did not see that far ahead. Like so many his age, he was certain what his future held. He was certain education was not a determining factor. I could tell my concern was just not real to him. I needed another approach.

"I tell you what, Bill. You are a big hunter, right?" Of course I already knew the answer. I knew this because for one, most of the students in the area were, and two, *Hatchet* by Gary Paulsen was the only book that Bill even picked up. He identified with the story. It was real to him.

"Oh, yeah, Mr. B. Just the other night, I bagged a ten-point buck from my brother's tree stand."

Hunting was not just popular at school. There was an actual form students could submit if they planned on missing school on opening day of the hunting season. I wasn't sure what this communicated to students: education is secondary to good game hunting? But hunting was a rite of passage in this rural community. Fathers passed on prime spots to their sons. Kids, and especially boys, were given guns at an early age. For many families, a good rifle put more meat on the table than a diploma ever did.

"Well, I have a proposition for you," I continued. "If you go back in there, go back over your answers, spend the rest of the hour giving it an honest try, I will buy you a Gary Paulsen book. There's one that's perfect for you. It's called *Tracker*, and it's all about a boy going hunting with his grandfather."

Bill looked at me as though I was joking. Not many people gave him gifts, especially books.

"Okay, Mr. B., that sounds all right," Bill said, still acting nonchalant.

As he sauntered back in, cool and unconcerned, I thought about our exchange. It was very important for him to keep up appearances. It occurred to me that Bill never seemed very concerned about his grades. In fact, he made it clear to all those around him that he did not pass *because* he did not care. This made sense. In fact, I saw similar behavior in many of my failing students. It dawned on me that failure was deemed socially acceptable, as long as there was an air of detachment. The point was made known to everyone: they failed because they did not try, and they didn't care. If a person failed after they *did* try, this reflected something entirely different. Then, the ownership was on them, and failure resulted from some defect. They could not pass because they were not smart or not skilled. For some reason, this all seemed perfectly acceptable in the world of the rural adolescent.

As I thought this through, I realized the importance of perception in both our worlds was very similar. We were both trying to impress others. We were trying to live up to—or not live up to—expectations and pressure. In Bill's case, I needed a way for him to learn in a safe environment. I needed to find a place where I could teach and he could learn, but without others around him seeing his effort. So, my plan was to live up to my bargain. I purchased *Tracker* for Bill. I even wrote a sincere inscription that ended with something like this:

> So, here is the promised book. Would you mind if we read it together? That way, I would get the chance to read it as well, and it would be yours to keep afterwards. I sure would appreciate it.

Bill and I worked out a deal. On Wednesdays, he caught a ride with his stepbrother, who could not pick him up until an hour after school let out. While he waited, he came to my room, and we read together. Every Wednesday we did this. He loved the story. He made connection after connection. At one point, the protagonist awakes on the morning of a big hunt, expressing his pure joy for the moment:

> John awakened before the alarm went off and sat bolt upright in bed. It was opening morning, deer season, and the old ways had come back, the old excitement . . . He kicked out from under the quilt and put his feet on the floor . . . John pulled his shirt on and went downstairs, two steps at a time . . .
> (Paulsen, 2012, p. 35)

I was raised in the city and knew nothing about hunting. But Bill went on and on about those mornings. He spared no detail, even telling me the ritual breakfast he and his father would share every year on opening day. Many times, Bill became the teacher as I asked about terminology and other elements of the story. During our time together, he related many hunting stories. I, too, shared connections. After we finished, I let him keep the book, as promised. Then a wonderful thing happened: we kept reading. It is because of Bill that my personal classroom library contains roughly twenty Gary Paulsen novels. Soon, we branched out into novels by Tom Brown Jr., Jon Krakauer, and Ben Mikaelsen.

Some students are so adept at crafting personas that we are fooled. For a long time, I saw Bill as a student who did not try because he just didn't care. Caught up in my own world of stress and test scores, I failed to see the lives my students were living outside of my class. Once I showed compassion and interest, I started to learn.

Bill reminded me why I began teaching in the first place—not just because my parents were teachers, or because I grew up in a house full of books, but because I wanted to connect with students. In fact, after my experience with Bill, I created a "Getting To Know You" survey. The survey asks the normal questions about email and contact information, but it also includes more personal questions about hobbies, jobs, sports, and leisure activities. I read student responses and highlight a few things that catch my eye. I pull out one a day for every hour. When I see that student, I make a simple comment. I may tell a student that I like some of the same movies or music. I might ask a student what super hero would she be and why. After the first month, I have had a quick personal conversation with each student in my room.

These little things by no means encompass all of who they are. But it provides an avenue: a way for me to approach them and get to know them a bit outside the educational realm. This has been one of the most valuable things I created. It shows them I am interested and that I care. Many times, these little interactions blossom. I keep a filing cabinet with a folder for each student. Most of the time, these folders get filled with sample essays, or tests, or behavior comments, but I also keep the surveys in there. I go back from time to time and pull out surveys. They are impressed when, in December, I bring up an episode of their favorite TV show. It goes a long way and translates into a better classroom.

By the way, after the final test that year, Bill, for the first time in years, ended the year with a score of proficient. But that was not the statistic that really spoke to me. Although I have come to understand there are far more important ways of determining a student's ability than growth reports, Bill scored the highest level of Lexile increase from the start of the year to the end of the year. Recently, a colleague told me something. He was going over the directions for the Lexile test with his class, explaining the categories and all the rest. When they were reviewing the growth report and target levels, Bill piped up and proudly said, "Back when I was a freshman, I scored the highest level of growth in Mr. B.'s class!" He even remembered the exact increase.

Bill is on course to graduate. I stay in touch with him. The family still owns the scrap yard, and Bill fully intends on moving right in. I can't help but think, with a diploma in his back pocket, he will have some options, and even some answers to those questions I posed all those years ago.

Reference

Paulsen, G. (2012). *Tracker*. Simon & Schuster.

FOR FURTHER DISCUSSION

1. Do your beliefs about the value of education contrast or coincide with those held by your family and community?
2. If school culture consists of shared symbols, rituals, language, and knowledge, how would you characterize the school culture of Bradly High School?
3. To what wider cultures does Bill belong? How does his membership in these cultures shape his school experience?
4. Which of Jeremy's strategies or techniques could you apply to your own teaching?

Adam Kennedy graduated from Grand Valley State University with a BA in English (Secondary Education) and now teaches English language arts to sixth graders in Maryland. During his four years, Adam has held the roles of department chair, Professional Learning Community facilitator, and teacher mentor. Adam realized he would be a teacher when, during a nightly reading of *The Giving Tree*, he asked his mother, "Why is the tree talking?" Since then he has been hooked.

The Rules
Adam Kennedy
Elk Park Middle School

Middle class, white, two parents, two kids, and one dog. The nuclear family. Cul-de-sacs and subdivisions. College degrees and SUVs. The mall. White people. This is my culture—the culture of suburban America. This is where I come from and, whether I want to admit it or not, this is a huge part of who I am. In the community where I grew up, everyone went to football games on Friday nights. On Saturday, many went to the country club for dinner. Then it was church on Sunday morning. When you turned sixteen, your parents took you out to buy a car. These were the rules. I never understood how these rules defined me because I had never spent any significant amount of time outside of my culture. I never saw the different expectations, belief systems, and behavioral norms that characterized other communities. I took my beliefs and my assumptions from my twenty-four years in southwest Michigan with me when I was hired for a job in Maryland. And for the first time in my life, I became a cultural minority. I saw firsthand how culture defines the actions, thought processes, and viewpoints of a community.

The place where I teach, Elk Park, Maryland, is different from my hometown in some pretty obvious ways: it has larger African-American and Latino populations (66% countywide), more poverty, and many more single-parent households. The surrounding county has more apartment buildings than houses. There also seems to be more emphasis on the extended family. I soon learned that threatening to call Mom or Dad might not do the trick. Kids have more responsibilities at home from an early age. A child might not have completed her homework, but she may have bathed and cared for a younger sibling, perhaps after sharing a room or even a bed the night before. Turning sixteen did not mean an automatic trip to the car dealership.

Beyond these broader cultural and socioeconomic differences, I also noticed things about the school itself that were new to me. I admit that my first impression of Elk Park was pretty bad. From my perspective, the place seemed to emanate negativity. In band class, students turned their trumpets into dented-up weapons.

In the hallway, students confidently opened lockers, looking for lunches and books to steal. And it wasn't just the behavior of the students: the hunched shoulders and glum discussions in the faculty lounge told me that my colleagues also felt demoralized. I felt that something was very wrong at Elk Park, and I began to look for explanations.

To me, the negativity seemed to begin at the very top. Our principal was regularly absent from school, and even when present, he often seemed uninterested in the daily happenings of our building. His health was failing. He was up against difficult state standards. And, after over thirty years in education, he just looked burnt out. Rumors swirled about his performance: he played favorites, he hired his friends as employees and made them untouchable, he refused to discipline either students or teachers. Tellingly, I once saw a student point to him and ask a friend, "Who is that old man?" Then there was the time at the faculty Christmas party, when during a conversation with him, I realized he did not recognize me. He had worked hard for many long years, and he had not always been negligent. Far from it, in fact. Older coworkers often talked about his past deeds in glowing terms. But now his attitude was poisonous, trickling into every teacher and student in the building. It hung over us. Why should we be accountable if the principal was not? Why would the students be accountable if we were not? And how could we meet the expectations of the community and the parents we served if no one was accountable?

But it wasn't just the administration. The parents seemed to mistrust us. It was as if they suspected we wanted to fail their children all along. One parent volunteer, while watching as a pep rally meant to excite our kids for the state test devolved into chaos, looked me in the eye and said, "Son, this place is a sinking ship. You need to get on a lifeboat." Another parent once withdrew his child after one day at our school, claiming his son reported that "no one here seems to care at all." Events like these quickly made me realize that animosity existed between the school and the community that it served. I struggled to maintain my positive outlook, and I began seeing parents as obstacles to learning. Dealing with them caused me anger and confusion. I did not understand what they wanted. I tried my best to view them as a potential resource and doorway into my student's lives, but too often, our conversations went nowhere.

At the center of this turmoil were the very real cultural and racial differences between the staff at Elk Park and the community around us. The staff at Elk Park consisted mostly of transplants coming from New York, Pennsylvania, Ohio, and Michigan. Very few of the teachers were from Maryland, and even fewer were African American or Hispanic. My experiences at Elk Park have taught me that race is still, at the very least, something that people notice, and still, at the very worst, something that people make judgments about. During times of stress or moments of failure, race can become a scapegoat for anger. By the time I arrived at Elk Park, there was plenty of anger. Test scores were low and fingers were being pointed. What was probably once a supportive and positive culture had disintegrated, leaving hostility between faculty members, administrators, and the community at large.

It would be wrong to say that everything was going poorly. In my classroom, I was running on adrenaline and excitement. I was a whirlwind of teaching, cajoling, and instructing. I felt confident about my own teaching, despite the negativity surrounding me. Not surprisingly, then, my first real interaction with a parent caught me completely off guard. It was a moment where I was at a loss as to how to act within my school culture. A moment when I would break the first unwritten school rule: keep it "strictly business."

I had been told that morning that I had an IEP (Individualized Education Program) meeting to attend. I confess that I did not know what an IEP was at the time; I was brimming with the type of irrational confidence that only comes from being truly inexperienced. It didn't even bother me that while on my way, I realized I didn't even know where the meetings were held or what was expected of me. I was not worried; I was certain I would have the answer to any question a parent might ask. I was late because I couldn't find the room (turns out it was in the attic, above the chorus room; I distinctly remember hearing "The Age of Aquarius" floating up through the vents). I had no idea what I needed to bring, so I took a clipboard just to have something to hold.

This particular meeting was about Andre, one of my most memorable and most difficult students. But at that time, just ten days into the school year, I was sitting at a table discussing a student I barely recognized. As the meeting began, each teacher discussed Andre's merits—he had a good sense of humor, he was eager to work, he was a creative thinker. Yet, I could see the mother growing angry about what we were sharing. The other teachers carried on as if they didn't see it. I became worried as my turn to speak drew near. Should I address the emotional state the woman was in? Should I be conciliatory? Or, like the rest, should I carry on and keep it strictly business? I had no idea how to act and was caught between my desire to comfort her and my need to follow protocol. I didn't want to seem like a know-it-all or break the unwritten rule of our school's parent-teacher etiquette.

I tried to remember what I had written on the Andre's comment sheet two days prior, something I had done quickly between writing an assignment and figuring out where the color copier was. As my turn began, I desperately glanced at my peers. They stared blankly back. I swallowed and started saying something about Andre's difficulty working with other students. Suddenly, his mother burst into tears. She was shaking and the table trembled violently as she slammed her hands down repeatedly on its surface. I froze, watching this woman cry and smash her hands onto the tabletop. In between sobs she kept asking, "What does it mean, my boy doesn't get along well with others! *He* shouldn't be the one who has to change!" I tried to clarify to her what I had meant, but she continued on, speaking over me and not listening. "My boy has tons of friends at home." I realized that it really did not matter what I was saying: she wanted to yell from the moment we began our meeting.

I didn't realize how poorly we had treated her up to that point, or how poorly the school may have treated her community in the past. She was surrounded by white, college-educated teachers who had no experience with the challenges that she faced every day. We must have come across as unforgiving and clinical. As we conducted the business of the IEP meeting, we somehow forgot the human side of education. I saw this repeated again and again: parents would come in to the office only to be spoken down to by unfamiliar people who showed little empathy toward them or their child. Unfortunately, instead of working to bridge this gap, our school personnel had tacitly accepted this way of acting, deepening the hostility between our school and our constituency.

After this meeting I promised myself I would never let the business side of education get in the way of doing what was right. Andre and I eventually grew incredibly close. I learned about his love of all things Pixar and his desire to become an animator. He even shared his super-secret script with me that he had written about the wild ponies of Chincoteague Island. The following year, as a seventh grader, Andre would find me every day by the busses, rain or shine, to give me a hug and wish me a great day. This job can never be, and should never be, "strictly business" when we are dealing with young people who need our support, love, and friendship.

We have to acknowledge racial and cultural boundaries, because only by admitting they exist within a community can we hope to cross them. I slowly learned that how our school treated parents was a huge problem. Andre's mother saw me as someone who had no idea where she was coming from. She saw me as young, white, affluent, unprepared, and worst of all, hostile toward her son. She was right, at least partially. When she looked around that table she saw faces like mine, people who were not members of her community. She saw outsiders, people who simply did not belong and did not understand the troubles she faced every day.

A big part of understanding students and teaching them more effectively is appreciating where they come from and who influences them at home. This is essential in being able to communicate honestly and effectively with parents and children. Perhaps an outsider like me can never completely understand a different culture, but by doing some research and asking some questions, I learned about the communities my students came from. I realized that most of our students received free or reduced-price lunch. Many came from single-parent households and took on adult responsibilities such as packing lunches and taking care of younger siblings. In some of these homes, college was a pipedream—just graduating high school proved challenge enough.

Had I known what I know now, I would have educated myself about the community I was entering, maybe even before the year began. I would have driven around the neighborhoods—in the daytime and at night—where my students live. I would have made calls home to introduce myself. I wished I had met Andre's mother before our meeting. I would have kept more specific, objective notes on student behavior, rather than trying to conjure it from memory later when I predictably had forgotten many of the details. These small considerations would have helped me talk to the desperate parent sitting across from me. It was early in the year, but cultivating a better relationship with Andre would have helped as well.

I continued teaching my first year. All around me, the status quo continued. Around Halloween, I began to have problems with an African-American student named Marcus. This was a new development. Prior to Christmas, Marcus was an up-and-down student who, depending on the day, was either somewhat unmotivated or engaged. He thrived in group work, where he could use his strong personality to lead others. But after Halloween, Marcus started throwing things. Or crawling around on the ground. Or hitting other students. He didn't respond to my prompting, and I knew he could do better. I immediately started writing referrals and detentions for him. This only exacerbated the situation, and he began to do things that seemed designed to anger me. At the time, I was unclear of why his behavior had changed. I continued to write behavior referrals, hoping he would earn some sort of detention, but little or nothing happened as a result. I had no choice but to carry on.

I was surprised when his mother finally requested a meeting. I sat down with her, and we talked about what was happening in class, but she refused to believe me. I made sure to apply the lessons I had learned from my experiences with Andre. I was honest, yet positive, and portrayed my belief that we could improve Marcus's behavior. I had detailed notes. I didn't dwell on past problems; I focused on what we needed to do in order to improve. Still, she sat back, crossed her arms, and aligned herself with her son. She claimed that the other students were provoking him, and accused me of singling him out. After all, he never had any problems in the past, so it must be my fault. The principal was called in, as well as other teachers, whose assessment of his behavior matched my own. I waited for the principal to step in, support me, and discipline the student appropriately. Yet, as Marcus's mother refused to accept our assessment and her anger grew, the principal sat wide-eyed and silent. Nothing was accomplished, the parent left and I realized I had broken another unwritten rule of our school: solve problems on your own, or "don't rock the boat."

I later learned that my colleagues criticized me for the meeting. I had forced them to get involved in my problems, and I had been unable to pacify a disgruntled parent. I had rocked the boat and now other teachers had to pay the price. What I had assumed would be a supportive meeting quickly turned into fingers pointing directly at me. Instead of a meeting about what "we could do to help Marcus," it became a meeting about "what Mr. Kennedy could do to make the problem go away."

Marcus's mother continued to call and email me with increasingly negative messages. She believed that I was the reason for Marcus's low performance and bad behavior. She was in constant contact with the principal, and I began to receive calls or emails from her at least once a day. The principal asked me what was going on, clearly annoyed that I had not yet taken care of the situation. Meanwhile, Marcus knew he had complete support from home, and with few repercussions at school, he felt he had carte blanche to do as he wanted in my classroom. As his behavior deteriorated and his mother continued to criticize me, I became increasingly resentful of her. My emails, originally polite and positive, grew to be short and antagonistic. At the time, I felt this was a personal attack, and I resolved to defend myself.

The principal was called in again. Clearly angered by having to sit in on this meeting, he was willing to do anything in order to appease the parent. The principal and parent discussed the problem as if I were not present. My principal refused to address me directly. I felt ashamed and hopeless. The meeting resulted in a preliminary discussion of moving Marcus from my classroom, which was just what he had been wanting all along. I was disturbed that Marcus might get his way, and I was upset that the principal was bending to an overly critical parent. I was also discouraged that my colleagues saw meetings like this as a burden rather than an opportunity to help a struggling student and support one another.

The next day, Marcus called me a racist for asking him to take his hood down and pick his head off the desk. "You never talk to anyone else you racist!" he screamed. I knew I was not discriminating against Marcus, but his accusation stung. It felt as though my consistency and fairness were being put on trial. I also felt betrayed by my administrator who seemed willing to make me a scapegoat. An emergency meeting was called, and his mother demanded that he be moved from my classroom. The principal agreed without so much as asking, communicating, or acknowledging my presence. By moving Marcus, my principal was temporarily solving the problem, but he definitely was not fixing it. In fact, he was failing to support teachers, complying with unreasonable parent demands, and worst of all, avoiding the complex and volatile problem of race.

Our principal would do anything to avoid negative attention, and a student accusing a teacher of being a racist definitely fit that description. Teachers, too, willingly compromised their professional integrity to stay out of trouble and to prevent unpleasant but necessary conversations about race, our community, and our school. We needed to talk about it: in both of my memorable encounters with parents during my first year, race played a central role, if not as the source of the problem, then as a catalyst that heated our disagreements to the boiling point.

Since my first tumultuous year, things have changed. I am now in my fourth year at the same school, a department head, teacher mentor, and presenter at regional and state conferences. Each year has been a step in the right direction, and each step has been taken because faculty members have been willing to look at their practices. They have been humble enough to admit that we can do better. We have learned that rules such as "strictly business" and "don't rock the boat" have no place in a career defined by how much one can give and how much one can help. Not everything is perfect, but our culture is changing. Teachers have taken on the responsibility of examining our culture by naming unwritten rules, confronting engrained practices, and demanding better of themselves and their co-workers. Many teachers identified the problem with parents that I experienced during my first year as crucial for our improvement. As a result, our community involvement has skyrocketed, and we are able to support and educate parents about the school lives of their children.

FOR FURTHER DISCUSSION

1. What elements contribute to the culture of Elk Park?
2. What role does race play in the conflicts that Adam experiences with Andre and Marcus?
3. Which of Adam's strategies or techniques could you apply to your own teaching?

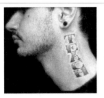

David Jagusch teaches high school English at an alternative high school in Detroit, Michigan. He earned his BA from Grand Valley State University and his MA from the University of Michigan. When he's not teaching and coaching his school's boys' varsity basketball team, David spends his free time writing poetry and playing guitar.

Lessons From the Slum
David Jagusch
Altius Academy, Kenya

Seventeen days after graduation, I was on an airplane headed to teach in the largest slum in Africa. Eighteen days after graduation, I was in a hospital, crying to go home.

It's hard to focus on the task at hand, to commit yourself to volunteer in a foreign region of the world, when you are vomiting and defecating in your pants—all from bad airline food. To make matters worse, the airline also lost my luggage, which was filled with the essentials of living in one of the planet's most impoverished regions—everything from malaria pills to Kerouac. I couldn't help but second-guess, and third-guess, even fourth-guess my decision to join a volunteer organization and come to this place. I spent the next three days in bed, a billet with a one-inch mattress, the wooden slats rearranging my spine as I rolled and sweated and dry-heaved and laid waste to the two extra pairs of underwear I had in my carry-on. I couldn't eat, I couldn't sleep, but I could cry. I came here to teach, but I had to first become a student; I had to learn life in the slum, and what better way than by lying in my own shit.

I lived in a home no more than a five-minute walk west of the slum, staying with a Kenyan family and a mesh of other volunteers also working through the volunteer organization: doctors, med students, and others giving time from their lives in hopes of extending the lives of those in the slum. As soon as my legs agreed, I began to explore. I tried to hide that I was gagging from the smell of the slum, my stomach still not quite right from the food poisoning. The composition of soil content was as follows: fifty percent human shit, twenty percent rotting garbage, ten percent animal shit, ten percent charcoal and ash, eight percent tears, and two percent earth. The passageways connecting thousands upon thousands of shanties formed a maze running up and down gelatinous hills, most not wide enough for two people to stand side by side. I tripped over sickly dogs gnawing on trash, whimpering next to roosters and chickens fastened with rusted bicycle chains to shanty walls, all surrounded by jungle-vine clotheslines dripping with clothes in the hot sunlight, decorating the slum in colors of brown, red, blue, green, and gray. The Kibera inhabitants responded to my presence differently, some looking away with indifference, continuing to go about their duties, recognizing that I did not belong. They cared only about the coming rain, which will cause their founda-tions to stink and flood. The children pointed and shouted *mzungu*, white person, while others repeatedly exclaimed *hellohowareyou?* When I responded, they only smiled, stared, snorted, and kept walking.

Altius Academy was a twelve-minute walk from my home-stay at a medium jaunt. The school served babies to grade eight, about 200 altogether. There was another volunteer placed at the school along with me, Laura, an Alaskan native who helped fundraise and supported various programs at the school. We would leave for the slum at quarter to eight, with classes commencing on the hour. After crossing railroad tracks and passing a half-dozen shanty homes that were eaten by fire, the men and women propping up scraps of sheet metal with half-burnt pieces of wood, we would wind our way along the main road wrapping around the northern portion of Kibera. We passed shops and street vendors and women selling fried bread, and pubs serving homebrew, and welders and butchers, all smelling of diesel, charcoal, and waste. Then taking a sharp right that cut through the muscle of Kibera, we would reach the school that consisted of three small buildings with sky-blue roofs, two with classrooms and a gathering area, one with a kitchen and empty space. An open area behind the buildings served as a soccer field, next to which was an uneven, shattered concrete slab with makeshift bas-ketball nets and a patch of tilled soil for a garden to provide food for the students. All of this sitting upon a small rise—Kenya is full of hills and slopes—overlooking the main area of the slum. Directly behind the school, a garbage pile taller than the school building.

After a week or two, the children grew accustomed to me, and they spent time after class asking questions about America: about the food, my life, my trip to Kenya, and President Obama. They were concerned about cabbage—whether Americans ate it, if I ate it, if we liked it in the States, how it's prepared—and they all echoed the sentiment: "Aren't we all lucky for cabbage?" They wanted to know about beans and rice and *mandazi*, *chapati*, and *ugali*. They could not imagine life without their cornmeal-based dishes, even wanting me to bring some back to the States to share. With elbows on their desks, heads on their hands, they looked up to the front of the room where I stood at the teacher's desk, perching myself on the edge for relaxed conversation, not the style of the typical strict Kenyan class-room instruction. They were fascinated by the fact that I owned my own car, that I could drive and didn't walk everywhere—"A big car or small car?" Very small I said, leading to the topic of public transportation, them thinking I owned my own airplane and that's how I came to be in Kibera, puzzled that I had to pay so much money to fly back and forth. Life is strange when people have money, they said.

After three or four weeks, my luggage finally arrived. To celebrate, I went to a Kibera restaurant for a heaping bowl of beans and *skooma* (a spinach-like cooked substance) and *chapati*, then from the market I purchased beer to have with din-ner and the evening. Walking into the Kibera restaurant, I received strange looks, my white skin already queer on the slum streets, and my visiting a local slum establishment beyond the comprehension of some locals. "Look at this *mzungu* coming to eat with us," one said as he stood from his table, staring with eyes wide and eyebrows down as I entered. Should I leave? Will trouble start? Is this guy looking for it? Maybe I should have left, but instead I said, "Beans and *chapatti*," and sat down to eat.

After about a month, I felt comfortable. My stress level was down, and I was teaching the full English course load at Kibera, alternating days between even-numbered grades and odd. I decided to take a weekend excursion of outreach service that was sponsored through the volunteer organization. Leaving the city by van and heading into rural Kenya, I noticed that the buses had disappeared, replaced by donkeys pulling carts with fifteen-year-old boys standing on two-wheeled teeter-totters, surfing over every rock, hole, and ditch like waves in the Pacific, with one arm bent out backwards for balance and the other swinging a whip or lash in the air, guiding one, two, or even three donkeys. Winding down the mountainside sliding along the borders of the Rift Valley, we passed a gray-coated baboon striding slowly uphill, and I could only imagine that his goal was to hitch-hike into the city in hopes of seeing a long-lost aunt about prospective business opportunities. We stopped alongside a moldy wooden outlook over the valley, with a gift shop full of sculptures of elephants and beaded jewelry. I looked down across the African country, seeing towns, camps, and areas of open, beautiful country, with mountains on the horizon in a blanket of haze. We made it down into the rift and then drove through a small town, the road jutting back into the country.

After another thirty minutes of driving, we reached the KCC community, a small plot of land along a country road, its school and kitchen built by past volunteers to provide slum children in the area with a free education and a meal for the day. The volunteers in my organization had donated money to expand the school to more grade levels, and the result was a new set of buildings. Here, out in the country, there weren't many children who were able to speak English well, a noticeable difference from those in the city. Playing, though, they still loved to do, demanding to be picked up and swung around, carried on my back and shoulders until they began hitting and kicking over who got to go next. After dancing and running and sack races, it was time for class to begin. I was assigned to grade three, to teach their daily mathematics lesson. I wrote problems of sums and differences on the blackboard, the students copying them down in their exercise books, one at a time coming up to answer a question in chalk as the entire class sang a rehearsed song of congratulations to every pupil who answered correctly. At the end of the lesson, I played with the children, snapped pictures of boys giving the lens a thumbs-up and girls shyly holding my hand. Before we left, the founder of the KCC project school, a New Zealander with sun-burnt nose and dirty legs, painted our hands and imprinted them on the side of a newly built classroom, freshly painted yellow, with our names underneath each print. It was, he said, a place to remember all the hands that have helped his dream and the dreams of each child there. These were classrooms constructed in a cornfield, providing children with infinite somethings in the middle of a thousand nothings.

The next day we made our way to a roadside town outside of Naivasha. There was an IDP camp not far down the road, located just past the town's outskirts. Our first stop in Naivasha was a bulk-food grocery store, where we purchased a couple hundred kilos of rice, flour, and fat, plus bags of suckers for the children. We heaved the bags into the van's trunk, then took them to a local hotel that allowed volunteers from our organization to package the food on their front porch. I scooped pitchers of flour from the hundred-kilo sacks into clear plastic bags, two others doing the same with the rice, two more carving up the fat from one gigantic slab into smaller chunks that could be readily used for cooking. Once the few large bags were broken down into a couple hundred little ones, we drove two miles down the road until we reached a grassy pasture full of weeds, cows, and goats. From a distance one could see a white, solid line in the middle of the plot. The line was a mass grouping of handmade tents: the IDP camp. Internally Displaced Persons, thousands of them the result of violence from the 2007 election, neighbors turning against one another, tribes who had lived in peace for years becoming enemies, killing and looting, plundering, stealing, squatting, and raping, all in the name of political opposition.

Many of the people forced to reside in the camps actually have homes, land, and possessions elsewhere in the country but have no way of getting them back. They are forgotten in their own country. Some of the tents came from the UN. Most of the tents were nothing more than grain sacks, torn open and sewn together with long ropes made from weeds collected in the surrounding grasses, muddy sticks and twigs for support, most no more than six feet high, the largest about seven by seven. There were no trees around to stop the wind, leaving the tents to whip and shudder, snapping and exposed.

Before passing out rations at the first section of the camp, we made a visit to the home of a fifty-year-old woman living with her husband and five children under the quivering sacks. Blind in one eye, she invited the six of us in. We clustered inside, forming a tightly packed circle sitting on the ground or on upturned buckets with our legs pulled to our chests. She wasn't able to speak English, so Izzo, a Kenyan social worker employed by our organization, sat with us and translated. Sitting with her hands in her lap, the woman told us where in the country she had come from and how she had lost the family farm. Izzo pointed to a handmade oil lantern, explaining how even one small flame produced enough smoke to blacken the grain-sack ceiling of the tent, melting the plastic twine and emitting a toxic fume as it did so. The jerry-cans some of us were sitting on were used to collect and store water from a well three kilometers from the camp. The cans, taken from an old chemical plant, once held toxic waste, which now mixed with their drinking and bathing water, causing the people to suffer from burning skin, tongues, and throats.

We then proceeded to passing out the food from the van. Two volunteers took all of the children away temporarily, luring them with sweets we brought for them. Izzo said it's better with them not around during the distribution. I remember wondering why: were they simply a distraction with so many of them running to and fro, or maybe it was more for the parents' benefit so their children didn't have to see the sadness in the lips and fingers of grown men and women standing in line, unable to provide for their own families, getting handouts. I noticed a variety of responses as we passed out the food: old women with old teeth and gums full of holes and brown stains smiling, saying *asante*—thank you—*asante sana*—thank you very much; young mothers, portraits of gloom, full of sickness; bachelors and fathers, both with blank faces and shame faded to indifference.

A few hundred yards away was a second section to the camp. As at the first, we made a home visit before distributing the food. The tent belonged to a mother of four: three boys out working somewhere, anywhere, in town or on a nearby farm that day to try and make a few shillings, and one four-year-old girl with crusted mucous covering her upper-lip and chin. She hung onto my legs as I sat on an upturned bucket, and she laughed uproariously when I tickled her belly and under her arms. The mother was able to speak some English, more than the last. She had lost both parents, both grandparents, and her aunt. She ran, along with her husband and babies. We didn't meet her husband, and I didn't feel comfortable asking whether or not he was still alive. Izzo explained that this woman seemed to be suffering from clinical depression. With no money for a doctor or medicine, she lifted up a scalded pot full of branches, roots, twigs, bark, and leaves floating in grayish-brown water, a traditional remedy for what was ailing her. She boiled the contents then drank the broth, hoping for at least temporary relief. There was a pile of weeds in one corner of the tent, thick stalks of fibrous strands that looked tough enough to make a towrope. Without enough food to go around, she cooks the weeds gathered from out in the pasture where the camp sets, mixes them with the little rice she has, and serves it to her children despite their protests of taste, smell, texture, and inability to chew or go to the bathroom afterwards.

The camp was located just down the road from a town that was a giant truck stop. Drivers transported everything from petroleum to cornflower. It's a welcoming place to girls desperate for money. With nothing else to do and nowhere else to work, they become prostitutes for the truckers passing through. What was worse was that they couldn't even share the money they earned with their families, because then questions would arise about its origin. Instead they would bury their money in the ground, or buy extra food in town for themselves and maybe a friend, or make themselves more appealing with new clothes and lipstick. When medical clinics visited the camps providing free HIV/AIDS testing, almost all the males went, just to make sure, but none of the girls did. They'd rather not know what's been given to them from countless nights spent in sweaty truck beds. There was an eleven-year-old girl in the camp who was expecting. I don't know what the others were thinking on the ride back to the home-stay, but I was discouraged

by the human race for creating or allowing such hopeless situ
world survive? How do those in the camps survive? How /
   Soon after, during lunch period one day at Altius Acad
work in the teachers' office, a small room containing two w
ken chairs and an open door to let in the sunlight. As I tried to wo
teachers caned damn near fifty students for the crime of speaking Swahili,
native language, on school grounds. As in most Kenyan schools, Altius Academy
permits only English. The teacher held the cane in his hand, a long shard of plastic
with a raised ridge down the middle to provide the maximum stinging effect.
He took each child by the hand, looked calmly into the child's eyes, like a Kibera
butcher at a meat counter, and asked, "How many do you want?"

I still I can't get over his tone of voice, asking as if the choice of how many
times he was going to strike them was a gift. None of the children dared to say
a figure below three, for an unreasonable offer was met with extra and increasingly severe hits. Most of the children responded quietly, the teacher making
them repeat loudly what he said. I think he wanted to hear their voices shake.
Then, after asking them if they wanted three or four slashes, he had them pull
their shorts and dresses taut over backs of their thighs so that his cane swing felt
all the more painful on their backsides. He didn't do consecutive hits in a typical
one-two-three fashion; he hit one . . . pause . . . wait . . . two . . . pause . . . wait . . .
three . . . pause . . . release. The pauses allowed the painful sensation to sink in
from leg to brain to tears. He held their arms tight against their bodies to stop
their natural reaction to raise their arm up to block the cane. This also served to
hold their bodies straight and rigid; if they were able to arch, wriggle, and curve
their bodies then they increased their potential to dull the lightening-flash cracks,
which to him was unacceptable.

I tried my damnedest not to gape and gawk, protest written all over my face,
and buried my nose in the book in front of me, twisting and biting the binding to
hold my tongue, pages rustling from my shaking hands as I began breathing harder,
big in-outs getting louder as the girls sucked in shrieks and the boys tried to act
older than seven years, trying to be stoic while others freely let out wails and tears
and jerks. I started to tear up as they stared at me through their own wet eyes with
quivering chins and knees. I began gagging. I was about to have my lunch come
up, not only in reaction to the sight in front of me but also in reaction to the other
half-dozen teachers present; it was my response to their response. All around me,
teachers were raucously laughing at each child's reaction. The loudest whooping
came when the teacher became overzealous and gave one strike too hard, bringing instant tears and howling from one of the older boys. When the teachers all
laughed, he let this one go with only the one hit. Between laughs, they talked to
each other—in Swahili—right in front of the jittering children waiting for lashing,
not heeding the irony that such talk on school grounds was the very reason why
the children now had welts, bruises, and bloody scabs. The instructor handing out
the beatings asked certain students to give him his "special handshake," so they held

heir tiny hands palm up as he slashed their tender skin instead of the back of
ir thigh. Lightheaded and sweaty under my shirt, I stumbled out of the room
nto the sun and found a corner in which to huddle and cry.

Why didn't I say anything? Why didn't I stand and scream and take that cane
and snap it across my knee? I'm a teacher, and part of my job is to look out for
the well-being of my students: not just educationally, but physically, mentally, and
spiritually. Why? Because I was told during my orientation that things are done
differently here, and that some things that happen in Kenyan schools are simply a
part of the culture, and that no matter how uncomfortable they made me, there
was simply nothing that I could do to change their way of living. It had been done
that way forever. So should I have accepted this as nothing more than a cultural
difference? I still complained, but while it was actually happening, I did nothing
except run away. To this day I still consider myself a coward.

As weeks continued to pass, I consciously spent more time getting to know
my students while at school, eating lunch with them instead of the teachers, pur-
posely not finishing my rice and telling them I was full, giving them something
extra to divide among themselves, a few grains to add to their plates of beans and
maize, anything to help fill in the voids in their stomachs. They begged me to
tell them more stories about home, about the cities, family, friends, schools, and
students. They wanted to know how different the rest of the world was, and if
there were any similarities in which to find hope. To them it all sounded so much
like a romantic fairy tale, each one of them with a different picture being painted
in their heads of the land over there. They were surprised when I told them that
America was also full of poverty—that not every place was shining and rich, the
image that the U.S. still tries to use as a marketing scheme trying to inspire the
rest of the world to follow its example.

It was often the most minute of details that left the largest impressions on me.
One afternoon while grading standard fifth-grade compositions, I came across a
written line that encompassed the Kibera child psyche: "If I grow up I want to
be like my parents." Not "when I grow up," not even "while," but "if," a personal
declaration frankly stating that their existence, let alone any sort of future, is not a
certainty. It was an unconscious but telling choice of words. Life being what it is, it
was just as possible, if not more possible, to die young than to survive until adulthood. There was no concept of premature death because, in the slum, death finds
its way just the same in a babe's coughing lungs or a grandfather's failing heart.

That one word made me realize that these children already held, deeply seated
in their minds, a truth that takes philosophers a lifetime to discover: life is fragility
and uncertainty. I now teach high school in Detroit at an alternative high school,
educating students that many consider the worst of the worst. I see this same
fragility and hopelessness. I see this same waste. It transcends oceans. Thousands
upon thousands of people lose opportunities because they are deemed unfit for
one reason or another, socially, economically, or racially. It doesn't matter if you're
in the ghettos of the United States of the slums of Africa.

FOR FURTHER DISCUSSION

1. In this narrative, David describes his first month teaching at Altius Academy, a world away from Western civilization and schools. How does David gain cultural competence in this setting?
2. What terms or ideas from our discussion of school culture can help us understand Altius Academy?
3. David writes that the KCC school, constructed by a volunteer organization, offered children "infinite somethings in the middle of a thousand nothings." Explain.
4. In the final paragraph, David likens his current school, an urban alternative high school, to the school in Kenya. Is this a fair comparison, in your opinion?

 After a 20 year career in the corporate world, Blaine earned his BA and teaching credentials at Grand Valley State University. He most recently taught at a school for underprivileged youth in western Michigan. When not teaching, Blaine enjoys reading, cooking, traveling, writing, and following his beloved St. Louis Cardinals. He and his son Connor live north of Grand Rapids.

Life Skills
Blaine Sullivan
Jefferson Alternative School

Everybody's first teaching job is challenging. Teaching is so difficult under the best of circumstances—if we're able to get it right, that is—and there is so much to learn. To say that college doesn't prepare us is often used as an indictment of our schools, but there simply *isn't* any way to really prepare us for every challenge that is headed our way.

For years, I had believed there was a teacher inside of me, and I tamped down the impulse to pursue it. The time just wasn't right: I had a family, a mortgage, and I worked too many hours already. How could I possibly even think about going back to school at my age? Finally, at the tender age of forty-something, I decided to take the plunge. I figured I could do it in three years and be settled in to a new career by the time I was fifty, with a teaching career of about twenty years if I remained healthy. What could possibly go wrong?

Friends raised eyebrows and asked if I had really thought about this. Yes, I assured them. Many people's response was, "Good luck finding a job when you're done." Thanks for your support. One of my friends cut right to the chase. "Why don't you do your mid-life crisis like most normal guys and go out and buy a red sports car? You could even go get a fake tan and bleach your hair. That way if it doesn't work out you can sell the car, shave your head, and wait for winter. Nobody will remember your fanciful adventure a year from now." Sage advice, I assured him. I ignored it. Classes were great. I loved the academic rigor and poured myself into every assignment. Often the only person in the room that could conceivably be regarded as a peer was the professor, and even so, I was often the oldest person in the room. One of my first instructors was a teacher at a local public school, and in time she began to urge me to do my student teaching in her classroom. We kept in touch, and I received my placement with her two years later. I kept working at my regular job, though I cut back on hours in anticipation of student teaching.

Two weeks before I was to begin, the earth shifted beneath my feet. My wife, Darcy, called and told me to meet her at the hospital; some blood work had come back abnormally, and they needed to admit her. The next day the doctor told us she had acute myeloid leukemia; that evening they would start chemo. Once in remission, Darcy would need a bone marrow transplant. I called my advisor at the College of Education and my mentor teachers to pull the plug on student teaching; Darcy was hospitalized for most of the next seven months. In time, she recovered enough for me to consider finishing my degree, but it seemed teaching was out of the question. We had planned to switch over to her medical insurance to let me focus on student teaching without having to work another job. But complications from her bone marrow transplant kept Darcy from working. So, I graduated without being certified, and soon after, I started a graduate program that allowed me to work and get certified simultaneously. All the gears meshed at the right time, and I spent the next year taking classes, student teaching for a full school year, and working at night to keep our medical insurance. Finally, that spring, I was certified to teach English by the State of Michigan. The job market was tough, and though I applied for lots of teaching positions, I impressed no one sufficiently to grant me an interview. I worked as a sub, and found I enjoyed not just high school but middle school as well. I looked forward to each day's challenge, not knowing what might come my way, and soon had my calendar booked through the end of the school year, as teachers apparently liked the job I was doing in their classrooms. In the fall I began subbing, but by mid-September we got news that Darcy's leukemia had relapsed. She began treatments immediately. In the midst of this I got a call to come interview for a teaching position. It was a different kind of school than I'd imagined working in, but after doing some research I liked the mission of the school and believed that the challenge would be good experience. The first interview went well, and I was called back for a second, which consisted entirely of a panel of students chosen by the faculty. I'm fairly confident in my ability to interview well, but this made me nervous. I knew that students have an innate ability to detect any hint of insincerity or bluster, but I felt I'd be fine as long as I answered everything frankly and honestly. A month passed, and I learned that they hired another candidate. One day, however, I got a call to come in for the final interview, this time conducted by administration of the school. I had not mentioned my wife's health problems to that point, and I didn't plan to. During the interview one of the panelists asked, "How well do you think you handle stress?" Here was an opportunity to separate myself from any other candidates, but it involved some risk. I took a deep breath. "Let me tell you about the last three years," I began, and briefly recapped my story. "Today, as soon as I leave this interview, I'm going back to the hospital to sit with my wife and wait for the results of her latest bone marrow biopsy. We don't know what it's going to show—remissions or more leukemia. You could say my stress level is pretty high today, but I'll leave it to you to judge how well I am handling it." I got a call the following day, offering me the job.

First years are difficult for almost everyone in teaching. The upheaval in my personal life made a stressful year more difficult by orders of magnitude. Before I accepted the job, Darcy and I discussed whether it was a good idea to start my teaching career in such trying circumstances. We made a list of pros and cons, discussed it some more, and came to the decision that all of the reasons not to begin teaching were based on fear: fear of her worsening health or even death, fear of dividing my attention between the job and Darcy and failing to do justice to either one, and fear of having eventually to choose between my job and family. It became clear that these fears would be present for as long as Darcy was living, and as she told me, "I didn't sign up for all of the sacrifices we made to get to this point just to chicken out because of something that might happen. Whatever's going to happen, will. Go for it. You'll be a great teacher, and you're a great husband and dad. This is what we've wanted for a long time." The only alternative we could see was to wait until she was gone to make the move, and we didn't expect that to happen anytime soon, so the only logical way to go was forward.

My school, Jefferson, is a residential school that welcomes students aged sixteen to twenty-four from disadvantaged circumstances. Most of the students come from Detroit, Flint, and Cleveland. Approximately eighty percent are African American. About three-quarters have been unsuccessful in previous educational settings, and one of the chief missions is to assist them in the completion of either a high school diploma or GED. The other main goal is to provide job training to prepare them for an entry-level position in one of several different vocations: culinary arts, carpentry, nursing assistance, facility maintenance, office work, security, and medical office support. They work through the program at their own pace, and a highly motivated student can complete it in a matter of months; others linger for up to two years. Not all are successful, but they have a remarkably high rate of graduation and employment.

I was hired as an academic interventionist, working with other faculty members to identify students who had or were in danger of falling behind. Through one-on-one meetings with individual students, students and other teachers, or a team of staff members including teachers, residential advisors, and counselors, we would confront the barriers to success as we saw them and try to arrive at a solution that met the needs of us all, most critically those of the student. Often the students participated actively in the meeting, explaining why they thought their performance or behavior had not met our expectations, and working with us to correct the problem. Sometimes, students were completely uncommunicative, not responding to anything asked of them, staring at the floor or glaring at one or another or at us. Almost all of Jefferson students have had difficult lives prior to enrolling in our program. Many have undiagnosed learning disabilities or emotional impairments that go a long way toward explaining, if not always excusing, low academic performance or disruptive classroom behavior. I was shocked at how willing many of the students were to discuss what they had been through. Students told me stories of cruel neglect and horrific abuse. Some had been routinely raped from a very young age; others had assumed the role of a parent to younger siblings while still preteens themselves. Most had struggled in school for a variety of reasons, and few had completed ninth or tenth grade, let alone graduated. Quite a few students had been or aspired to become gang members at some point in their lives; several had sold drugs at one time or another, and it seemed that the vast majority had been regular drug users as well. I suspect that the abuse, coupled with the bleak economic circumstances, had a great deal to do with their decision to self-medicate with drugs or alcohol. One of the most heartbreaking admissions I heard from a student was, "Until I came here, I never knew an adult who really gave a damn about me." Such comments were not common, but I have heard them more than a few times. The school building itself is an old public high school that has had an extensive remodeling in recent years. It is a fully modern facility, with computers and web access in each classroom, along with projectors and document cameras available for whole-group instruction. Class sizes are kept small, usually between twelve and sixteen students, because so many need individual attention and because of the behavior of so many of the students. In addition to classrooms for both academic and vocational instruction, we have a recreation facility, health and wellness center, and a cafeteria that serves three meals a day, seven days a week. Students live in dormitories on campus, and much of their time and activities are structured to minimize opportunities for aberrant behavior—though where there's a will, there's a way. They are restricted to campus when they first arrive and are gradually allowed more privileges as they demonstrate the ability to adapt to and follow the rules and norms of campus life. Since students arrive and depart each week, there is a system of support and mentoring that occurs organically; more experienced students are housed with new students to help them adapt. Sometimes, of course, this arrangement has the opposite effect. An eager arrival with a positive attitude can quickly be soured by the influence of a jaded, negative roommate.

The first thing one notices about the students is how *loud* they are. This is due to a number of factors. First is the desire of many teens to make themselves noticed. In addition, working-class African Americans in particular seem culturally inclined to talk more loudly and demonstrably than other groups. During the fifteen-minute breaks between class periods, the din can become deafening, despite the constant redirection of staff to use "indoor voices." Since so many of our students have not been socialized to display the same level of deference and respect for others that broader society favors, the noise level tends to ratchet ever higher.

Nor does it subside once class begins. My manner is fairly laid back, but simply standing up in front of class does not convey the message that it's time to be quiet. Over time, my approach has become firmer, but even a martinet would have difficulty. I learned that a gentle but firm style works best, not unlike holding a hamster in your hand: relax too much and he will escape, but squeeze too tightly and he will bite back. The students are much more interested in their own conversations than they are about learning math or reading skills. That is true of most students in most schools, but our students either lack the experience to understand how things work or simply don't care enough to subordinate their immediate desires to the longer term good of learning math skills. Often the attention spans are vanishingly small and vary greatly from one day to the next. One of my colleagues once said that they are like preschoolers in adult bodies, driven by teenage hormones. Moods, attitudes, and motivation levels change daily or hourly, more mercurial than I have ever seen.

One student of mine, Latonya, was particularly moody and had repeatedly been written up for using profanity in class. I hadn't had much trouble with her but knew her reputation well. One day on the way into work, I heard a story about the Civil Rights Act of 1964; it was the anniversary of its being signed into law. Figuring that my students were always interested in delaying the start of math class (I had transitioned from interventionist to math teacher), I thought it might be interesting to talk a little about this and hear from them what it meant to them. My first-hour class were all African-American students, and so I began. About two minutes into my lesson, Latonya burst out, "Why the fuck are you talking about this in a fucking math class? Does this have anything to do with math? I come in here every day to learn math, and you stand up there *talking about something that doesn't even apply to me!*" I tried to explain why this should matter to them, but by then the genie was out of the bottle and I knew a losing battle when I saw one. I transitioned quickly to multiplying fractions.

Students sometimes sought extra help, which I was always happy to provide. One young woman struggled with math, which she still needed to graduate from high school. She came to me after I redirected her for sleeping during an assembly. She explained that since I cared enough to wake her up, maybe I also cared enough to help her with math. She came to my room during lunch, after class, and even asked me to correct the problems she worked on in her spare time. After several months of relentless work, she passed her math requirement and literally ran to my classroom, burst in, and shouted "I passed! I passed! Mr. S., I passed!" and gave me a hug. Another student sought help from anyone who would help before she took her GED math test. When I began working with her she added on her fingers, but a few months later she was confidently solving algebra problems. She was committed to her own success and asked for help when she needed it. I can't think of a better formula for success.

I found many of my students unable to make the connection between effort, preparation, and success. Late last fall, I asked one of the students in a GED class why he wasn't working on anything.

"I got nothing to do," he replied.

"Then why are you in this class?"

"I passed the pretest yesterday, and I take the state test (GED test in reading) next week. So I'm all good."

I knew him well enough to know he was a sports fan. "Did the 49ers make the playoffs this year?" I asked.

He took the bait. "You know it. They going all the way."

"What do you think they're doing this week?"

A look of confusion crossed his face. "What do you mean?"

"Do you think they're practicing, or are they out relaxing by the pool?"

"Man, they putting in new plays, and lifting, and getting ready for next week's game. Don't you know nothing about football?"

I smiled and paused a couple beats for the connection to sink in. "Do you think you could do anything like that to get ready for your playoff game next week?"

He grinned and shook his head. "Ain't got nothing to do with it. This ain't football, man. I told you, I'm good."

Predictably, he did not pass the test, and two months later we had much the same conversation when he was scheduled to try again.

I discovered that many of the students did not see preparation as something that would help them improve their scores. To them it was a matter of luck, fate, or a good feeling. "I'm feeling it today Mr. S. I'm gonna pass it." Or more commonly, a look of discouragement on the day of a test. "Today just ain't my day. No way I'll pass." Too often the latter became a self-fulfilling prediction.

Part of the cause of problems for Jefferson students lies in the tremendous influence of commercial rap music and the culture it promotes. It emphasizes the need on the part of males to be tough, powerful, and often indifferent to the emotions and needs of those around them. For young women, nothing is more important than being sexually available to men. Whether or not our students truly buy into these stereotypes, they act them out almost constantly when they have an audience. There is a tension, I believe, between what they feel they should say and do and what the rap culture tells them. Mainstream rap also expresses and reinforces their antagonism toward law enforcement; most of the male students have experienced police discrimination themselves or know a friend or relative who has. I have been told that I cannot possibly understand because I haven't had the experiences they have, and I think they're absolutely correct. I always try to explain that I am not trying to diminish or devalue those experiences, but to give them the tools to succeed in society.

Our students can be quite rude, to each other and to staff. I have been called many names. I have learned that the f-bomb can be used as every single part of speech. I listened in amusement one day as a student ranted about what an awful teacher I am. "How can anyone stand to get up every morning and go to a job they are so *bad* at?" he asked repeatedly. Less than two weeks later, he asked me to explain something he hadn't yet grasped. After doing so, and he confirmed his grasp of it by practicing it on a dozen or so problems, he exclaimed, "You are the only person that has ever explained that in a way I can understand. I get it now! You are the best teacher ever! Did you hear that, everyone? Listen to this man— he is a *great* teacher!" All spoken without a trace of irony, and to my tremendous satisfaction.

I also learned never to argue with a student. I knew this before, but at the other schools where I had subbed or student taught I had recourse to explain my thinking if someone questioned something. Students might consider my argument and even accept it if I made it compelling. At Jefferson, though, students resisted mightily, and I found it was easier and more effective to simply agree and return to the topic at hand.

"Mr. S, math is stupid."

"It is, isn't it? So what would you do next on this problem?"

"You have an ugly tie on today Mr. S."

"Yes it is. I picked it out just for you. Do you need to multiply or add first?"

"Why do we have to have all these rules? They're stupid."

"We all have rules to follow. Yes, some of them seem stupid. Which number do you need to multiply next?"

During my first year at Jefferson, my wife's health continued to worsen. During one hospital stay, she was walking to the bathroom when her femur snapped and she fell. She would never walk normally again; two surgeries, many months, and countless hours of therapy enabled her to walk a few steps with the aid of a walker. Two months after the femur fracture, she developed pneumonia, blood poisoning, and an acute infection that had her in ICU for twelve days. We doubted she would survive, but she did. The administration, faculty, and the students at Jefferson were incredibly supportive of me when I was at school, and even when I chose to take time off to be with her.

Much of our time teaching focused on life skills, or what one colleague called "middle class values." These lessons included such skills as how to get along with others in the workplace, and what is appropriate to wear and say and do. A major battle was to keep students from putting their heads down and checking out during class. Generally speaking, most of our students saw nothing wrong with treating school like a cafeteria—they took what they want and left everything else. This included rules involving the dress codes, class behavior, effort, and substance abuse. If they felt the impulse to do something, they most often did it, at least for the first few months on campus. There were consequences, but some students reached the point where it no longer mattered to them. Disobeying gave them the sense of control, though most admitted that they had not been very successful when they allowed themselves to be governed by their impulses.

There was a lot of posturing and persona-making at Jefferson. Among the boys, this most often followed one of two tracks: they styled themselves as a tough-guy gangsta rapper or as the ultimate ladies' man. The former is targeted to the other boys; the latter to the girls. The tough guys will adopt a brooding affect and refer to themselves as "The O." (original gangsta), or a "savage." Most have tattoos, some with gang affiliations. Interestingly, I never once really felt threatened around any of the students, even when I broke up fights. Most of them were more interested in creating the *perception* of being tough rather than doing anything to prove it.

Part of the tough image was not being perceived as stupid. As a result, most students avoided asking for help, or being seen receiving help from a faculty member. For a time when I was doing interventions, word circulated among the students that anyone who went to see me for help was "slow" or "special ed." In truth, most of the interventions had more to do with behavior and motivation than academics per se, but that mattered little to the grapevine. Curiously, the culture from which so many of our students came seemed to dismiss educational achievement and to belittle those who earn it. Many of the classroom antics disappeared completely when I worked one-on-one with students. Without an audience, they were free to appear interested and engaged; but in front of their peers, dissing the system was the correct play.

Understandably, the culture at Jefferson took an emotional toll on staff and faculty. Turnover was high. The program ran year-round, so there was little time for teachers to recharge drained batteries. Successes were celebrated, and when students succeeded—and they did so in surprisingly high numbers—it was and is the greatest feeling possible for a teacher. Most of our students got it, eventually. Graduation was almost euphoric; for many it was their greatest achievement of their young lives. Though I was on leave of absence during graduation week, I left the hospital room long enough to attend the ceremony. It restored some of the energy that I had lost in previous months. Students who had been rude and obnoxious a few months before shook my hand and thanked me for getting them to this day. One young man eagerly waved me over to him and introduced me to his grandmother. "This man is the most important reason I'm here today," he told her, holding up his diploma.

Still, the daily grind at Jefferson became almost unbearable as Darcy's condition deteriorated. Most students knew what was going on, but I didn't make excuses because I didn't allow them to. When the leukemia returned once again, I understood that despite the last-chance endeavor to wipe out the disease with one more round of chemotherapy, the odds did not favor success. When she developed pneumonia two weeks later, I requested a leave of absence to spend as much time as I could with her. Her doctor wept as he told us there was nothing else he or anyone else could do for her, save making her comfortable. We said goodbye to our many friends at the hospital where she'd spent so much time—nurses, PA's, aides, and doctors—and we drove home one last time.

She died ten days later, on my birthday, surrounded by family and friends. The pain she'd felt for so long was mercifully gone. Her last week she had been inundated with scores of visitors; I turned no one away, because her friends were so dear to her. Though I had expected her death, indeed had spent countless hours thinking about what it would be like *someday,* I could not have predicted how hard it would be in the event.

I returned to work two weeks later. The first days were hard but tolerable. The hardest part came at the end of the first day when I was packing up my stuff to go home. "What am I going to tell Darcy when she asks how my first day back at work went?"

When I returned after Darcy's death, I explained to all of my students why I had been gone. Most were sympathetic, and I received several cards signed by many, many students. But the honeymoon with the students passed quickly. Soon they were back to their normal behavior patterns, rude comments, and lack of productivity. I could feel that my patience was wearing thin when a few students justified their inappropriate behavior with comments like, "You just don't understand—I got stuff going on. Real stuff, man. Life is hard." No kidding, I thought.

Sometimes it crossed the line from rude to grossly insensitive and hurtful. One day, a couple weeks after I returned, a student who was very close to completion—and had been boldly disruptive for several days—was the last one to leave class. It was the last hour of the day and it had been a difficult one for me. I heard the door close, and then immediately open again. Then the voice of Tyler, the student who had spent most of the hour talking. "Well, I think I'm going to go home now to be with my wife." I was too shocked to be angry. I knew who it was, though I didn't see him. I'm glad that he didn't say it to my face; I let it go for the time. The next day wrote him up and he was removed from the class and sent home.

I love teaching. I love interacting with students, and anticipating what each new day will bring. I knew it was going to be hard to go back to work after the funeral, but I felt it was the right thing to do. I decided I would not make any hasty decisions; I would give it a few weeks to see how it would go, and only then decide. My colleagues and the administration were very supportive, and encouraged me to hang in there. Within a month, I gave Jefferson notice of resignation, though the Tyler incident had very little to do with my decision. My son was struggling in school himself, and the emotional demands of teaching at Jefferson were so high that I simply had nothing left by the time I got home. My tank was empty every night, and it wasn't fair to my son to always draw the short straw. Working as a teacher while navigating the grieving process can be done; it happens every day. Perhaps if I had been teaching in another school, where student behavior was less challenging, I'd still be there. Almost certainly if I'd been further along in my career, it would have been easier to have made it through. My colleagues at Jefferson were amazing and encouraging, but they also told me after I'd made the decision that they didn't see how I could have stayed. As I've said, it's a tough place for a teacher to work. Paradoxically, when I returned to the school a few times to see people or pick up my paycheck, it was the most difficult students who came up to me to tell me how much they missed me, or thank me for help I'd given them.

For the time being, I am subbing when I want to work, and taking days off when I need to. The ability to focus solely on being a dad is gratifying, and I'm still in the process of healing as I write. I hope to find another teaching job. I believe I would be welcomed back at Jefferson anytime there was a vacancy, but I'm not sure I want to teach there again. Time will tell.

As driven as I was to become a teacher, it seems less important right now. My son is the most important factor, and as long as I can help him achieve to his capability, I will do that. I miss teaching when I'm not there. I very much want to have a classroom of my own again, with students who are eager to learn, and a subject about which I am passionate. All of these are not mutually exclusive goals. I now have experience as a teacher, and it is in a school that is recognized as a difficult teaching experience. No doubt I would get good references from Jefferson; all the administrators told me as much, and I believe them. The fire is still there—it just needs a little time to glow as brightly as it did a few months ago.

FOR FURTHER DISCUSSION

1. In what ways do Blaine and the students at Jefferson Alternative School defy traditional definitions of teacher and student?
2. Describe the school culture at Jefferson. What factors does Blaine suggest are responsible for this culture?
3. After a long journey to certification, Blaine lands his first job at an extremely challenging school and loses his wife during his first year of teaching. What does his story suggest about the teaching life you are undertaking?

3

SCHOOL CLIMATE

Introduction

Robert Rozema

Over the past decade, I have been inside of dozens of public schools in west Michigan. As a content area supervisor in a teacher certification program, I evaluate teacher assistants and student teachers completing their field placements in secondary schools of all kinds—middle and high schools, large and small, suburban, rural, and urban, impoverished and affluent, black, brown, and white. It is common for me to visit two schools on the same day, often within an hour or two. On these days, I sometimes experience a kind of whiplash, as I jolt between starkly contrasting schools within a short period of time.

An early morning observation might take me to Hillcrest Middle School, a diverse urban school that has hosted dozens of teacher assistants from my university. I have been to Hillcrest over forty times during the past three years, and I always leave feeling positive about the school. It begins in the main office, where the receptionists humor my request for a school map—my frequent visits have not improved my abysmal sense of direction. The hallways are clean, bright, and decorated with student projects. There are large, wide-open spaces for students to work together and to socialize. Without exception, the teachers at Hillcrest have welcomed assistants and student teachers from my university, mentoring and modeling with professionalism and care. The students share in the sense of community. At the beginning of every class, they are invited to share good news with classmates. The behavioral problems that sometimes characterize urban schools do not seem to exist here, thanks perhaps to a school-wide emphasis on discipline, order, and respect. Not everything is perfect, but the vibe is undeniably right.

My next visit later that morning, however, might be at Northern High School, a large urban school just a few miles down the road from Hillcrest. My trouble begins on the outside: the school has multiple entrances, all locked, and even after countless visits to the school I am forced to negotiate with a security guard in order to get in. Once inside, I sign in at the main office, where a receptionist eyes my video camera and tripod with suspicion, despite the permission I have obtained, painstakingly, from both the school and district administration. Here, the hallways are narrow and poorly lit. I notice two more security officers on my way up the stairs, and during my observation, a *code yellow* is announced over the intercom. My teacher assistant locks the door, draws the shades, and carries on teaching. Her cooperating teacher is excellent, but other teachers in this building have been examples of what *not* to do. Once, as I observed a teacher assistant at Northern struggle with a particularly disruptive class, her cooperating teacher leaned over, gestured at the misbehaving students, and whispered to me, "Crack babies." I know that the majority of teachers at Northern would be horrified by her behavior, but still, I cannot help but feel dispirited when I leave the building.

The contrast I am describing here could be understood as a difference in *school climate*. Like school culture, school climate is a big idea that can be difficult to define. In fact, as the opening chapter points out, school culture and school climate have been used interchangeably by educational researchers for many years. More recent research, however, has sought to distinguish the two terms, and most discussions of school climate now subsume it into the larger category of school culture (Van Houtte, 2005; Schoen & Teddlie, 2008). Even within this context, however, school climate differs from school culture in notable ways. To begin, school climate has to do with perception—how teachers, administrators, and students *perceive* their school environment. In this way, school climate is a psychological construct, subtly different from the more anthropological idea of school culture. And while school culture refers to a combination of numerous elements, school climate is used more holistically to describe the overall environment of a school. Hoy (1990) provided a helpful definition: "School climate is the relatively enduring quality of the school environment that is experienced by participants, affects their behavior, and is based on their collective perceptions of behavior in schools" (p. 152). In describing the school climate of Hillcrest and Northern, my opening examples, I could use single words: *healthy* or *positive* for Hillcrest; *unhealthy* or *negative* for Northern.

Of course, my perception of both schools is subjective and may not reflect how students, teachers, and administrators actually feel about their schools. Even after multiple visits to both campuses, I remain an outsider, and as such, I cannot see the whole picture. Moreover, even insiders—students, teachers, and administrators— have differing views on the climate of the school, and these individual perceptions are shaped by their experiences and contexts. Making broad statements about the overall environment of a school is, then, potentially problematic (Van Houtte, 2005; Van Houtte & Van Maele, 2011). What conclusions can we draw about my impressions of Hillcrest and Northern—not to mention the dozens of other schools that have evoked similarly strong responses from me? Or, to put it another way, if you are new to teaching, can you trust the gut feeling you get about your school as you pull into the parking lot, walk through its hallways, and unlock your classroom door?

In a word—yes. While your feelings about your school will always be subjective, there are several external factors that may be contributing to your positive or negative perception. The first of these is school safety. A safe school is one in which students and faculty feel physically, emotionally, socially, and intellectually secure. For many students, the fear of physical violence—most often in the form of bullying—is a daily reality, particularly in urban schools with impoverished populations (Mayer & Furlong, 2010). Not surprisingly, schools with more violence also have lower academic performance and increased absenteeism (Astor, Guerra, & Van Acker, 2010), both of which contribute to a negative school climate.

In this era of Columbine and Sandy Hook, both solidly middle-class schools, teachers can also feel physically unsafe at school. While only four percent of teachers nationwide are victimized by violence each year (National Center for Education Statistics [NCES], 2013), the presence of metal detectors, security guards, and lockdown protocols can make teachers uneasy. Media coverage of school shootings has escalated our fear of being harmed or killed at school. When individual teachers perceive a school to be dangerous, even when it is safe, the school climate can suffer (Roberts, Wilcox, May, & Clayton, 2007). In my experience at Northern High School, for instance, I encountered security guards and a lockdown procedure, both of which heightened my anxiety. In reality, these measures may indicate that the school is taking important steps to reduce school violence (Gregory, Cornell, & Fan, 2012).

Your perception of your school may also be influenced by the social, emotional, and intellectual security of your students. There is no greater threat to this security than bullying, a more pervasive and more severe problem than physical violence alone, though bullying often involves physical aggression. Bullying in all of its forms—physical, verbal, emotional, and cyber—has many harmful effects on its victims, damaging their ability to learn in the short term and increasing their chances of psychological disorders in the long term (Wolke, Woods, Bloomfield, & Karstadt, 2000). Notably, bullying also affects students who witness it—about two-thirds of all students, according to one study—making them more prone to range of mental and emotional disorders (Rivers, Poteat, Noret, & Ashurst, 2009). If you see bullying in your school, and particularly if the bullying goes unpunished, you may feel that your school is an unsafe environment for your most marginalized students.

Thankfully, research indicates that schools can take steps to reduce bullying. Schools with consistent rules and supportive adults have fewer incidents of bullying. When students perceive that rules are administered fairly and that adults will listen to them, the school becomes safer (Gregory, Cornell, Fan, Sheras, Shih, & Huang, 2010). In fact, these two factors—the structure of the school rules and the interpersonal relationships that a school fosters—form the *social system* of a school, a key part of its overall climate. In my visits to Hillcrest, I have noticed how well the social system works: school rules are explicit, governing in-class interactions (students stand to address the teacher) and out-of-class procedures (students walk on the right side of the hallway). Some of the teacher assistants I supervise have even complained about the rigidity of the rules, which after the freedom of college life can make Hillcrest seem like boot camp. But students also know that the teachers and administrator are interested in their lives and available to help, evident even in small classroom procedures, such as the sharing of good news. Gregory et al. (2012) labeled this kind of climate—an effective balance of structure and support—as *authoritative*. This is not to be confused with *authoritarian*, a school climate in which structure is overemphasized and support is nonexistent. Other possible school climates are *permissive*, which characterizes a school with no discipline but lots of support, or *indifferent*, a school without structure or support (pp. 402–403).

In addition to the safety and social system of a school, other more tangible factors may influence its climate. Most teachers recognize that the condition of their school building—new or old, well-maintained or in disrepair, orderly or chaotic—can affect its climate, but to date, little research has examined this connection. Some studies of the physical environment of schools have attempted to correlate the features of school buildings with incidents of school violence. One study conducted in Kentucky, for example, concluded that a disordered school environment was associated with an increase of teacher-reported crime (Wilcox, Augustine, & Clayton, 2006); another Michigan study found that students and teachers perceived *unowned* portions of the school building—public spaces such as bathrooms, for example—to be more dangerous than other locations in the school (Astor, Meyer, & Behre, 1999). Other research has found that a deteriorating school building can negatively affect student learning (Berner, 1993).

Another way of thinking about the physical environment of your school, however, might be to consider how its architectural design shapes the learning that occurs within its walls. Many public schools in America were built during the baby boom years following World War II. By the new millennium, the average age of a school was forty-two years, and forty-five percent of all schools were built in the period from 1950–1969 (NCES, 1999). Schools built during this era followed a basic formula that maximized utility and minimalized cost. Northern High School, for example, was constructed in the late 1960s. Like many school buildings of this era, it features individual, rectangle-shaped classrooms meant for twenty to thirty students. The chalkboard or whiteboard occupies one side of the room, and the teacher typically stands in front of the chalkboard to deliver lectures from behind a podium. Desks fit best when configured into long rows, impeding collaboration between students. Class materials are relegated to the side walls, typically stored in bookshelves and filing cabinets. Technology may be present—perhaps a television mounted into an upper corner, a data projector affixed to the ceiling, or a desktop computer—but it is controlled solely by the teacher. In addition, the teacher usually has a larger desk in the front or back of the room.

With little variation, the school as a whole is organized around these individual classroom containers, which branch off of narrow hallways that are typically segregated by discipline. In these types of schools, public spaces are utilitarian and limited: there is a gymnasium, an auditorium, a media center or library, and a cafeteria, but no other spots for collaboration or socialization. These kinds of buildings might be considered *factory schools*, and their architecture itself sends a message about learning. Factory schools "embody the transmission model of learning: the teacher has the knowledge, and in assembly line fashion transmits that knowledge to the students. Then students are tested as to whether they have retained the knowledge that has been presented to them" (Upitis, 2004, p. 20). To be sure, not every teacher in old school buildings lectures all of the time. Many use progressive, student-centered pedagogies, despite the architectural restrictions. Even when the desks are screwed to the floor, some teachers are managing to use collaborative learning.

But today, many new schools are built to reflect modern ideas about teaching and learning. The climate of these schools differs substantially from the factory schools of the last century, and if you are lucky enough to teach in such an environment, here are a few things that you might notice: first, the idea of collaboration is everywhere: there are large, open places where students can work together and socialize, along with a variety of multipurpose rooms for specific projects. The spaces are sometimes named with familiar, community-oriented language: the *living room*, the *backyard*, and the *town square* might all be located within a new school, alongside a cafe that provides nutritional snacks and beverages throughout the day. A new school may even adjust its schedule to encourage collaboration: a high school down the road from me, for example, has a period called *collaboration* built into its daily schedule. Collaboration also informs the way classrooms are laid out within the building—not in separate wings as in a factory school, but in interdisciplinary clusters around public spaces, a design that encourages cooperation between teachers in different subject areas. Teachers have multiple workspaces for planning with colleagues. Within classrooms themselves, collaboration is encouraged by modular furniture that can be arranged into any formation. The teacher is no longer alone at the front of the room: there are whiteboards on every wall for student and teacher use.

Students are also using technology, another key feature of new school architecture. In factory schools, student-accessible technology is typically restricted to stand-alone computer labs that house twenty-five to forty desktop computers. Teachers lose time traveling to and from the lab, which is always hot from the computers and noisy from the whir of their fans. Modern schools, however, spread technology throughout the school, doing away with isolated computer labs in favor of student laptops, netbooks, or, more rarely, tablets. This technology accompanies students from class to class (and often to their own homes), allowing for more meaningful integration of technology into all subject areas. A wireless network lets teachers and students share files, project content through data projectors, access media, and print materials via wireless printers located throughout the school. In its reliance on technology, the new school is what Kitchin and Dodge (2011) labeled *a code/space*—a social space that is created and mediated by software. The technology is everywhere, but ironically, it may be less noticeable than in a factory school.

Beyond the technology, you may also notice greater attention to features that have long concerned architects: natural lighting, traffic flow, green spaces, visual patterns, and more. If the hallmark of the factory school is the crowded, window-less hallway, the new school uses windows throughout the building to provide natural illumination throughout the school season. It provides multiple pathways to different areas, alleviating hallway congestion and noise. The enclosed stair-cases of the factory school have been replaced by wide, open stairs that are easy to access and easy to monitor. Green spaces such as open courtyards, gardens, and atriums are incorporated into the structure, providing views of nature and allowing students easy entrance to the world outside. Inside, rich visual textures replace the industrial cinder blocks of the factory school. Textures might include student artwork, school symbols, and visual allusions to local history or culture. All of these patterns are intended to stimulate the minds of students (Upitis, 2004). Taken together, the architectural features of a new school create a warm, inviting school climate that encourages student learning.

Whether you teach in a classic factory school or a new school, whether you are teacher assisting, student teaching, or in the early years of your career, it is important for you to gauge your school climate. We think the stories in this chap-ter will help you do so, chiefly by showing you how two new English teachers, Tami and Kristyn, learned to identify and respond to their own school climates. Before you read their stories, though, you may want to try one or more of the following exercises, designed to get you thinking and talking about the environ-ment of your school.

- **Write.** When we talk about school *climate*, we are using a metaphor drawn from meteorology and other scientific fields. Take a few minutes to describe your school using your own original metaphor. Go beyond "if your school was a tree, what would it be?" to find a deeper, more illuminating comparison. Then share your metaphor with your colleagues or classmates.
- **Role Play.** In a large or small group, assign one or more of the following roles to individual colleagues or university classmates: first-year teacher, substitute teacher, veteran teacher, freshman student, senior student, African-American student, and LGBT student.

  Colleagues: assuming that all individuals are instructors or students at the same school, answer the following questions: How do you survive in this school? How do you succeed in this school?

  Classmates: assign the same role (e.g., LGBT student) to all individuals, and using the context of your own field placement, answer the following ques-tions: How do you survive in this school? How do you succeed in this school?
- **Visualize.** On a separate piece of paper, draw a map of your classroom or school as a whole. The map may be realistic, with accurate representations of

desks, classrooms, and hallways, or it may be symbolic, with your choice of words/images representing the psychological/environmental aspects of your classroom or school building.

References

Astor, R. A., Guerra, N., & Van Acker, R. (2010). How can we improve school safety research? *Educational Researcher, 39*(1), 69–78.

Astor, R. A., Meyer, H. A., & Behre, W. J. (1999). Unowned places and times: Maps and interviews about violence in high schools. *American Educational Research Journal, 36*(1), 3–42.

Berner, M. M. (1993). Building conditions, parental involvement, and student achievement in the District of Columbia public school system. *Urban Education, 28*(1), 6–29.

Gregory, A., Cornell, D., & Fan, X. (2012). Teacher safety and authoritative school climate in high schools. *American Journal of Education, 118*(4), 401–425.

Gregory, A., Cornell, D., Fan, X., Sheras, P., Shih, T., & Huang, F. (2010). Authoritative school discipline: High school practices associated with lower bullying and victimization. *Journal of Educational Psychology, 102*(2), 483–496.

Hoy, W. K. (1990). Organisational climate and culture: A conceptual analysis of the school workplace. *Journal of Educational and Psychological Consultation, 1*(2), 149–168.

Kitchin, R., & Dodge, M. (2011). *Code, space: Software and everyday life.* Cambridge, MA: MIT Press.

Mayer, M. J., & Furlong, M. J. (2010). How safe are our schools? *Educational Researcher, 39*(1), 16–26.

National Center for Education Statistics (NCES) (1999). *How old are America's schools?* U.S. Department of Education. Retrieved from http://nces.ed.gov/

National Center for Education Statistics (NCES) (2013). *Indicators of school crime and safety: 2012.* U.S. Department of Education. Retrieved from http://nces.ed.gov/

Rivers, I., Poteat, V. P., Noret, N., & Ashurst, N. (2009). Observing bullying at school: The mental health implications of witness status. *School Psychology Quarterly, 24*(4), 211–223.

Roberts, S. D., Wilcox, P., May, D. C., & Clayton, R. R. (2007). "My" school or "our" school? The effects of individual versus shared school experiences on teacher perceptions of safety. *Journal of School Violence, 6*(4), 33–55.

Schoen, L. T., & Teddlie, C. (2008). A new model of school culture: A response to a call for conceptual clarity. *School Effectiveness and School Improvement, 19*(2), 129–153.

Upitis, R. (2004). School architecture and complexity. *Complicity: An International Journal of Complexity and Education, 1*(1), 19–38.

Van Houtte, M. (2005). Climate or culture? A plea for conceptual clarity in school effectiveness research. *School Effectiveness and School Improvement, 16*(1), 71–89.

Van Houtte, M., & Van Maele, D. (2011). The black box revelation: In search of conceptual clarity regarding climate and culture in school effectiveness research. *Oxford Review of Education, 37*(4), 505–524.

Wilcox, P., Augustine, M. C., & Clayton, R. R. (2006). Physical environment and crime and misconduct in Kentucky schools. *The Journal of Primary Prevention, 27*(3), 293–313.

Wolke, D., Woods, S., Bloomfield, L., & Karstadt, L. (2000). The association between direct and relational bullying and behaviour problems among primary school children. *The Journal of Child Psychology and Psychiatry and Allied Disciplines, 41*(8), 989–1002.

Tami Teshima graduated with a BA in English (Secondary Education) from Grand Valley State University. Since then, she has taught high school English and middle school language arts. Her teaching experiences have taken her to various places, from Northern Michigan to Cape Town, South Africa, to the gulf side of Florida. She now resides in San Jose, California, where she spends her leisure time hiking along oceanfront trails, eating good *pho*, reading great books, and obsessing over crafts on Pinterest that she will likely never attempt.

Loving and Leaving
Tami Teshima
Quest Alternative School

While many of my classmates sought to teach in beautiful school districts in posh suburbs or wealthy cities, I thrust myself into the teaching world desperately hoping to work with at-risk students. To me, these students were a forgotten part of our school systems. Off the radar and often lagging behind academically, at-risk students are the ones who are "let go" in order to meet adequate yearly progress (AYP), for poor behavior and a myriad of other social issues. I wanted to work with these students, the ones no one else wanted to teach, to help them foster a love (or at least a tolerance) for education. As an English teacher, I even dreamed of helping them to see the usefulness of literature.

My dream of working with at-risk kids came true during my student teaching semester. I was placed at Quest Alternative High School, an alternative school serving three districts in Northern Michigan. The school was a much better fit for me than the affluent high school where I did my student assisting the previous semester. Quest sat a mere fifty feet from a major traffic artery. The dilapidated building, a former furniture warehouse, had been halfheartedly converted to a school by the districts that fed into it. Smelling dank from the black mold the landlord insisted was harmless, and lacking appropriate heat and ventilation during Michigan's bipolar seasons, Quest's worn walls provided bare-bones accommodation to its 120 attendees.

Ranging in ages from thirteen to twenty-one, many of Quest's students came to the school having been expelled from their home districts. Others had dropped out but decided to return to school to pursue their high school diplomas. A good chunk of them were jailed during the evening and released during the day for school. All of them came to Quest with serious baggage. Many lived day to day wondering when they would eat again, if they would have a place to come home to, or if the utilities would be working when they arrived. Some students were drug or alcohol addicts and lived with parents who were also addicts. A surprising number of students were already parents themselves. Though the physical environment of the building was dismal, Quest was a place of comfort to these students, a safe environment in which they could learn and grow without worry. And even with the challenges of at-risk students—and there were many—I felt that Quest provided exactly what I wanted. It was no cakewalk, but student teaching in an alternative school proved to me that these were the students I wanted to be with.

So I was pleasantly surprised when one of the social studies teachers at Quest took a job at a local middle school and left an opening at Quest. I applied immediately, keeping my fingers crossed that my performance during student teaching had impressed the principal, John. After a quick phone interview—I was finishing my student teaching in South Africa as part of an international studies program—he hired me as a social studies teacher. I was elated! Never mind the fact that I would be teaching a subject that was not my content area. I felt fortunate enough just to get a job.

Throughout college, I was told that the first few days of school are the most important for establishing routines and procedures. While I did listen to this advice, I assumed that since I student taught at Quest, things would be easier for me. I had developed a strong rapport with many of the students, and many of them were excited when I returned as their social studies teacher. I learned quickly that excitement does not exactly breed obedience. Within a few short days, I was verbally assaulted and locked out of my classroom. Personal items disappeared from my desk. Students straight-faced refused to do anything in class, preferring to sleep, text, or talk to someone else who had made the same choice. At one point, a student walked into my classroom and punched another one square in the face while I had my back turned. Without exaggerating, I can say that my classroom resembled the beginning scenes from *Dangerous Minds* or *Freedom Writers*. I felt like students were plotting sinister ways of getting rid of me.

Within a week, I was a wreck.

Desperately trying to fix the situation, I recalled what one of my professors had said about classroom management. His suggested that if situations like this arose, I should "tighten it up." He claimed that it would fix things in the long run, even if it meant that the students may be a bit "resistant." Never the type to be completely discouraged, I came in and "tightened up" my classroom. Opening Pandora's box may have been less tempestuous. Hunkering down on discipline in a normal classroom is challenging, let alone in a classroom of very angry students. I held my ground, and despite the backlash (and the profanity-strewn rants thrown in my direction), things eventually calmed down.

This is not to say that things became easy. Working with 120 at-risk students is no simple task, even when your classroom management is stellar. Horrible language became a part of the classroom, a part that, like many other things, I started to let go. I also stopped worrying about mildly disruptive behavior, such as students talking or wandering around while I taught. I had bigger fish to fry— namely, stopping fights. A physical altercation broke out about once a week, unless we were able to catch wind of it before round one commenced. I kept my ears open, listening for any sort of warning signs that would indicate a fight. If one did break out, I was like a deer in headlights, not knowing what to do, other than to start screaming hysterically at the top of my lungs. Luckily, the rapport I developed with the students came into play in these situations. The older boys would (gently) push me out of the way and break it up so that I wouldn't get hurt.

Drug dealing occurred regularly at Quest, and I kept my eyes peeled for any indications of a transaction. Students talking about meeting at a "certain place" at a "certain time" with "cash only" tended to catch my attention. Occasionally, it happened right in my classroom or directly in the vicinity. While I never witnessed it, there were rumors that the couch in my classroom was a hot spot for drug deals. As soon as I heard this, the couch magically made its way from its comfy spot in the corner to the school dumpster. That did not deter the most enterprising of our dealers, however. Drugs still found their way through our halls. Sometimes, a teacher would find a plastic bag on the floor in the computer lab. Sometimes, other students would discover ground-up powder in a line on the bathroom counter. Other times, the police would come in with dogs to sweep the school for drugs. As the German shepherds sniffed at lockers and backpacks, the students would shift nervously, wondering who would be escorted out of school and into the police cruiser that day.

And, in the midst of this hostile climate, I was still responsible for their education.

I went to college to become an English teacher. I indulged in novels for fun, crafted essays about literary technique in my sleep, and reveled in creating innovating and engaging lessons about characters, setting, and all of the elements of a good story. When I took the position at Quest, it did not register with me that the things I loved to teach would not be the things I *would* teach. I had five preps— current events, world history, economics, humanities, and world civilizations. While I did have a minor in political science, the nuances of political thought and foreign policy did not exactly help with high school world history. I had no idea who Charlemagne was or the significance of the law of diminishing returns. Struggling to understand the material, I found myself at school until at least five or six every night, and I continued working at home until I went to bed, trying to figure out what I was teaching and how I would teach it for all five of my classes.

To compound the problem, I had moved back into my parents' home. They lived thirty minutes north of my school and were delighted with the idea of having me back home again. Their supportive nature kept me motivated and inspired throughout my academic career and helped me to achieve success along the way. However, they did not understand why my days were so long, or why I needed to, after a sixty-hour week, return to school on the weekends to continue planning. It is difficult to explain this to anyone who is not a teacher, even to people like my parents, who support the profession. Eventually, I had to move out, both to alleviate the pressure at home and to cut down on driving time. This provided me with an extra hour a day to do productive things, like reading the text I'd be teaching that week or planning an activity for the students. Even with these minor adjustments, though, it was clear that my work had become my life.

I sat at my desk, long after the students and all of the staff, save the custodian, had gone home. I had to read, then reread, and often reread again the textbook to make sure I understood the material. Then I attempted to make an engaging activity to help the students understand the material as well. Unfortunately, I had very little interest in any of these subjects, and as hard as I tried, the quality of the activities and assignments so failed to meet my personal standards that I became frustrated with myself and started over. The custodian would often prompt me to go home and get some rest, especially once it became dark. I would heed his advice and go home, only to sit at my dining table to continue working until the late hours of the night. Even in my sleep, I would dream about teaching, and wake up in the middle of the night with an idea that I had to write down immediately.

Socially, I practically became a pariah. I started losing contact with my friends, who had scattered across the state after graduation. We tried to maintain our relationships despite the distance, but my job made communication difficult. I continued working through the weekends, the time when my friends used to visit one another. The once-abundant phone calls became less frequent and soon tapered off completely. To have my friends come visit me was nearly out of the question. Piles of laundry accumulated around my apartment, threatening to take over the place. Dishes remained unwashed, until I resorted to paper products to allow myself more flexibility in time. My kitchen was stocked with only a few beverages and condiments in the fridge, a bag of pizza rolls in the freezer, and stale boxes of cereal in the cupboards. It was a bleak existence, but it was the only existence I could muster up the energy to maintain.

After school one day, my principal, John, came in to sit with me for a minute. Concerned with the amount of time I had been putting into school, he came in to check on me. He asked me one simple question:

"What are you doing for yourself?"

I was a little dumbfounded by his question. John was a wonderfully supportive principal who did everything in his power to make sure I had what I needed to be successful. More so than mine, his life at school and outside of school were intertwined tightly, and he was deeply entrenched in his job. So when he asked me this question, it threw me off a little.

"I'm asking you as a means of asking myself as well—what are we doing for ourselves to make sure we're good, healthy educators?" he said. After a long discussion, we concluded that in order to be good teachers, we needed to stay at least partially separated from the job. Turning into an education hermit was probably not the healthiest choice, and teaching where we taught, it was our responsibility to maintain our emotional well-being, modeling stability for students who might not have a responsible adult figure at home.

John's discussion with me exemplified the support system of teachers and administrators at Quest. During my first year, I was privileged to teach alongside of my former cooperating teacher, Kelsey. Many schools will set up mentorship programs for new teachers, but very few new teachers are allowed to continue working with a teacher who already knows them. Being able to teach alongside

Kelsey was both helpful and a little embarrassing. Kelsey knew when to coddle me and when to push me if something needed fixing. She would never even hint that she was disappointed, even if she were, and her support throughout that year gave me confidence I would not have had otherwise.

The support network also included two other teachers, Linda and Ted. Linda, our middle school teacher, had worked in alternative education for her entire twenty-five-year career. Linda worked with a group of about ten to fifteen middle school students all day in a self-contained classroom. From my perspective, her dedication to her students was apparent in everything she did. Her lessons were engaging, her classroom management was flawless, and her ability to reach the students was like something out of a movie. When she offered me advice or ideas, I took them and ran. Ted, our math teacher, was also an alternative-school lifer. While his career was significantly shorter than Linda's, he had taught in a jail previously and worked only for a brief stint at a regular public school. His quick wit and easygoing nature made him a favorite among the students and helped me to keep my chin up and to laugh a little at myself during that first year. Between John, Kelsey, Linda, and Ted, I had a strong support net of individuals who cared a great deal about the students, the curriculum, and about me.

Unfortunately, not every teacher at Quest was like Linda or Ted, and the actions of a few changed our school climate for the worse. A handful of teachers seemed to spend most of their time either ignoring students or gossiping relentlessly with them. In his documentary film *Waiting for Superman*, Davis Guggenheim refers to these teachers as "lemons," ineffective teachers who are frequently bounced from school to school since the unions make it impossible for them to be fired. While the film's portrayal of unions has been criticized, I did see teachers who simply did not do their jobs. My first year taught me that these teachers have the power to corrode the climate of the school, souring the way their colleagues and their students regard the school itself. Students are not always the most reliable sources, but there were rumblings among them that certain teachers would take them out to smoke during lunch breaks. Or that certain teachers gossiped about colleagues and students. Almost every day, I heard "I don't know why you are so mean about (fill in the blank). Mrs. So-and-So said that we could do that in her classroom, and that you're the only one who cares about (fill in the blank)." While I struggled to wrangle in my classes, other teachers outside of my support system were sabotaging me in an effort to maintain their "cool guy" status.

The ineffective teachers at Quest did more than damage my ability to manage my students. They also hurt my ability to maintain high academic standards. When I finally got a grip on my curriculum, it frustrated me to hear from the students that they were "not doing anything" in other classes. Grades seemed to be assigned arbitrarily on a "like" or "dislike" basis. Tests were given with answers. Excuses were made. Flabbergasted, I went to John, who was aware of the situation but whose hands seemed tied by the local union and district superintendents. To me, this seemed unreasonable. In what profession is it acceptable for someone to do a mediocre job? Was it because we taught at an alternative school where no one seemed to care?

Despite the negativity of the surrounding climate, I was doing my best to maintain a happy environment within my classroom. On St. Patrick's Day, I donned the brightest orange and white shirt and the largest shamrock-antennae headband I could find. Prancing around school during last period, my homeroom class and I were busily picking up papers for our recycling program when I noticed two official-looking men in the front of the school. I assumed they were probation officers, as many students had random visits from theirs. My students pointed out that they were not, in fact, probation officers, but both of the superintendents of our districts that I had yet to meet, even months into teaching.

Thinking nothing of it, I ignored their presence and carried on. Back in my classroom, we were deep into our discussion of recycling when a superintendent popped his head into my room and beckoned me to join him in our back office. The students' eyes widened nervously, and I followed slowly, still not sure who this person was. In the back office, he very carefully explained to me that three of our ten staff members were being laid off. I began to panic immediately, knowing I ranked lowest in seniority and experience. While tears welled up in my eyes, he informed me that I would be spared and would teach course recovery instead of a regular academic class the following year. Two of our support staff and one of our science teachers would be let go.

In shock, I wandered back to my room where students, their faces streaked with tears, sat waiting for me. They had heard from another teacher, wrongly, that I had received the boot. After I pacified their concerns and sent them home for the day, our principal, John, called for an emergency staff meeting. The mood was both somber and angry. While everyone was upset that we had to lose any staff, a handful of veterans argued that new teachers like me should be let go. Rookies, they claimed, would easily find new work. I was owed nothing and had not earned the right to stay. Again astonished at the level of unprofessionalism in such a dire situation, I sat in shock, unable to say anything. The meeting adjourned, and I knew the odds were not in my favor.

Realizing that I had nothing to lose—my job was likely gone anyway—I decided to make the best of my current situation. I had finally secured my classroom management skills and figured out a system to help me plan my lessons. Once I established that, I worked to improve my rapport with the students. This was easiest to do with my afternoon homeroom class, which consisted of only four students. During homeroom, we had specific tasks to accomplish. Once a week we had to do homework and grade checks, and once a week we had to go to group therapy. This consisted of discussing a given topic, such as substance abuse, relationships, or coping strategies in a group setting in order to teach appropriate social behavior. Aside from that, I had free reign to do what I pleased.

So I started a recycling program at the school, and my afternoon homeroom and I delivered the papers, plastics, and cans to a local recycling center. During these times, we made small talk in our school van. I learned about my students and often had conversations about their lives. Because of the small class size and our strong bond as a class, we did a lot of things that many other classes could not. We could take quick trips to Dairy Queen for ice cream or to Lowe's for supplies to make prom decorations. I trusted my students to make good decisions about what they did with their time, and if any of them were to disrespect it, they checked each other, attempting to keep the bond of the class intact.

By the end of the school year, Quest's attendance had dropped significantly. My humanities class, once consisting of twenty students, dwindled down to three that showed up on a regular basis. But because of the small class size, I was able to do projects and assignments with them that I could not dream of doing with other classes. Utilizing our limited technology, I showed the students how to make a digital story and gave them disposable cameras to capture concepts and ideas from our units of study. Once they learned all of the different elements, they were set to go on their own and were actually excited to come to class. We completed a terrific unit about human rights based on the movie *War Dance*. Together, we hovered around my laptop and watched the documentary about children in Uganda. The students would stop the DVD as they pleased when they had a question or a comment, and our discussions sometimes took up the entire period. The students asked to do other case studies on other countries like Uganda, and produced some of the best quality work I have seen as a teacher. The students valued this time with me and with each other, and worked hard to maintain the strong bond within the walls of my classrooms.

My students and I became closer. My seniors did not hesitate to remind me that they were graduating—or if I had a bad hair day for that matter—and would soon be gone. Knowing they would soon leave, the connection I had with them was much different, a much more mature bond formed by their age and their knowledge that everyone (themselves included) messes up. When I stumbled over myself, teaching the content I still did not know, they patiently waited for me to gather my thoughts. More than a few times, I had to stop instruction and, grinding my teeth, admit that I needed to relook at the material. In many of those situations, the students would push their tables together and have me sit with them as we went over it, learning it together. We joked around and laughed at one another frequently. When it came time for prom, the girls and I had running bets as to who would win—one of them, or me? The prom queen elected that year *still* reminds me that *she* won, and got the crown. All of this provided a much better environment that afforded me the opportunity to teach and for the students to learn.

As graduation approached, I found myself getting sentimental about my small group of seniors. The mood in the school turned to one of excitement, both on the part of the students and the teachers. Being a newcomer, I shared in the joy but couldn't help feeling that I had only a small part in the students' success. My short time at Quest had only allowed me to make a good connection to a handful of the seniors, and I had not had enough time to teach them all that I wanted them to know. So it came as a shock when one of my seniors approached me and asked me to be her "special person" at graduation.

Because Quest's students needed second, third, and tenth chances, John asked that the seniors pick a "special person" to present them with their diploma at the graduation ceremony. He stressed that the individual should be someone who influenced them in a positive way and provided them with love and support throughout their school years. Many of the students picked parents, grandparents, siblings, or other family members—people who had always been a part of their lives. And for some reason, this student chose me, the lowly first-year teacher.

I spent a lot of time talking with her about this decision. By my reasoning, she should have picked a family member or someone of greater importance than me. She insisted that I do it and refused to change her mind. Ultimately, I asked why she had picked me in the first place.

"You spent time with me and made sure I understood everything. You were patient and made things fun," she explained. "But most of all, you made me come to school and you would never let me fail."

To this day, her answer still shocks me.

She was right. I would not have let her fail. Ever. We spent much of the year trying to work through her issues at home and elsewhere to make sure that she made it to school. A smart, fiery young girl, she represented the school on the county's Youth Advisory Council and played on our various sports teams. Between her academic and extracurricular activities, she and I both knew that she was college bound. But when she became pregnant at the end of the year, she realized the magnitude of her situation and considered abandoning her college dream. We continued to look into community colleges and technical programs, and I helped her apply to Baker College at the end of the year. Not knowing how the next nine months would play out, we both acknowledged the difficult road she needed to travel, but I offered her all of the help I could think to give her. I thought I was just helping her out, giving her an extra boost of confidence and a good push in the right direction. To her, it was much more than that. When she explained this to me, suddenly, all of the trials, troubles, and flat-out failures I had experienced throughout the year became nothing more than tiny blips on my memory radar. I did something right.

And as I watched her and my other seniors walk across the stage on graduation night, I knew that the ups and downs of the year were not for nothing. To say I was simply reaffirmed in my decision to teach is a mild understatement. In this moment, I knew that this was my calling. This was what I was meant to do.

Year Two

Fired up and filled with creative energy, I spent my summer plotting my next school year. An edict had been handed down by the districts proclaiming that we all were saved! No layoffs would be necessary after all, and better still, I would finally teach English. I whiled away my hours, dreamily concocting projects, assignments, and read-alouds that would accompany the literary units I chose. In an effort to stay ahead, I created online curricula for all of my classes—English 9, 10, 11, and 12. In the meantime, I took a position as the summer school teacher to earn extra money, supervising three students as they completed coursework through Michigan Works, a program in Michigan that provides employment for teens and adults who have limited job opportunities. For three weeks I picked them up in the school van, helped them complete their work, and for the second half of the day, they worked with our custodian to fix things around the school. Between online coursework snafus, sleepy students, and one really horrible school van break in (Note: police officers do *not* appreciate civilians playing with the K-9s), the four of us had a few learning experiences. Luckily, this provided me with the time to work on my online classes while the students received high school credit. By the end of our three weeks, I had my classes nearly completed, and two of the three students worked hard enough to complete nearly fifty percent of their classes.

The school year quickly approached, but the fate of Quest was still unsettled. While our staff survived the layoff scare, the possibility of losing an employee or two after the FTE (Full-Time Equivalent) count was still a distinct possibility. Moreover, the district's budget shortfall made us all wonder if any of us would have jobs in the near future. The faculty felt afraid and powerless. Still, we took to the new year with energy and excitement. This time around, I knew what I had to do in order to maintain order and peace in my classroom. *Never again,* I thought, *will I have the same predicament as last year.*

Retrospectively, my thinking made sense. My classes consisted almost entirely of returning students, so my job seemed exponentially easier. Repeat students, however, present a double-edged sword. You can maintain previously made connections with certain students, but you might also reopen old wounds.

One particular student and I had not been so friendly the previous year. He was a constant behavior problem for me, refusing to do *anything* I asked—to wake up, to sit down, to leave the room, to take a chocolate bar out of my hand. The year started off with the same shenanigans, but this time he upped his game with horribly disrespectful behavior. When I redirected him, he cursed at me; when I asked him to take out a pencil, he threw folders, pencils, and chairs at me. Sometimes, he flatly denied my requests, accompanying his refusal with a laughing fit or a long nap afterward. After a while, I had him removed from my class on an almost daily basis. We figured out that while, yes, he did not enjoy me as a person or a teacher, he especially did not enjoy me as a woman. In this student's culture, women are generally treated as inferior. Though this explained a lot, I could not tolerate a student treating me in such a way, especially in a classroom full of students who were borderline to begin with. John and I talked about him, trying hard to devise a plan to improve our relationship. We worked out reward systems, time-outs, and alternate assignments, but nothing worked. Ultimately, the bomb exploded in one verbal exchange in which he called me the worst name you could ever think to call a female.

Yes. He called me *that* word.

While he claimed to be discussing the character of Beneatha in *A Raisin in the Sun*, the other students and I both knew his actual motives. After spending a few days on mandatory vacation (as I like to call it), he spent a good portion of the rest of the quarter working in John's office during my class. Since he would not respond to me, John spent time with him, trying to figure out how we should proceed. Still, he refused to comply, and he eventually returned to my class, as stubborn as ever. We were all out of ideas and plans. I spent the rest of my year trying to work with him, but the juvenile court system eventually caught up with him and he was removed from school before anything could change. A probation violation landed him in a juvenile detention center, and after that, he rarely came to school. To this day, I think about that student and how I could have done things differently. I realize now that I will never connect with some students. While this realization is disappointing and difficult, teaching simply does not supply us with a never-ending supply of likable students.

This student, however, did not represent what the rest of the year was like. Teaching English instead of social studies brought a breath of fresh air into my life. The planning and developing of curriculum became much easier, and the balance in my life was restored. My one-on-one time with my students increased, and for a few of the classes the students picked out novels based on interest. Being picky myself, I still managed to sneak a few classics into the curriculum. The students sharply refused *Frankenstein*, one beast of a novel, initially. However, once we started rolling with it, the students took to loving it. Many connected with its central idea—abandonment after creation—simply based on their own life experiences as children of drug addicts, alcoholics, and abusers. *To Kill a Mockingbird* also sent a jolt through my freshman class, my only mixed-race class, provoking serious discussion about stereotyping and judgment, something they had experienced not only with race but also as students at an alternative school. The security camera installation in my room sparked serious paranoia among the seniors, who claimed "Big Brother" had caught up with them. I finally felt that I was hitting my stride.

As I gained confidence, I also discovered a funny correlation existed between the quality of my teaching and the number of other jobs I was asked to take on. Since I had worked so diligently on my curriculum, my students were both learning and organized. John saw this and slowly started handing me different jobs that he trusted me to complete. At first, I was asked to coach volleyball, an innocuous task to some, but to me, with a team of twenty at-risk girls, it ended up being a nightmare. Between potential girl fights, truancy issues, and my players' preference for smoke breaks over running, the season ended poorly. I also became the new coordinator of our clothing closet, which supplied clothing to needy students. Meanwhile, Kelsey had taken a position at a local middle school, and her former responsibilities became mine. I now represented Quest on our district's formative assessment team, working with a phenomenal group of teachers to turn middle school and high school standards into student-friendly language and to develop multiple types of formative assessments for the classroom. In addition, I replaced Kelsey as the lead administrator of the ACT. Many sleepless nights and wads of hair were lost in the process of maintaining the paperwork, confidentiality, and promotion of such a huge test. A tremendous amount effort went into preparing the students, all of whom were entirely ill-suited for a test of this importance. I put a huge effort into trying to get the students to actually show up to the test. We made many bribes to get them there, an endeavor that proved to be successful.

Beyond the school itself, I also volunteered to help students with their community service hours to finish probation by doing restorative work around the school and the community. Frequently, I would stay after on Thursdays to participate in the teacher advancement program provided by Michigan Works that helped students learn how to cook and how to provide for themselves. The students would watch movies, play games, or just sit and read in my room while I worked. Meanwhile, I tried to have a semblance of a life outside of school. In a feeble attempt at a social life, I joined an environmental organization and ran a homeless shelter at my church. I began presenting at conferences and doing other work outside of school to make me a better teacher. This also seemed to me like an excellent opportunity to purchase a gym membership and to buy a dog to provide me a little cheer when I arrived home from work. What this really added up to was exhaustion.

Still, my job made me happy. The students, though a bit emotionally draining, were great and my curriculum was fun to teach. We created soundtracks to novels, performed readers' theater, and discussed current issues. I continued to develop close relationships with many of the students, one in particular with whom I am still in contact today. A frequent school skipper, this student was so far behind in her work that she faced the possibility of at least another year of high school. At the age of eighteen, she wanted nothing more than to be done. I would tease her, saying that I would come and drag her out of bed and force her to come to school if she continued in her ways. When she would disappear for a few weeks, she would return and apologize. On one particular occasion, I heaped on the guilt, chiding her, "I'm not angry. I'm just disappointed." Strangely enough, she returned to school for a few weeks in a row after that, claiming that when she thought about not getting up for school, she saw my head floating above her saying, "I'm not angry. I'm just disappointed."

Shortly thereafter, she was found carrying illegal substances and sentenced to ninety days in jail. Now too far behind to recover, she moved to a nearby city to get a fresh start. I made a few calls and had her enrolled at an alternative school where a mentor of mine was the school counselor. A year later, very late at night, my cell phone blasted in my ear. It was this student, wanting desperately to tell me that she had graduated high school. She apologized for the late call but said she needed to let me know since I had helped her so much. It was another moment that solidified my decision to stay in the profession, a moment sprouted out of this school year.

While I felt good about my teaching, the overall climate of the school was still poisoned by a small group of teachers who seemed intent on demoralizing the staff. Their griping polarized the staff, and from my perspective their complaints were baseless—they resented documenting their lesson plans, coming to work early, and attending professional development workshops. Their ultimate goal was for everyone to hate the system. What I really started to hate, though, was the idea that people like this could be employed and able to work with students who need strong adults in their lives.

One afternoon, I overheard a colleague talking to a group of students. He was advising them to hurt another student in an attempt to "let him know his place." After discussing the issue with John, I realized my only recourse was to give a written statement against my colleague to document the incident. But John told me that doing so risked a lengthy and potentially damaging fight against a union that already protected this teacher. Having almost lost my job once, I backed down, knowing there would be no way to prove what had happened. Meanwhile, the districts also made it known that with the budgetary situation, Quest might not be open in the near future. We again risked layoffs to our short-handed staff. We were also refused money to improve our run-down, ill-equipped building. Instead, outdated textbooks and barely functional furniture was bestowed upon us, as if they were magical gifts given to children on Christmas Day. I became increasingly frustrated.

The students started to take an emotional toll on me as well. While my year was significantly better than the previous, it also brought with it a new level of connection with the kids. Because I lived in a neighborhood with many of them, they would frequently visit while I was outside gardening or reading. Many would ask if I had any food; others would come to be in a safe place on my lawn with me. I could see them walking down the street with their parents, who struggled to walk in a straight line and used their children as a means of propping themselves up on the trek home from the gas station. I employed one student to let my dog out while I was still at work. During one of our conversations, she asked if I would be home over the weekend. When I asked why, she grew quiet.

"My mom didn't pay our heating bill and we have no heat or hot water at my house. If I get cold, can I come watch your dog?" she replied.

Stories of discovering parents passed out in the bathroom, needles stuck in their arms or a bottle of open pills spewed about the room, swirled around my classroom. Students without homes, not sure where they were going to sleep that night, tried to make arrangements to sleep on friends' couches. Teen moms missed significant chunks of school because they could not find reliable or safe day care. Hot meals provided by the school were often a student's only meal. Students came in with bruises and cuts from what I can only assume was a serious beating the previous night.

By the end of my second year, I knew I stood at a crossroads. Continuing at Quest would mean a career filled with intrinsic reward, working with students who desperately needed a good teacher. It also meant unlimited creative freedom in my classroom—no fear of censorship or prescribed curriculum for me. Initially, these positives seemed to outweigh the negatives of the job. But the longer

I worked there, the more I realized that teaching at Quest would always mean watching superintendents and school boards ignore marginalized students to save money and employ ineffective teachers to pacify the union. It would always mean watching the students suffer at the hands of people in power, while I lost sleep with worry about them. I knew something had to give.

In July of my second year, I applied for a job in Pasco County, Florida, where I now teach middle school language arts. I left without warning. John knew my intentions at the end of the school year, but upon returning in the fall, the students were blindsided with a new English teacher. I received many emails from them in the following months, asking what happened and why I left. Guilt still plagues me, knowing that I left them without so much as saying good-bye. On my way out, however, I decided to be brave and stand up for my students. In my exit interview, I let the districts know how I felt, how abandoned my students had been by them. I burned every bridge I had in an attempt to do the last good thing I could think to do for the students.

When I think back to my two years at Quest, it fills me with much joy. On one particularly bad day this past school year, one of my former students contacted me, asking me to be her special person at her graduation. She was in her junior year when I left, and after completing the past two years without me at the school, she came to the conclusion that of all of the people in her life, it had been me that pushed her to finish. Despite my absence for the past two years, she persevered through many obstacles in an effort to uphold the standards I set for her. Other former students still contact me. They enjoy filling me in on their lives and letting me know about their successes. News of graduation, college, a full-time job, or the completion of a novel continue to fill up my inbox. Sometimes, they grumble about how they dislike their new English teacher. I preach about giving him a chance, but secretly, it makes me just a little happy.

FOR FURTHER DISCUSSION

1. Describe the school climate at Quest. What factors contribute to the climate?
2. If you were hired to teach at Quest, how would you cope with the emotional stress that is often involved in teaching an at-risk population?
3. Beyond the challenge of teaching marginalized students, what other issues at Quest frustrate Tami? How does Tami address them?
4. Citing the movie *Waiting for Superman*, Tami blames the union for protecting "lemon" teachers by making it nearly impossible for them to be fired. Based on what you know about teacher unions in your state, is her criticism valid?
5. Why did Tami ultimately choose to leave Quest? Do you think she made the right decision?

Kristyn Konal graduated with honors from Grand Valley State University with a BA in English (Secondary Education). Since then, she has worked with several school districts around her hometown in Michigan as a substitute teacher, summer school instructor, and interventionist for at-risk youth. When she isn't teaching or exploring graduate opportunities, Kristyn enjoys experimenting with new recipes in the kitchen, traveling with friends, and spending time outdoors with her two rescue dogs, Abbey and Cooper.

Why the Hell Would You Teach *There*?
Kristyn Konal
Clark Middle School

One of the first values my parents instilled in my sister and me was open-mindedness. We were taught to remain objective and observant when encountering new people, places, or experiences, and to draw conclusions only after unbiased reflection. I struggled with this notion of objectivity when I arrived at Clark Middle School at 6:35 for my first day of substitute teaching of the new school year.

If ever a building perpetuated the notion that school serves as a prison for adolescents—and most of us are able to recall the comparison made between public schools and oppressive penitentiaries in *The Breakfast Club*—this one succeeded incomparably. Renovations to the structure appeared to have ceased sometime in the 1970s, and the indisputable fragrance of chemical cleaners and mildew assaulted my nostrils within seconds of walking through the aged double doors to the office. To further reinforce the feeling of imprisonment, each window was accessorized with steel or iron bars. In addition, the classrooms were crammed with more desks than appropriate for the dimensions of each room—at least from what I could see on the way to my classroom—and the empty but noticeably narrow hallways were claustrophobic, even without the swarm of students rushing to their next class. I came to this building by *choice,* and I wanted to leave as quickly as possible. How could the students be expected to arrive at school with any excitement or desire to learn in such an environment?

It was only after my discussion with the principal, a towering man with a warm smile, that I learned that this was one of the least-funded schools in the Metro-Detroit area. He had glanced around him and, as if he had read my mind, remarked that if he had the resources, he would fix the school up himself so that this building invited students in and enticed them to stay. He suggested that perhaps then he would have fewer issues with absences and greater participation in extracurricular programs. Although I felt it would be inappropriate to comment on the principal's prediction aloud, inwardly I agreed.

I was long-term subbing for Mrs. Wilson, and I hoped that her room would exhibit some homey characteristics, even if nothing could be done about the school's exterior. At least the teachers could use their own materials to make their individual classrooms a place where students actually want to be, I reasoned. But I was sorely disappointed. The interior of the room surpassed the hallways in bareness. The walls were the sickly yellow of decaying antique books—the first image that flashed across my mind was the bedroom from Charlotte Perkins Gilman's "The Yellow Wallpaper"—and lacked any sort of picture, poster, or display of student work. No vegetation, color, or evidence of life could be found. At first, I thought perhaps I had entered the wrong classroom, since in the place of desks or tables sat the elevated tables with sinks characteristic of science classrooms. The principal, however, confirmed that I was in the right room.

I am rather ashamed to admit that my initial reaction involved a silent admonition of Mrs. Wilson, despite my parents' lessons in objectivity. I wondered how any teacher could believe that a room with the sterility of a morgue would be conducive to learning. I hoped that my future classroom would cultivate a spirit of confidence and optimism, and I believed that a nurturing classroom environment was crucial. The establishment of a healthy classroom environment takes place on the first day of school, the very minute, in fact, when students' eyes absorb the details of the classroom itself. A multitude of information can be conveyed about the teacher, the school itself, and the expectations of the students in the seven to ten seconds it takes to scan the classroom. For instance, my thought process upon entering an English 11 classroom from a neighboring district later that year went something like this:

Pink chair covers, pink drapes on the windows, pink daisies on the desk . . . this woman really loves the color pink! It looks like a bottle of Pepto-Bismol in here! She is the first teacher I've seen, though, who provides chair covers and seat cushions for her students; that's really quite thoughtful. I'm sure they appreciate it. Those satirical posters about teaching satire are pretty amusing, which more than likely means she's got a sense of humor. Her students probably like that. I can see by the assortment of posters, eCard prints, and photographs that she's a fan of David Tennant, Martin Freeman, Benedict Cumberbatch, and Tom Hiddleston. We'd get along famously! I bet this open "fangirl" display has provided many debates about the actors themselves, as well as the merits of the TV series and films in which they appear. There's another opportunity for her to bond with her kids right there. I bet these pictures provide some great material for free-writes, too. She's got her classroom rules clearly displayed on that wall— "Give respect, and you'll get it back twofold; come to class prepared and ready to work; discussion is fantastic, but please don't interrupt those who are talking; please keep all electronic devices away until told otherwise. Thank you." They know she won't allow disrespectful behavior to go on in her room. Oh look, she has her desks arranged in groups of three and four—probably for writing workshops—and each group has a lamp placed in the center of it. I wonder how often they use them. She probably uses them as a source of ambient lighting as the students write. That's what I would do. I think the students would like a break from the harsh lighting in here from time to time. She's also stacked a class set of dictionaries and encyclopedias in the back. Do all English rooms here have those? It's good to see a classroom with resources readily available. I see her students made movie posters advertising various Shakespeare plays. How cool! These are really well done. The students must have enjoyed working on them. I bet they like this class; it seems like they have a fun, caring, relatable teacher to work with . . .

Students make assumptions about their teacher based on the décor and arrangement of the classroom and, subsequently, make predictions about how they will interact with the teacher and their classmates. If students imagine that their classroom experience will be agreeable because their teacher appears interesting and amiable, then these positive feelings will blossom into a productive, supportive, and enthusiastic classroom climate as long as the teacher works to establish rapport with her students. In short, first impressions are critical in making or breaking the foundation needed for an optimistic, nurturing, and successful classroom—and on a larger scale, school—environment.

I know that establishing this kind of environment depends to some degree on money. I recalled what the principal mentioned earlier that morning regarding this school's appalling lack of state funding, and I thought about the implications of those words. For me, a long-term substitute who had visited many underfunded schools, these words evoke images of poorly maintained buildings, antiquated textbooks—in some cases no textbooks at all—and sparse resources. In addition, smaller budgets entail smaller salaries, which in turn translate to decreased disposable income available for teachers. Many pay out-of-pocket for the tools and materials needed to transform their classrooms from inhospitable cells into comfortable havens. Even something as seemingly minute as extra pencils or individual binders for each student can make a remarkable difference in the classroom. Not only do these amenities promote a healthy work ethic and organizational skills, they also help to build trust and respect between students and teachers. Unfortunately, too many times their significance goes unnoticed until, out of financial necessity, these small comforts disappear altogether. I surmised that this—an insurmountable financial strain faced by the classroom teacher— must be the key reason behind the bleakness of Mrs. Wilson's room. Before I could speculate further on the matter, the sound of the principal's voice gently pulled my attention away from my private meditation, and I found myself once again gazing at the vacant laboratory tables.

"I know it's a bit odd, holding an English class in a classroom built for chemistry, but Mrs. Wilson has been in this room for the past two years and it seems to serve her well. The kids are less likely to lean back in their chairs, anyway. They don't want to topple over that far off the ground! Anyway, call me or the assistant principal, Mr. Rawlson, if you have any questions. You have first hour prep. Your next two hours will be seventh-grade language arts, followed by one section of eighth-grade composition, and then two more sections of seventh grade language arts."

He left with a nod and a morsel of advice for a novice teacher like me: "Don't be afraid to get strict with these kids. The moment they act out, call them on it. The minute they get disruptive, call a security guard to come get them or call Mr. Rawlson directly and he will escort them from the room personally. Put your foot down. If you don't, by God, these kids will eat you alive."

With that less-than-comforting speech on my mind, I scanned the desk for the sub plans. As a student teacher, I had become quite practiced at writing sub plans, detailing everything from lesson plans, to the location of worksheets and other class materials, to contact information, to student helpers. While I doubt that any normal person would wish to read three to four pages of information about the classroom, I tend to err on the side of caution. These, however, were the lesson plans I received:

"Hello, and thanks for coming in today!
Seventh-grade L.A.: Continue to work on short story. They started it yesterday.
Eighth-grade Comp.: Begin persuasive essay.
Call Rawlson with any questions.
—W"

What? What type of short story are they working on? Tall tales? Horror stories? Science fiction? Do they have any samples they can reference? Do they have any rubrics or have they discussed the parameters of the assignment? How about the eighth graders? Do they have any resources available to them? There must be a resource book, a textbook, something around here somewhere.

I scoured the room for materials, but with no success. I opened every drawer, cupboard, and closet, only to find a handful of empty folders and the binder for emergencies and evacuation procedures. After looking for class sets of textbooks in the library, teachers' lounge, and resource room, I decided call another English teacher in the hopes that I might borrow a class set of writing guides or textbooks. Fortunately for me, the young male teacher in the classroom above mine answered his phone and promptly descended the stairs with a class set of seventh-grade literature books in tow. In my experience as a substitute teacher for multiple districts, I have conversed with a handful of skeptical teachers who claim that students fail their classes because they have no desire to put forth an effort. One educator I encountered from one of the larger school districts in the area explained:

When students say, "I don't understand the assignment," it's a load of malarkey. What they really mean by "I don't understand" is "I don't want to do the assignment." It's an easy way for all of the accountability and responsibility to come off the shoulders of the kids and get placed back on the teachers. If we don't hold their hands through every step, every paragraph, it isn't going to get done. So, really, the kids know that by saying, "I don't understand the assignment" they'll get a free ride out of everything we give to them. They're just plain lazy and used to getting everything handed to them. I don't buy it, and I don't allow that excuse in my classroom. If they don't get it after the second explanation, well, by that point it is out of my hands. If they don't do their work as a result, that's on them. They have the resources; they just refuse to use them.

While I know this is true of some students, not every student who fails a test, skips an assignment, or flunks a course is lazy. I believe that if educators provide thorough and consistent instructions, students will work harder. This uniformity and attention to detail also help to build trust with students; it relieves some of the stress and anxiety they feel over not knowing what to expect. Then, when they succeed at a tough but clear assignment, their attitudes toward the class, the school, and even education as a whole can change for the better.

So, what were Mrs. Wilson's expectations for the short-story writing assignment? When I asked the seventh-grade students to review the guidelines for their short stories, I discovered that they were supposed to be writing works of horror fiction. The only details they had discussed with Mrs. Wilson was that it had to "contain something scary; be school appropriate; and be longer than half of a page single-spaced, handwritten." A few students sighed that they "had no clue where to start."

So I scrawled the elements of horror fiction across the whiteboard, asking the students to take notes so that they had something to reference as they worked on their own stories. Of course my request was met with several grumbles, but I stayed enthusiastic, enjoying how I could use material I created during my student teaching, and hoping that my energy would breathe life into the groggy group of students sitting before me. In addition to the mini-lesson on horror fiction, I provided them with a brief list of adjectives, nouns, and verbs that might be used in a horror story. I also passed out the textbooks so that the students would have a sample short story, alongside a diagram of the basic story arc. Aside from having to remove six students from the classroom, two for an escalating verbal altercation and the remaining students for throwing temper tantrums because I refused to let them sleep, eat their lunches, or text during class, most of my seventh-grade students worked diligently all hour.

The eighth graders, however, were a different matter. To say that they behaved inappropriately fails to describe the scene accurately. The boys were rowdy and boisterous, several of the girls entered the room announcing their most recent sexual exploits, and one couple slid to the corner of the room and proceeded to kiss so vigorously that they might have been cannibals devouring each other's flesh. I asked politely, but assertively, for the students to sit down and get ready for class. Not a single body moved. Not a single voice lowered. Using a level of volume and force that I had not utilized since my role as a drum major of the high school marching band, I demanded that the students please settle down and take their seats immediately. Four or five responded. I boomed again, "Sit down and take your seats, NOW!" Two more students quieted their voices. The veteran math teacher next door heard the commotion and tried her luck with the students, but they ignored her as well. I thought that perhaps the presence of Mr. Rawlson, the recognized school disciplinarian, might grab their attention and bring some order to the classroom, but again I was mistaken. Mr. Rawlson stood at least six-and-a-half feet tall and had a voice like thunder, and the students *still* refused to listen. It was not until Mr. Rawlson threatened suspension for insubordination and physically removed seven or eight students from the classroom that the teenagers finally took their seats and ended their conversations.

The eighth graders made it clear that the social system of the school was not functioning. The students did not respect the authority of the teachers, and many of the teachers seemed not to care about the students. While respect and accountability are first learned at home, I believe that teachers and administrators must cultivate these qualities in our students. When teachers, administrators, counselors, and other staff members exhibit the characteristics we wish to instill in our adolescent students, they lay the groundwork for building a school climate that promotes cooperation, empathy, and integrity. For instance, a school that effectively utilizes team teaching demonstrates to its students how to communicate and collaborate with colleagues, skills that are not only beneficial to students as they work through their education but will also help them to become caring, resourceful, and valuable citizens in our democracy.

I can only imagine how time-consuming, frustrating, and physically and emotionally taxing it would be to attempt to teach accountability and respect within an already packed curriculum, and I wondered if perhaps Mrs. Wilson, in addition to the financial strains she and the other educators at Clark were currently experiencing, was struggling with this very problem. Every teacher I have ever spoken to mentioned "problem classes," those particular combinations of conflicting personalities paired with discipline problems and emotional issues that blend together to create a perfect storm. These kinds of classes can test any teacher, regardless of her resourcefulness or determination. I guessed that my eighth-grade composition students were going to be my "problem class" until Mrs. Wilson's return, and that they would likely continue their misbehavior unless Mrs. Wilson could get appropriate support from her colleagues and administrators.

While the veteran teacher remained in the classroom, I asked the students about their writing assignment. They had already read an article about discrimination and were required to write a persuasive essay about one method the school should use to fight discrimination in society. In essence, they had to explain the meaning of discrimination, detail the pain it causes those being discriminated against, and argue why their method of eradicating discrimination was the most effective one. Many students needed a review of the meaning of discrimination. One student described it as "hating on people because they are too stupid to have good fashion sense," while another maintained that discrimination involved "feeling sorry for ugly people because you know they'll never be happy because no one wants to marry someone who's hit."

While some students were able to articulate the meaning of discrimination clearly, and therefore were able to detail some excellent examples of prejudice in their writing, I was shocked by the number of students who struggled. Perhaps discrimination was all too real for these students, who attended an impoverished school with few resources and little support from the community. Or perhaps they were simply apathetic about the world around them.

Student apathy occurs in every school, but I found it hard to believe that all of my students were indifferent or oblivious to their surroundings. I was certain that some of the students recognized how their school differed from the schools in other districts; however, I suspect that the significance and degree of difference was somehow lost on them. Even though my students frequently had to go without, they could not comprehend the extent of their deprivation. They consistently had no books, laboratory supplies, writing utensils, and extracurricular activities. Students and colleagues told me the school had no music or visual arts programs. In addition, they only had five sports programs available to their students—football and basketball for the boys, cheerleading and softball for the girls, and co-ed track. There were no community service groups, student leadership councils, or honor societies. According to accounts from teachers and administrators, the school used to have an array of sports, clubs, and other extracurricular activities to help promote student success and community service. Years ago, the school boasted a highly competitive performing arts program that won awards for their musicals and student stage productions.

Sadly, as the school lost funding from the state, it lost support from the community as well. Parents, neighbors, friends, and relatives of students and staff alike stopped participating in fundraisers, attending events, or donating their time to the school. The once steady stream of monetary support and school spirit slowed to a trickle until no choice remained but to terminate programs and slash the budgets for supplies and equipment. It seemed to me that the deterioration of the once-thriving school programs led to the decay of the school's morale and the unraveling of the once-positive relationship between the school and its constituency.

To say that Clark currently has a bad reputation is an understatement—it, like the other schools within the same district, has been called a dropout factory that produces criminals, junkies, and prostitutes. When I told people that I accepted a substitute teaching position at Clark, a friend and fellow teacher exclaimed, "Seriously? Clark? Why the hell would you take a job *there*?" I wondered if teachers and administrators had internalized this negativity—if in fact, it was possible to maintain a positive outlook at all while teaching at Clark.

The students attending Clark have, in recent years, been characterized as troubled children, problem students, and at-risk youth. Michigan Educational Assessment Program and ACT scores, student grade point average, and graduation rates at Clark and its adjacent high school have declined steadily. And without the support of community members, the school maintains little hope for improvement. The district board of education must hear the voices of its community members before it can change policies and implement new procedures for the betterment of its students; booster clubs need funding, advertising, and participation in order to sustain successful programs; students need the encouragement of their neighbors so that they have the volition to try new activities and stay involved with community service projects.

In short, schools need both moral and monetary support from the community in order to promote student success through the provision of both tangible resources (books, journals, computers) and intangible ones (hope, encouragement, communication). These commodities assist in leveling the playing field for impoverished districts and ultimately closing the achievement gaps that exist among varying schools. The discrimination that occurs with facilities like Clark can diminish as long as students are provided opportunities to demonstrate that they can be just as competent as students from more privileged districts. Without a symbiotic relationship between a school and its community, however, the outcome that remains is a vicious cycle that perpetuates inequity. This inequity, in turn, fosters feelings of negativity and lethargy throughout the various members of the school population, further undermining any attempts to create and maintain a healthy school climate.

Even before my encounter with the eighth-grade composition class, I had my suspicions that the vitality of the school climate was suffering. My first experience with the veteran math teacher next door further fueled my qualms when, after the students began writing at reasonably steady pace, she pulled me aside to inform me that this group was the worst of the day. Why she felt the need to underscore how unruly the students were reported to behave was beyond me, especially since they were currently working with relatively minimal distractions. "The craziness you just witnessed," she began, "is a regular happening around here. Maybe you can get them to settle down some, but I would anticipate headaches for as long as you're here. Make sure you have the behavior referral forms ready and some Motrin or something in your bag. You'll need it with this group of characters."

I was shocked by her frankness, as well as how reproachfully she spoke about the teenagers who were sitting no more than ten feet away from her at the time of our conversation. This seasoned educator, Mrs. Brown, then proceeded to expound on precisely how migraine-inducing Mrs. Wilson's students could be. Mrs. Brown further revealed that Mrs. Wilson lost all control of the eighth graders weeks ago, and proved "totally inept" at regaining it. According to Mrs. Brown, while all of the eighth graders were unruly to an unprecedented degree, Mrs. Wilson's composition class proved to be the worst in the entire school. "Her class is completely out of control, and I don't know how she allows the noise level in her room to get that high. It's pretty bad that *I* have to shout over *her* students while *my* kids are taking notes. I shouldn't have to be concerned about *her* degenerates disrupting the learning going on in my classroom." With that, Mrs. Brown left for her classroom, looking back over her shoulder to remind me to call her if I ever needed assistance with my students. I thought that Mrs. Brown's comments were as unnecessary as they were unsolicited, and I hoped that she was merely venting out of frustration in that moment.

Often, I hear teachers, students, parents, and peers recall the ugly side of middle school. They typically discuss the insecurities and emotional pains experienced during adolescence, remembering bullying or the general awkwardness of the teenage years. I shudder slightly as I recollect my own middle school experiences with bullying and ostracism, recalling my fervent wish to enter adulthood and thereby distance myself forever from the pettiness and cruelty exhibited by my peers. During my lunch break in the teachers' lounge one afternoon, I was exposed to viciousness among faculty members, and faced the stinging reality that cattiness and malevolence do not necessarily abate with age.

What I thought was the initiation of a pleasant conversation about my work at Clark Middle School quickly morphed into a verbal onslaught of Mrs. Wilson and her supposed lapse in work ethic. It began innocently enough: Mrs. Brown asked about the students and if I was enjoying my time at Clark now that the students proved less rambunctious than they were my first two days in Mrs. Wilson's room. She then remarked that Mrs. Wilson had always prided herself on cultivating manners and respect in her classroom, but that this year she seemed entirely preoccupied with other issues. Mrs. Brown claimed that Mrs. Wilson, who had been her friend for many years, must be on the verge of a nervous breakdown.

"Either that," she said, "or she doesn't give a damn about her students or her career now that she's achieved tenure." She proceeded to list off every mistake Mrs. Wilson had made that year, from allowing students to swear in her classroom without punishment to "defying school rules" by giving the students permission to use their cell phones in class. "Not only does she let her kids use their phones on a regular basis," she began, "but she has a reputation for checking her phone constantly throughout the day as well. How can she be so disrespectful, so oblivious to the impact that has on the kids? Does she realize the sticky situation she puts everyone else in? I cannot tell you how many times I've heard 'but Mrs. Wilson lets us' from her students. What a pain in the ass she is this year!" She also stated that she planned to bring a thorough record of all of Mrs. Wilson's faults to the administration.

At this point in the conversation I attempted to change the subject, but another party prevented me from doing so. The social studies teacher next door, Ms. Stockton, joined in with the bashing, exclaiming that Mrs. Wilson was one of the worst educators she had ever had the misfortune of working with. In addition, this teacher said that if I ever needed any assistance with Mrs. Wilson's students, I should ask her, because Mrs. Wilson certainly failed at maintaining control of her classroom. "It truly is a shame," she sighed, "for such talent to be wasted like that. She seemed so promising when they hired her in, so smart and full of ideas. We were all snowed, I guess. I really don't know what the hell her problem is. She's certainly let those kids run her classroom into the ground in record time. They were animals to begin with, and she's just fueled the fire with her incompetence."

"One thing's for certain," Mrs. Brown chimed in, "I wouldn't trust *her* with my classroom for second. Who knows what she'd let my kids get away with! I've worked hard since the very first day of school to promote self-discipline, respect, and integrity in my classroom, and her devil-may-care attitude would undermine all of my efforts."

"What's more," added Ms. Stockton, "her complete disregard for the standards set by the other teachers in this school has seeped its way into her attire as well. We try to teach these children something about professionalism, about taking pride in your appearance—Lord knows we have enough issues with the dress code to worry about already with those damn yoga pants and boxer shorts—and she shows up every day in jeans. Jeans! I mean, they're fine for spirit week and science labs, but what in the world are jeans doing in an English classroom?"

Ms. Stockton proceeded to carry on about respectability and how the school principal from her first teaching assignment would have reprimanded her thoroughly had she arrived to her building wearing anything less professional than a full suit. At this point in the conversation, Mrs. Brown turned to me and said wryly, "It's terrible when you know the kids are better off with a sub than they are with the regular teacher. Maybe she won't come back and they can give you Wilson's class. You can't screw it up any more than she has already and, who knows, perhaps you'll actually do something to *improve* the students in her room."

Offended and at a loss for words, I excused myself from the table as politely as possible and headed back to the room, content to finish my lunch in solitude. I've experienced discontent in the workplace and the occasional gossipy vent session before, but I did not think I could stomach that much open hostility toward another teacher.

As hard as I tried to push it out of my mind, the episode from the teacher's lounge vexed me for the remainder of the day. I made an attempt to work productively, but I proved entirely too distracted to grade essays or compose emails to parents. Instead, I halfheartedly straightened up the room—pushing a chair in here, replacing a book there—and pondered where such animosity among the educators here originated.

Surely, some sort of major disagreement had to occur for that much venom to come from Mrs. Brown's mouth; that level of disdain does not magically appear out of thin air. What happened? What did Mrs. Wilson do to anger her so greatly? It really couldn't be as simple and petty as jealousy, could it? I mean, Mrs. Wilson couldn't be that poor of a teacher, right? Did Mrs. Wilson attain tenure much quicker than Mrs. Brown? It isn't like they even work in the same department, so I see no reason why Brown should feel as though she is in competition with Mrs. Wilson. I wonder if Mrs. Wilson is aware of how her neighbor feels about her? How would you even work under those conditions, having to share a wall with someone who relishes the chance to criticize your every move?

A knock on my door from an unexpected visitor disrupted my thoughts. Little did I know that this visitor, an English teacher from Clark High School, would provide me with more insight into the world of Mrs. Wilson's classroom than I ever expected to obtain during the course of my employment in the Clark district. His name was Mr. Kryzynski, and he had been Mrs. Wilson's mentor teacher when she first started working at Clark Middle School. When Mr. Kryzynski inquired as to how I was enjoying my time at Clark, I hesitated with my response, telling him that I was uncomfortable with the role of the drill sergeant. And then, with some trepidation, I asked him about the relationship between Mrs. Wilson and Mrs. Brown. I did not want to add to the already smoldering hostility rising within the building, but I could not curb my curiosity. I needed to know what initiated the toxic interaction, and if something could have been done to prevent it. Mr. Kryzynski confirmed my suspicions that the bitterness between the two teachers had more complicated origins that mere jealousy.

"The problem with this district, and particularly Clark," started Mr. Kryzynski, "is that the administration—whether knowingly or unwittingly, I can't say for certain—actually encourages competition among its staff in place of cooperation. They give out so many various awards for classroom achievements—stuff for student progress, best teaching practices, most creative assignments and all of that—that nobody wants to share ideas or help each other out, which I think is really juvenile, personally." He intimated that most of the honors were merely symbolic, but that the school does provide a small bonus for the teacher who consistently meets and exceeds AYP and the standards set in their professional growth plan.

He further explained that Mrs. Wilson's supposed flightiness was the result of multiple stressors colliding at once, a dangerous mix of financial hardship, emotional turmoil, and psychological strain brought on by unsympathetic colleagues: "She's got a one-year-old at home," Mr. Kryzynski explained, "and is currently going through a divorce. To make matters worse, her" soon-to-be-ex-husband is a teacher within the district, so everyone sees all of their dirty laundry. The attitude around here is that she should simply suck it up and deal with it. I will admit, she has been less focused on her lessons, but I believe it is totally justified. People like Mrs. Brown, though, maintain that a stronger person, a person more dedicated to her career, wouldn't allow her situation at home to affect her work."

Everything clicked: the stark room, the sparse lesson plans, the apparent lethargy, the judgmental colleagues, everything. Mrs. Wilson was not the stereotypical exhausted, self-indulgent teacher like those depicted in films like *Bad Teacher* or *The Breakfast Club*. Her personal life paired with the unhealthy school climate carried her past the emotional threshold. Mr. Kryzynski's final words sum the situation concerning Mrs. Wilson and Clark Middle School absolutely: "This, *this* is what happens when teachers don't receive the support they need—monetarily, administratively, socially, or otherwise; they are forced to cope with so many problems that they build and build to the point where they become insurmountable. At that point, a nervous breakdown is inevitable."

So the question remains: what happens to the students when their educators—their leaders, mentors, and role models—have been thrust off the precipice? What happens when an unhealthy school climate festers, without any sign of significant change in sight? The cycle continues, and the students fall farther behind those who have experienced a positive, nurturing educational setting.

FOR FURTHER DISCUSSION

1. Describe the school climate at Clark Middle School. What factors contribute to the climate?
2. What steps did Kristyn take to manage her difficult eighth graders?
3. How does Kristyn account for the hostility between faculty members at Clark?
4. What steps could teachers and administrators at Clark take to improve its overall climate?

4

CURRICULUM

Introduction

Lindsay Ellis

What comes to mind when you think of *curriculum*? When I started teaching eleventh-grade English, I was given a list of books to teach. I was told to start the year with *Brave New World* by Aldus Huxley and then to teach *Frankenstein* by Mary Shelley. Because the school was new and, as a result, quite small, I didn't have any experienced colleagues teaching the same class. In the two weeks before school began (I was hired in August), I voraciously read and drafted discussion questions and essay assignments for the novels. Though I enjoyed this autonomous and creative work, I admit that I longed more than once for a fairy godmother teacher-friend with a chronologically organized file folder of daily lesson plans to share.

During those two weeks before school began, I was writing curriculum. I had to figure out what I was going to do when students walked into my classroom each day. What would I say? What would I ask them to do? Each day on the calendar was like a blank stage. The actors were going to assemble, looking to me to define and to direct the scene. More than once that first year, I had nightmares about being in a play whose script I hadn't memorized. I was on the stage, the audience waiting for me to say my lines, and mortified.

So as I drafted lesson plans and assignments that August, I was trying to avoid being caught not knowing my lines. I didn't merely want to fill our time with junk, however. I didn't want students to continually ask, "What are we doing today?" as they trudged through the doorway and took their seats. As I reread the novels, I thought about what ideas and skills were valuable and useful to me as an English major in college and in graduate school. I thought about what I wanted students to know and to be able to do by the end of the semester and the year. I tried to create an increasingly complex series of tasks that would teach the understandings and skills that I believed my students would need in twelfth grade and in life. Yes, I made lists of vocabulary words as I read. I also drafted questions for reading quizzes that would both motivate students to do their homework and spark deeper thinking in preparation for discussion. I came up with a list of essay questions for the exam in December. I did what I knew to do at the time to teach English.

Today, in the middle and high schools where I coach pre-service interns, new teachers are rarely just given a novel and told to teach it. Ours is the era of learning standards and standardized assessments. Curricula is sometimes written by committee. In many districts, curriculum is seen as too important to be left to the hand (or whim) of just one teacher.

So what is curricula? A curriculum is a set of plans for what students will learn and how they will learn it. I say *set* of plans because, like an architect's drawings, a curriculum includes large-scale overviews of learning objectives, medium-scale plans for activity sequences, and small-scale plans for resources and word choice when teaching orally and giving instructions in writing. A curriculum should include a purpose, specific content, a sequence, teaching methods, a list of resources, ongoing assessments, and possible adaptations as the teacher learns more about students' unique needs and learning potentials (Fink, 2003; Lattuca & Stark, 2009).

Unlike architects, however, curriculum designers are working with people, with *agents*. One of the most exciting, frustrating, and sometimes overlooked aspects of education research is that human students and human teachers are so infinitely complex and creative that they don't behave in predictable ways. Humans aren't inanimate pieces of wood that can be assembled by architects with exact precision according to the laws of physics. Though our bodies are made up of chemical compounds, educators cannot expect to work like scientists who combine chemical compounds under stable conditions and get the same result every time. The conditions in which teachers teach are changing minute to minute. The variables at play in each student's mind and body as she learns (or does not learn) are immeasurably many. This unpredictability is why we talk not only about *intended curriculum*—that is, the plan as it is drafted, or what teachers hope that students will learn. We also pay attention to the *achieved curriculum*—the knowledge, skills, and attitudes that students actually learn and remember some time later (Cuban, 1992). We are always trying to write intended curriculum with the best chance of becoming achieved curriculum.

Closing the gap between intended curriculum and achieved curriculum requires a deep knowledge of students and how they learn. Making sure that this achieved curriculum is actually useful to students requires deep and careful thinking about what matters in society, in work, and in life. Curriculum writing requires the synthesis not only of psychology and sociology but also the philosophical and the practical. Humans aren't computers (in fact, computers are better at being computers than we are), so curriculum needs to teach students more than recalling facts and computing numbers.

Curricular architects must begin by deciding what knowledge, skills, and understandings are valuable. Teachers in some subject areas (like science and history) must challenge themselves constantly to think about curriculum as more than a body of knowledge that students should know by the end of the year. Deciding *how* to teach what we value is equally challenging. That is the challenge in my own favorite subject: the teaching of writing. Writing is less a body of knowledge and more of a discipline: a skill, an art, and an act. Though writing well does require specific knowledge of the conventions of grammar and genre, the challenge in drafting curricula for the teaching of writing is to put fluency, purpose, conventional grammar, artistry, and genre knowledge together as students use writing to learn or to express their learning about each of their subjects.

Several teachers have written extensively about curricular design in teaching writing. Nancie Atwell (1998) begins her now-classic book *In the Middle* by recounting how prepared she felt when she faced her first classroom of students because she arrived armed with detailed, well-researched curricular plans developed under the guidance of her former professor James Moffett (1968/1986, 1973). Atwell planned to give her students a sequence of increasingly complex writing tasks: writing to oneself in a journal, writing to a single audience in a letter, then writing for a more complex audiences. Atwell felt confident and prepared. The curriculum was tried and true.

What Atwell discovered, though, was that her students, at least some of them, were not engaged or interested in her sequence of assignments. She came to believe that giving students more choice and more autonomy would better foster the skills, understandings, and knowledge that actual writers possess—how to choose a topic, choose words, sentences, and their organization to communicate meaning to a unique audience within the conventions of a chosen genre.

To teach what she believed her students needed to learn, Atwell created a writing workshop in her class, teaching the students *how* to work as a writer but not giving them strict assignments about *what* to write. Over many years of refining her workshop method through observation and reflection, she added more prewritten curricular content back into these workshops. The curricular content that she added explicitly taught students what she understood about writing that they did not. This sounds simple, but her deep and flexible curricular planning required careful observation of the gap between, first, her own understandings and actions as a writer and, second, what her students didn't yet understand and do as writers. In other words, her curriculum could only develop on the heels of her work as a writer, in relationship to a particular population of students.

Some teachers who have read about or tried Atwell's workshop approach doubt its transferability from her teaching context (small class sizes in a small school) to theirs. In the 1980s, when she drafted her curricula, Atwell's first concern was not whether her students successfully scored well on high-stakes tests. She was not seeing six groups of thirty students per day. Under different teaching conditions, critics argue, her curriculum is not possible to implement, but proponents still celebrate her attention to making sure that what is being taught is actually what is useful to individual students.

The complexity of curricular design is evident when comparing one approach to another. While Atwell advocates teaching students how to work as a community of self-directed creative writers in school, another well-respected curricula writer advocates immersing the whole class in one unified unit of activity. Using the principle of scaffolding, George Hillocks (1995) conceives of curriculum as an environment within which students tackle an increasingly complex series of tasks. Teachers must set the stage, creating the multisensory environment that will inspire students' creative engagement. By building skill with simpler tasks as the unit progresses, students develop the understandings and abilities needed to complete final projects that require multiple steps. Hillocks' research suggests that students improve as writers within this curricular structure (Hillocks, 1995). However, research also suggests that a majority of teachers do not use his methods (Smagorinsky, 2009). Hillocks (2009) has weighed in on the influence of his work, expressing frustration that the curricula he has so carefully constructed is not being well implemented. For example, some teachers do not create an adequate environment before giving assignments to students. They do not scaffold their way through the smaller tasks that students will need to combine in order to complete the final project.

Others besides George Hillocks are frustrated that teachers are not implementing the most effective curricular resources available. Many public school districts, including the one in which I live, have drafted and now require teachers to follow a common curriculum across schools. In my city, this means that all sixth graders, whether they are in a Spanish-speaking class in an immersion school or an English-speaking class in a majority African-American neighborhood, are answering the same comprehension questions on the same novel during the same week. Such standardization expresses hope, on the one hand (shared by administrators, curriculum coaches, and teachers working on a curriculum-writing team), that the most effective resources can reach and teach every child. Standardization also expresses fear, on the other hand, that without standardization, teachers will not deliver the most effective resources to their students.

Is this hope realistic? Is this fear pragmatic? Is it true that one curriculum can foster the learning of every child across a district? Are individual teachers too busy actually teaching, grading, and talking to students to also research and write their own effective curriculum? These are important questions, hotly debated.

Tellingly, even when educators agree that curricula should be given to teachers, they have a hard time reaching consensus about what that curricula should be. Two controversies, in particular, return again and again. First, some argue that curricular standards should list what students should know and be able to do at the end of a school year, while others argue that curricula should map a set of issues to tackle and problem-solving heuristics to understand (Applebee, 1997). Second, some argue that students' learning (and the effectiveness of teachers' work) should be discernable through testing, and therefore that if teachers effectively implement curricula, then students will succeed on a test. Others argue that the kind of student learning that is valuable to career and quality of life in a democracy is not discernable on a test, and therefore teachers' delivery of high-quality curricula may not result in students scoring well on a test (a test that measures knowledge and skill not actually helpful beyond succeeding on that same test; Wilson, 2006; Hillocks, 2002).

In the face of these controversies, you may be thinking, "just tell me what to do! Give me examples of clear success to emulate or clear failure to avoid." What we find in the narratives that follow, however, are early career teachers who are assessing and trying to teach within the zones of their students' unique learning potential, to use the curricular materials at hand, and to simultaneously adapt to the curricular cultures of their unique school settings. Indeed, the "right" curriculum (*what* to teach) at any moment must be determined as the intersection of the potential of the learner, the material resources available, and the knowledge of the teacher, within the cultural context.

In order to focus our attention on curriculum, this chapter offers three narratives written by new English teachers like you. Like you, they must decide what will be taught in their classrooms—by assessing their students, themselves, their resources, and the context of their teaching. We think that the variety in these narratives proves that a one-size-fits-all curriculum is a myth, and we invite you to read them as examples of the kind of critical reflection that should accompany curriculum design. Before you do so, you may wish to complete one of the following activities, meant to focus your attention on the curriculum of your middle or high school.

- **The Tale of the Textbook.** The commercial literature anthology plays a major role in secondary English language arts curriculum. Textbooks published by Pearson, McGraw-Hill, and other publishing companies are the primary source of material for many English teachers. For this exercise, borrow a commercial literature anthology from a sibling, a local middle or high school, or your university library. Then, examine it using the questions below, which are drawn from Arthur Applebee's (1991) study of commercial anthologies.

  When was the anthology published? What is the anthology's intended grade level?

  The selections in an anthology can be organized chronologically, thematically, geographically, by genre, or by a combination of these. Check the table of contents to see how your anthology is organized. What assumptions about the study of literature are revealed by the organization of your anthology?

  Survey the selections included in your anthology. How many genres are included? How many contemporary authors? How many women writers and writers of color? What assumptions about the study of literature are revealed by these selections?

  Nearly half an anthology is composed of instructional apparatus—questions before and after the selection, along with a range of additional materials. Find one select and focus on the questions following it. How many are *recitation* questions calling for a single correct answer? How many are *authentic* questions that yield multiple possible responses?

- **The Write Stuff?** Working alone or in small groups, critique the writing assignment shown in Figure 4.1, taken from a middle school English language arts classroom. Would you use this assignment in your language arts class? What kind of curriculum would produce this assignment?
- **Close Reading the Core.** The Common Core State Standards (CCSS) for English Language Arts can be found at http://www.corestandards.org/ela-literacy. Although the CCSS do not mandate particular materials, the standards currently guide the development of curriculum across the nation. Scrutinize the standards on reading and writing. What kinds of reading and writing are privileged? What kinds of reading and writing are deemphasized? What kinds of curriculum and assessment will the CCSS yield, in your opinion?

Figure 4.1 Short Story Assignment

Directions: Using your short story notes and your endless imaginations, you will create a fictional short story. Your story must contain the following elements:

1. Length: 1,000–1,500 words
2. Title (original)
3. Plot (introduction, rising action, climax, falling action, resolution)
4. Characters (protagonist and antagonist)
5. Setting (time and place)
6. Point of view (consistent throughout the story)
7. Conflict
8. Theme
9. Cover (see attached information)
10. Two elements from the options below

Options:

1. Suspense
2. Symbol
3. Irony (verbal or situational)
4. Flashback
5. Foreshadowing
6. Tone
7. Introduction of a second conflict within the storyline

***You must follow the project due dates and guidelines to receive full credit. Use the following pages to help you budget your time and create a masterpiece.

References

Applebee, A. N. (1991). *A study of high school literature anthologies*. National Research Center on English Learning & Achievement. Retrieved from http://www.albany.edu/cela/reports.

Applebee, A. N. (1997). Rethinking curriculum in the English language arts. *The English Journal, 86*(5), 25–31.

Atwell, N. (1998). *In the middle: New understandings about writing, reading, and learning* (2nd ed.). Portsmouth, NH: Heinemann.

Cuban, L. (1992). Curriculum stability and change. In P. Jackson (Ed.), *Handbook of research on curriculum*. New York, NY: Macmillan Library Reference.

Fink, L. D. (2003). *Creating significant learning experiences: An integrated approach to designing college courses*. San Francisco, CA: Jossey-Bass.

Hillocks, G. (1995). *Teaching writing as reflective practice*. New York, NY: Teachers College Press.

Hillocks, G. (2002). *The testing trap: How state writing assessments control learning*. New York, NY: Teachers College Press.

Hillocks, G. (2009). A response to Peter Smagorinsky: Some practices and approaches are clearly better than others and we had better not ignore the differences. *The English Journal, 98*(6), 23–29.

Moffett, J. (Ed.). (1973). *Interaction: A student-centered language arts and reading program, K-12*. Boston, MA: Houghton Mifflin.

Moffet, J. (1986). *Teaching the universe of discourse*. Portsmouth, NH: Boynton/Cook. (Original work published 1968)

Lattuca, L., & Stark, J. (2009). *Shaping the college curriculum: Academic plans in context*. San Francisco, CA: Jossey-Bass.

Smagorinsky, P. (2009). Is it time to abandon the idea of "best practices" in the teaching of English? *English Journal, 98*(6), 15.

Wilson, M. (2006). *Rethinking rubrics in writing assessment*. Portsmouth, NH: Heinemann.

 David Jagusch teaches high school English at an alternative high school in Detroit, Michigan. He earned his BA from Grand Valley State University and his MA from the University of Michigan. When he's not teaching and coaching his school's boys' varsity basketball team, David spends his free time writing poetry and playing guitar.

Kibera Sings
David Jagusch
Altius Academy, Kenya

My first day teaching in Kenya was nothing I expected; but then again, I didn't know what to expect, so I suppose all went according to plan. The students couldn't have been more different than those I taught in the States. They had an authentic desire to learn, they were polite, they wanted to read aloud, and they wanted to answer my questions. They had no fear of being wrong. They stood to address me formally as *teacher* or *sir*. They carried my supplies for me, erased the blackboard for me, even pulled my chair out for me to take a seat.

I began my day by teaching English, grade seven. I started with just this one class, but as I became comfortable and assimilated, I took on grades four through eight for the rest of my stay. It went quickly; the lessons were focused, as all lessons in the slum are, straight from the textbook, which more closely resembled a coloring book compared to the cinderblocks of paper and glue back in America. I couldn't help but be amazed. Growing up in the slum, children were fluent in at least three languages: Swahili, English, and their tribal dialects. America seems the only place where children don't grow up speaking more than one language as the norm. We engaged in close-reading exercises, applied interpretation to short stories, learned vocabulary, and practiced multiple adjectives in singular description, for instance: the scrawny, pale-faced, ink-filled teacher.

Next, I became the sixth-grade science teacher for their lessons before lunch, getting a refresher on blood vessels, arteries, capillaries, and veins taking oxygen to and from all parts of the body. I made them look into each other's eyes, watching capillaries, then squeeze their arms until veins came popping. We then examined pulse rates by running, the boys in their pale blue shorts and girls in their dresses, sprinting around the building, me alongside as they listened and felt their hearts go *thump-plump* to remind them that they were, in fact, alive.

For the final lesson of the day, I taught seventh-grade science on a topic that I have little knowledge of and even less experience with: the female reproductive system. We discussed uterine walls, ovulation, vaginas, and menstruation. The thirteen-year-old boys and girls were more stoic and scientific than I was when they talked about insertion and penetration, subjects I never thought I would teach, but I suppose it was good practice so I can tell my son or daughter about placentas and afterbirth, just so they know what they're getting themselves into before they decide to give it a go.

About a week into teaching, the reason I stayed in the slum presented itself: music. Before classes commenced, the students formed ranks by grade level, babies up to grade eight. The principal then chose one level to lead the music. The entire student body began to clap in unison a four-four time signature. Then a solo rang out over the beat, sung by a sixth grader in Swahili, her voice that of a Kibera princess repeated by the rest of her class until finally the entire student body joined in, call and response accented by the naturalness of body percussion. Boys so young projected voices so deep. Girls connected their hymns to the sweet chorals of ancient birds; I closed my eyes and was lifted in spirit. In that moment, I was home. For half an hour, songs blended together into continuous praise, an opera of youth.

Not until the singing was almost finished did I notice Kibera's residents beginning their daily redundancy of survival. I realized that the students weren't just singing in ritual, they were singing to Kibera—not above, not at, not around, but *to* Kibera. From midway into Kibera, on a ridge overlooking the southern half of the slum, along the railroad tracks, students gave a daily morning gift to Kibera more nourishing and filling than toasted bread and tea, taking all minds off the smells, off the streets running with shit after last night's rain, off the crumbling walls and leaky, roasting, rusted tin roofs. With songs of worship accented by all the *Hallelujahs*, the gift of tranquility and forgetfulness floated down like butterfly wings, resting softly on the shoulders of Kibera, flapping softly into ears, washing away the infection of poverty, dripping down in little falls onto fingertips and feet, leaving imprints of humanity amid the slum. The children, the music, and the sun all made me a better person. I was witnessing beauty in true human form, naturally created. I had to turn away and hide my eyes so students and teachers wouldn't wonder why I was crying.

From that moment, I began concocting plans to fundraise and start a music program at Altius. First, I met with a Kiberan man named Dennis, a musician and church music instructor, to plan what types of instruments and materials were needed. He promised to get estimates so that I could figure out the amount of money to be raised. I wasn't able to do this task because, being white in Nairobi, most storeowners would try to make me pay more. The biggest obstacle that we foresaw was finding a teacher for the program once I left; the salary for an instructor would not be able to be raised every year to come. The next week, the principal and head pastor of the school held a meeting with the staff; all agreed that my music plan could be implemented, the only struggle being that of hiring an instructor and procuring extra funds for salary. I called up a local piano man to look at an ancient piano housed in the adjoining church that we'd be able to use for the program. I then headed to downtown Nairobi with an employee of the volunteer organization to quote the instruments and books. The plan was beginning to fall into place. Music could come to the school and to the children, allowing them to play and sing.

Just as I was in the midst of planning the music program, another volunteer, Mary, started a women's education program. The program was intended to educate girls and women of all ages on reproductive health and to empower women as individuals. I helped write the curriculum and provided any assistance she needed, whether it was running errands or looking for supplies and donations. The first event was held at Altius for our female students and women in the nearby beauty school and surrounding slum. Even though it was a rainy Saturday on which the girls and women could have been working, nearly the entire female population of Altius was in attendance, another tribute to the value they placed on education. Of all that happened during the event, what remains clearest in my mind are the slips of paper we passed out allowing them to write down questions they were too shy, embarrassed, or afraid to ask aloud. Many of the questions were along these lines:

"My father is raping me and threatening to no longer pay my school fees or to stop giving me food or to kick me out of the house if I tell anyone. What should I do?"

And: "What should you do if your family is forcing you to go out and have sex with strangers for money to bring home?"

I walked back to the house slower than usual that day, crying behind my sunglasses.

Students of Kibera had to take midterms and finals, similar to testing in the States, on which students receive a score no matter if they study in the ghetto of downtown Detroit or the mansions of Grosse Pointe. After midterms were completed, I graded the eighth-grade composition portion of the test in which students had to write a two-page creative response completing the following prompt: "You have just arrived home after school. While taking a cup of tea, your father . . ." and the rest was up to them to complete. Most wrote of their fathers coming home drunk, hollering and yelling, beating and breaking things, smashing the house and family.

One essay in particular branded my memory. The student wrote that her father walked in the door, demanding to know where her mother was. Her mother was out to see her sister. Their son (the author of the story) wrote that his father was furious, wanting dinner, smashing the tea thermos to the floor, locking the son and siblings outside in the rainy cold. When the mother came home, bewildered as to what was going on, the father flung the door open and started throwing punches, knocking his wife and sons starry-eyed, the kids shouting for the neighbors, for anyone, for help. The father then dragged the mother into the house. By the time the son came to and walked back into their shanty, he saw his father with a *panga* (a machete) hacking away at his mother's neck until her head became fully detached from her body. The son passed out. She was bleeding like "a running water flow," he wrote. He then awoke to police taking his father away for life; he and his brothers and sisters were now orphans. I showed this essay to one of the head teachers. She gave a nervous chuckle and said that for the compositions the students were supposed to be as creative as possible as she kept her hands busy twisting a pen to hide the shaking. This was *too* detailed: all stories blossom from seeds of truth.

About two-and-a-half months into my stay, I was still in the collecting stage of starting the music program, dealing with the headaches and aggravations of gathering funds from halfway around the world to purchase instruments and books. I could not teach well without resources, and the communities that I saw were consistently thirsty for education. I saw this when I headed out to a rural Maasai village with another volunteer named Kristen, an elementary school teacher from Canada. Our aim was to help the teachers in any areas they wanted, providing them with strategies and suggestions, many of them not having any formal teaching training. I was apprehensive about going, excited to see open African wildlife away from diesel and shanties and flaming garbage piles, looking forward to quiet sounds and time to relax and think, yet nervous to experience, yet again, different ways of life.

We started by observing three teachers, some of them naturals, especially one, a man in his thirties with an exuberant smile. Other teachers we observed seemed confined to the textbooks they had, and like American teachers, worried about teaching to the government exams. Though these villages were small, they administered the same tests as the city and slum schools. Echoing debates back at home, they seemed to be trying to cover too much at one time, resulting in the students learning nothing at all. The classes were also larger than those of the Kibera slum, some with more than fifty children coming from kilometers around. The students stared at Kristen and me in curious, sideways glances and grins.

The first workshop that we led for the teachers concerned mathematics (Kristen's forte, not mine) and discussed the conceptual differences between digits and representations. One teacher in particular was hesitant and questioned why they needed these new strategies, why they couldn't simply open the textbooks and provide students with what was written on the pages in front of them. Through an open discussion, this group would have made Socrates proud by asking each other questions, until they realized that education is a useless commodity if one is unable to transfer and apply what is read in books into real-life situations, whether in dusty bean-fed villages or muddy bean-fed cities. Overall, the first day was a success with all the teachers acting again like students, excited to learn, laughing at their own mistakes, and eager to guide the youth of their tribes, their villages, and their country. Kristen and I experienced the greatest joy of teaching when we saw the smiles of understanding stretch cross their faces. Seeing this in adult teachers was in certain ways more rewarding than teaching young people. It was proof that regardless of age, education was valuable and satisfying.

For the next two days, we observed the rest as the staff and held two more workshops. The second of the three focused on English, and I took the lead for this one. Kristen and I did a sample lesson demonstrating subject matter and instructional strategies, the teachers eagerly wanting to answer my questions and laughing in jest at their classmates who gave wrong answers. They were engaged as they shed their role as teachers and took on the role of students.

One older Maasai teacher with sagging ears had eyes that came alive and sparkled. He was a sage who understood education and all its possibility and mysticism. When we observed him, however, he was highly animated, telling jokes with all the maturity of a twelve year old, the sheer opposite of his stern demeanor outside of the classroom.

As a final workshop, we addressed the topic of assessment: why as teachers we do it and what it can be used for. I was aware that my personal philosophies were an undercurrent in our discussion, my disdain for government standardization ringing through. But my opinions weren't even necessary. The teachers eagerly shouted and raised their hands and voices, their own distaste for the tests that they were forced to give dripping from their tongues. "Just because you fail a test doesn't mean you're not smart!" they argued. I should bring them to speak to Congress.

Upon arriving back at the home-stay in Jamhuri, I found out there had been a snag in the money collection for the music program. The online bank account that we were using had been frozen, the reason being "suspicious activity" because money was coming in from multiple locations. Even after providing them with the documentation to prove the legitimacy of our program, they still refused to reopen the account with frozen donations inside. I had no idea what would happen with all those donations, because the bank didn't trust our music program in the slum. I suppose that they would rather know that the money was staying in the country in case they needed another bailout.

Another time I was grading, this time a standard fourth-grade examination composition, I came across a jumbled mess of words and letters with maybe one in every thirty discernable as English. I assumed the student had misunderstood the assignment, writing a composition for English class in Swahili, but when I handed it over to one of the Kenyan teachers and asked if my assumption was correct, she shook her head. Her eyes moved up and down the page for minutes until responding with, "This is very serious." I then realized that this was not Swahili, but instead confused English. The student who authored the piece was called to meet with us in the teachers' office where we sat. He was a meek child with a smooth face and delicate features. He came to the door with folded hands and a bent head, not knowing the reason for his summons, but right in his assumption this was not a social visit. The teachers asked if he could write down the alphabet for us. Once past the letter F, his pencil tip began dragging, scraping the page, unsure of the order, the shapes, and sounds of what was to come next. When asked, he couldn't explain what he wrote in his composition. Maybe he was too embarrassed and knew he was in trouble, or perhaps he didn't know what he was trying to say. His head sank lower to the ground the longer he stood in the office, watching his own feet kick at pebbles and dirt, afraid to speak above a whisper. He feared being punished and beaten, the common result for poor classroom performance.

The look of helplessness on his face as he walked out of the office galvanized my desire to teach.

After he left, the teachers and I began brainstorming what could be done to help him. I presented the concept of learning disabilities to them, discussing the possibility of it not being a simple matter of smart or stupid. After all, his oral language was pristine in pronunciations and lexicon, but there was a gap somewhere when it came to the processing of sounds. But in a place like Kibera, where adults struggle to provide children with basic food and shelter, there were simply no resources for students with learning disabilities. Nonetheless, lack of resources aside, the teachers responded with genuine heartache and concern, willing to take their own time to work with him through his challenges, refusing to give up, believing that he could be anything so long as he didn't become discouraged. Remaining hopeful and resilient, they refused to let another child become one with the street, just another boy of the shadows, shaking and hungry.

After nearly three months of dealing with all the headaches from the banks and online systems, we finally reached our fundraising goal. I headed downtown to the music district, a street full of shops selling instruments, electronics, stereos, and televisions. DJs, club owners, and aspiring musicians gathered there, scheming to get their hands on the newest expensive gear. After bartering and negotiating, my friend James helped me to purchase a keyboard; several acoustic guitars; drums various in size, shell, and head; and a variety of shakers. We placed orders and exchanged money for stamped forms and receipts; everything was to be collected the next day and taken directly to the school. I was proud and amazed that we actually accomplished it. Each and every donation had come from everyday people: teachers, students, friends, and family in the United States, all with their own financial burdens and stresses back home. There were even donors who I had never met, who still gave, believing that improving education in a person's life, no matter how insignificant it may seem, is still better than making no difference at all.

The next day we picked up the instruments. We headed to the main street where we purchased the majority of our instruments. My favorite were drums from a locally owned no-name-brand manufacturer, simply an old man in the back corner of a shop with tools, wood, twine, and leather, a man who carved guitars by hand and shaped drums, stretching wet hides taught to dry, ornamenting shells with fur and wide thread stitching. We purchased four such drums, two large and two small. Two were covered with dark brown, soft fur, and the other two with a mixture of white-black-gray fur, each with woven straps to be slung over shoulders and braced under the arm, allowing both hands to beat rhythmic dances, chants, and hymns.

On all of these outings, James had been of the utmost help by searching, pricing, and guiding me through Kenyan commerce. With every errand I needed, with every trip, he made sure that the prices I paid were accurate, and that I wasn't lost in fast-bartering Swahili tongues and rapid gestures. The least I could do was pay his bus fare and give him lunch money for each of his trips, the days being so hot and dry. He was proud and modest, for it was usually already late in the day when he would tell me that he hadn't been able to take breakfast because he simply couldn't afford enough to eat. I could tell at lunch that day that he was afraid to order more than what I had, but at my insistence I was glad to see him exhale in contentment as he bit into an extra order of *chapati* followed by slurps of pineapple soda. Riding back to Kibera in a vanload surrounded by bags and boxes, the outcome of the giving power of love, I sat back with my eyes closed and let the breeze through the soaring van window fill me with the breath of Africa.

Arriving back at Kibera, I experienced true magic: immediately after pulling through the school gate, we parked, slid the door open, and the students swarmed, most not knowing what was inside the van. Only a few of the older students from my upper classes had caught word that music was on its way to the school. A buzz arose at the sight of the boxes, packages, and bags all bulging with potential. I perched in the open door, handing out the loot, feeling sorry that there weren't enough instruments for every student to be able to hold, carry, and play at the same time. The excitement was humming through their bodies and voices as they all fought to touch something new, something that would allow them to create, something that would allow them to transform their lives into song.

Instantly, music and dance, like a flashing savannah dust storm, swept over the schoolyard. No direction was needed, no permission, no orders; it was as natural to them as going without breakfast, lunch, and dinner. One of the older boys, with a new drum under his arm, began a beat and called out a chant, and in no more than a few seconds every drum, *kayamba*, and shaker joined in with compliment-ing rhythms. There were no written notes or sheet music, no practice or instruc-tion, simply the music living in their depths as integral to their survival as heart or lungs. Those without instruments grabbed hands with friends, stomping, clapping, singing responses, or screaming with joy. The youngest ones spun in circles, letting the colors of the world blend with the harmonies in the air.

Until that moment, I had been unsure. I had been constantly asking myself, "What is Africa to me?" Then I had an answer. It is when those who have nothing reject sorrow and come together in one song, when the sounds of children's joy accept the moment and nothing more, when the song of life overcomes death. Africa to me is when Kibera sings.

Before we could begin music classes, I needed to spend a day working on the guitars we purchased. I need to adjust the bridges and actions of the guitars, to tune and to clean them. Fortunately, I had time immediately, because the school term happened to be ending on this day. For the children, it was not a day of rest, however. When I reached campus in the morning, I saw students all around the schoolyard with buckets, rags, and dirty water, washing the schoolroom floors, windows, and walls. Children were sweeping dirt, rinsing desks, ensuring that the beginning of the next term would serve as a reminder that in a world of filth and grime, education is still knowledge, pure and clean.

I couldn't help but chuckle at this cultural contrast to the United States, reinforced as I watched little school children hand-washing, older students in bare feet standing ankle deep in mud, painstakingly reaching to get windows and classroom building corners spotless. Meanwhile, some students back home were ruining textbooks, desks, tables, chairs, floors, and walls, refusing to notice the janitor's slow step behind them bending and laboring with an arthritic back, picking up what they leave behind as they laugh and spit and look away. But not here. This was everyone's school, everyone's home, everyone's opportunity. There was no work below anyone's station; no work too dirty, sticky, or full of stench; no one's hands better or worse. All played the same role, boy and girl, young and old, student and teacher, everyone working together with no complaints or protests. It was a chance to be together and get something accomplished; another way that education made them all equal.

The first guitar class consisted of all older students, two eighth graders, two seventh graders, my friend James, and Mac, the school security guard and groundskeeper. Already knowing their eagerness, I was still impressed with how adeptly they took to instruction. Some caught on quicker than others, James especially, and a boy named Byron, from seventh grade. Like beatnik boppers, they were able to pick up and blow, the instruments as natural feeling to them as clapping, able to let the tunes flow and pop. After a basic introduction of string names, guitar parts, and holding, we began with strumming techniques. Next, the first chord I taught was G-major, only one student having trouble with his finger placement and spacing, unable to arch his fingers so not to mute the other strings. Upon helping him, using my hand to guide his own, I noticed the rigidity, the calloused stiffness in his joints. His were the hands of a boy not knowing childhood, already the arthritic hands of a laborer permanently curled tight to his palm from long, heat-filled afternoons after school swinging an ax or wielding a pick and spade.

I wished some girls had shown up on that first day. One of the boys made the observation: "It's not like with boys—girls don't have free time during the day." On top of work outside of school that boys and girls both do—going out to supplement their family's income by street vending, begging, or working small jobs—girls were also confined to claustrophobic shanty walls, backs bent in muddy alleyways doing family laundry, scrubbing floors, preparing meals, or looking after babies and siblings. There was not a single house-girl or washerwoman you couldn't hear singing songs of redemption and forgiveness while they worked.

After not even a half-dozen guitar classes, we grew from an average class size of seven students to over twenty. Students couldn't come to every class because many had to work after school, but their effort and desire was clear. Having such a large number of students and only five guitars, I had to split them into groups of four. Not a single one of them minded: the children of Kibera knew the importance of sharing, knew that everyone having a little is better than an individual having it all. Their fingers, joyful in noise, sounded like angelic hymns.

The boys became uncomfortable when for the first time girls showed up. But I was ecstatic. Their discomfort was heightened when most of the girls, their fingertips toughened by years of scrubbing, were able to play the guitars better. Fortunately, the students were willing to become teachers; they helped each other strum and pluck, boys and girls together holding hands in one goal, one purpose, for one hour able to forget their hunger, aches, and worries.

In my introduction to music class, I taught younger students musical terms and notation—staffs, quarters, halves, wholes, and time signatures. A week earlier, a shipment of recorders and music books had arrived. Compared to the guitar class that was composed mainly of students from the upper classes, in the introductory class there were many young students, over half being below the age of ten, wanting the chance to blow and make sounds they had never heard. I had a hard time teaching the notes and proper fingering with them all creating shrieking, high-pitched noises.

I was asked by an adult sitting in on the lesson, "Isn't this too hard, too beyond what they can remember, what they can learn?" No. Never. Nothing is beyond the open mind, nothing beyond the willing. Tomorrow they may not remember the musical lines or spaces, but if they keep trying, keep playing, keep creating, they will grow in theory and practice and song. Age is irrelevant. The world needs to have confidence in what youth can do and achieve, in what they can be—nothing is beyond them, nothing is impossible, nothing is too difficult for the hands of those willing to try.

FOR FURTHER DISCUSSION

1. What is the significance of music to David, to his students, and to the community within which the school is located?
2. How does David's approach to teaching music compare to what we know about the school's approach to teaching English and math?
3. What can teachers learn about creating curriculum from David's experience?

Sierra Holmes lives and teaches in her hometown in West Michigan. She has a BA in English (Secondary Education) from Grand Valley State University. She is currently earning her MA in English and enjoys participating in the Lake Michigan Writing Project summer institutes. When she is not at school, Sierra spends her free time with her family, friends, and very spoiled pets. She can often be found scouring the shelves of local bookstores for new additions to her classroom library.

Going Gradeless
Sierra Holmes
Lakeview High School

I loved English in high school because my teachers gave me books to read that meant something to me and encouraged me to write about things I found important. They made me feel like I had a voice, and when I decided to be an English teacher, I wanted to make my students feel that way, too. I wanted to be responsive to who they were and what they needed. Of course, I had no clue how to do that. To learn, I began reading everything I could get my hands on about teaching. Because all this was going on in 2005 and 2006, I read lots of articles by people who were staunch advocates of "higher" standards, data-driven instruction, and teacher accountability for student achievement on standardized tests. I paid close attention to their words and came to understand their arguments, but even then, when I was only just taking my first hesitant steps into the world of teaching, I knew that model didn't make sense to me. It didn't reflect the experience I'd had as a student in several wonderful English classes. It didn't honor the deeply important teaching that my own outstanding teachers had done while I was in their classrooms.

Luckily, those articles weren't all I read. I also began devouring books about educational philosophy. I read about teaching reading and writing. I read about assessment. I stayed awake late into the night, curled up in my loft with a flashlight, devouring the words of Don Murray, Don Graves, Tom Newkirk, and Tom Romano. My shelves, already stuffed with novels, buckled as I added books by Linda Christensen, Jeff Wilhelm, Linda Reif, and Peter Elbow to the tops of the already too-tall piles. These teachers argued passionately for a different approach to teaching. They believed in the value of subjectivity and the importance of engaging with students in the learning process. Theirs was a deeply responsive pedagogy, one that honored teachers, students, and the life-changing nature of the work they do together in the classroom. Finally, I saw my own experience as a student reflected in their stories, and I knew that they were on the right track. Through reading and reflection, I grew determined to be an advocate of responsive teaching, at least as much of an advocate as I could be without yet actually being a teacher. I also grew determined to become an opponent of attempts to standardize and control teachers, students, and learning.

I took that determination into the only real place I had to voice it at the time, my education classes. While some of my professors encouraged my ideas, my peers often dismissed me as an idealist, as if there were something wrong with that. I would dive headfirst into a heated discussion about the most appropriate methods of writing assessment, only to be told by a classmate that it just wasn't realistic to think kids were going to care enough about their writing to do it if they weren't being graded. Another testified that the kids she was working with just wouldn't revise unless they were forced to do so. "It's a good idea," they'd say, "but it just won't work with real kids."

I graduated from college as determined as ever to become a teacher whose pedagogy matched her knowledge that kids naturally want to be engaged in learning that they find meaningful. I wanted to find a school where I could experiment with my teaching in order to discover the most effective ways to help my students invest in their learning. I wanted to be able to assess in a way that would match the way I taught and reflect my students' desire to be heard rather than judged. I also wanted to make my classroom decisions based on what made sense, not on what policy said I was supposed to do. Basically, I wanted to teach in a way that was responsive to my students and their needs. But I was worried. I knew none of these things was going to be easy.

After all, most schools, thanks to a variety of laws and incentives, were barreling down a slippery, data-laden slope, creating common curricula and assessments with the assumption that those were necessary to show that teachers were teaching and students were learning. These schools also assumed that common assessment data meant something important, and that if all teachers did the same thing, students would all learn the same thing. They were developing often elaborate behaviorist systems to reward and punish students, teachers, or both for achievement or lack thereof, however they defined it. None of those things were compatible with how I wanted to teach, and I knew it. But I didn't know of any schools that were doing anything differently. Any, that is, except one.

While I had been studying to earn my teaching certificate, big things had been happening in my hometown high school. While other schools were running headfirst into the data trap, often with the help of some version of Richard DuFour's (1998) Professional Learning Community model, the staff of this district had gone in a different direction entirely. The teachers there, including those who had been so important to my own excellent high school experience, knew that it didn't make sense to begin trying to improve a school by looking at achievement on common or standardized assessments, because most meaningful learning is highly subjective. By only testing those things that teachers can agree on, most standardized assessments are by nature unreliable measures of students' unique learning trajectories. The teachers at my high school also understood that even on valid assessments, achievement is a product of teaching; if better learning is the goal, improving teaching has to be the focus. For those reasons and others, the staff had decided to create their own professional development model from the ground up, and avoid worrying about data altogether. They began by reflecting on moments when they as teachers had connected strongly with their subject areas. They examined those experiences, and used the common threads they found as the basis for a new vision statement:

> In an environment which recognizes that learning is relational, students will engage in the complex questions that face them—in the world, the work-place and continuing education—and use the perspective and skills of each field to address these issues.

Next, the teachers broke off into four professional learning communities, each charged with the task of researching one of the four key aspects of the vision: relational learning, workplace education, continuing education, and global educa-tion. They read and discussed countless research articles, decided what was most important about their topic, and then presented their findings to the rest of the staff at a retreat organized by the school improvement team.

By the time I arrived for my interview, the staff had begun to discuss how to put the knowledge they had amassed into practice more consistently, across both teachers and subject areas. They were determined to do that, however, without mandating common lessons, techniques, or assessments. They knew that those things could only lead to superficial changes, and what they really wanted was to change the culture of the school in a deep, meaningful way. They wanted to increase learning by building professional capacity and by helping teachers to become more responsive to the needs of their students. This school's improvement process had left the door open for me to be the kind of teacher I'd always wanted to be. When the principal, one of my former writing teachers, called to offer me a position teaching in his English department, with a few additional sections of Spanish in the middle school, I did not hesitate to say yes. It was a no-brainer. Somehow, I'd ended up right back in the right place.

Almost as soon as I accepted my position, I realized that getting a teaching position was by far the simplest part of having one. Next came getting ready for the school year, and that part was far more complicated, in a good way. Nobody was going to drop a binder full of lesson plans, curricular pacing guides, and com-mon assessments on my desk. Nobody was going to hand me a rubric and tell me I had to use it to grade my students' writing. My new colleagues responded enthusiastically to my late-August requests for information about what the heck I was supposed to be teaching in a few weeks, and handed me folder after folder full of everything from background information on novels to assignment sheets for essays. But unlike at some schools, where I would have been told not just what would be taught, but also how and when, the other English teachers told me what was in the curriculum, and told me to feel free to steal or not steal their materials as I saw fit. It was up to me to decide what to do, and it was up to me to choose how to best assess it. I had the freedom I'd always wanted to teach the way I wanted. Now I just had to put my beliefs about meaningful, responsive teaching and assessment into practice. That sounds simple enough, but I wasn't at all sure how to start. Still, armed with the firm conviction that just by luck I was bound to get at least a few things right, I was more than ready to try.

Barely a week into the school year, my fifth-hour freshman English class had already stolen my heart flat. They and their classmates oozed personality, and their spunk and liveliness made our class a blast to teach. One of the first things we did together was write personal narratives.

I went out of my way to make that early high school writing experience a good one for my students. We looked at sample narratives and discussed what made them work. We did plenty of quick writes to come up with ideas. I conferred with students while they wrote, offering feedback as necessary and helping them past spots where they got stuck. I talked students through their first feeble attempts at sentence combining and offered examples to help them begin to consider issues of mechanics in writing. I demonstrated the peer revision process, and provided them with plenty of time to go through it. Then, finally, they printed their papers for our read-around.

The read-around was scheduled for a Friday afternoon. Normally, the last hour of the day on Friday could be a bit hectic, but this week, the kids were geeked to hear their classmates' stories. After our reading time, I asked them all to pull out their papers and put the desks in a circle. Anyone who has ever watched twenty-seven kids try to make a circle out of thirty desks in a very crowded classroom knows it involves a lot of pushing, pulling, sliding, jumping over, and ducking under desks, books, backpacks, and people. It also involves a lot of wincing and pleas to be careful on the part of the teacher. This time was no different in any of those respects, but it was different in that I'd never seen it all happen so fast. Those desks were in a tight circle, filled with freshmen, in about two minutes flat. After a quick discussion, we decided that whoever had possession of Blake's skateboard would read, which despite Adam and Levi's many attempts to steal it away, meant Blake would begin.

Since I'd been reading their papers over their shoulders all week, I had a pretty good idea what was in each one, and I knew who the strongest writers were. I knew some of the papers that would be read that day still needed work, but I was eager for the authors to see the impact of their writing on a real audience. I watched and listened carefully as Blake began his story about the bond skateboarding had helped him create with his uncle, layered over a story about skateboarding in a bank parking lot. There were some issues with Blake's paper. He had summarized a few key scenes in a way that detracted from the overall quality of the story, and in some places, even after the revisions he'd made, it wasn't completely clear which story he was trying to tell. Some of his verb tenses didn't make sense, and I knew there were still some other mechanical issues, too.

But that didn't stop the other kids and I from being captivated by the way he described the feel of a skateboard under his feet. There was good writing in Blake's paper, despite the issues, and even though he still had a long way to go, I was pleased with how far he'd come. I'd seen the original draft. This was an improvement. *It'll probably be a C or so*, I thought, *but that's okay. When he revises some more, he's going to end up with a really nice paper.* I couldn't wait to help him work his way through that revision.

When Blake finished reading, we all *oohed* and *ahhed* over his story. Then he glanced around the room, picked the next reader, and, in a practiced motion, wheeled his skateboard back and sent it rolling across the empty interior of our circle to Jonise, who stopped it with her foot, and became our next reader. Over the course of the hour, we laughed a lot, and even cried a little, as the kids read stories about everything from crazy escapades with their friends to family members dying from cancer. We finished up just in time for the bell to ring, and they left their papers in a helter-skelter pile on the front table on their way out the door. I went home that evening, eager to absorb their words.

When I was done grading my class's papers, I was left with some As, Bs and Cs, and a very few lower grades, only because the authors had not finished their stories or had not revised at all, despite my best attempts to help them do so. On Monday, I passed those papers back, with my comments, of course, and reminded all the kids several times that they could revise, no matter what grade they'd received. I thought for sure many would do so. By leaving the door open for them to revise, and therefore change their grades, I thought I'd downplayed the grades themselves. I thought the kids would worry less about their grades, because they would know those grades didn't have to be permanent. They would think about their writing instead, and take the opportunity to make that writing better. But I soon realized that I was wrong. Most kids didn't revise, and those who did had very different reasons than I'd hoped.

"Ms. Holmes," Marianne asked me as she dropped a revised manuscript in my hands, "could you look at this and tell me if I changed enough to bring my paper up to an A?" It knocked the wind right out of me. She, like the others who had chosen to revise, did so because of the grade, not because of any desire to make the writing itself better. And the kids who I'd most hoped would revise weren't even motivated by the prospect of improving their grades, much less by a desire to improve their writing or be understood more clearly. They didn't revise at all, and for that reason, they missed out on the learning opportunity they so desperately needed. My intentions had been good, but this system wasn't at all responsive to my kids or their needs. I'd goofed up. This was my first clue that my relationship with grading needed to change. Fortunately, I was free to make that change. I just needed to figure out how.

More quickly than I could blink, the first semester ended and the second began. Along with it came new classes and the opportunity to teach the same curriculum for a second time, something I'd never done before. Luckily, I had Thanksgiving weekend to think about what I wanted to do differently this time around and what I didn't. When my new group of freshman English students walked through the door on Monday, I was ready to go. This time, I would put off grading their writing as long as possible by responding to several drafts first. I would be lying if I said I didn't have some concerns about the new system. After all, doing it that way meant the grades in the grade book—the ones parents, students, teachers, and administrators could pull up at any time—would be few and far between. Also, all my carefully cultivated beliefs about engagement and kids working because they wanted to were about to be put to the test. Would I be able to keep my students invested enough to keep up with their work when they weren't being graded on it regularly?

Three weeks into the start of the semester, we had reached a milestone: my kids were turning in drafts of their personal narratives for the first time. I stood behind my desk a few minutes before the bell rang and smiled stupidly as they dropped their stories into a pile in front of me. Even the hours and hours of reading and responding that I knew I'd be doing that weekend didn't stop the excitement from bubbling up in my stomach. Even the anticipation of cramped hands and strained eyes couldn't dull my sense of privilege. Being handed their words, their stories, was not only part of my job, yes, but it was also a tremendous gift. I stood there savoring the moment, silently promising myself that I'd never lose sight of what it meant. They were trusting me by giving me their papers, and I was determined to respond to their writing in a way that would prove I deserved it.

The last paper landed on top of the pile just as the bell rang. Its author, Nicolle, returned to her seat to pick up her things, spending an inordinate amount of time zipping her pencil into the pouch, tucking her papers into her folder, and sliding her bookmark into her novel. She was doing a dance I'd come to recognize as that of a student who wants to talk to a teacher about something, but is a bit shy about asking. I wasn't surprised. Nicolle, one of the quietest students I'd ever met, was always shy about speaking up. I decided to make this easier on her.

"What class do you have next?" I asked.

"Science," she answered quickly.

"Do you need a pass, or do you think you can make it?"

"I think I can make it." She looked nervous. I tried to figure out what might be on her mind. "Umm, Ms. Holmes?"

Here it was. "Hmm?"

"You said you're not grading our papers yet, right?"

"Right. I'm just going to read them and leave comments."

"Okay," she sighed in relief. "Mine is . . . I don't know. It just isn't right. I think the beginning is okay, but I'm not really sure about the rest of it."

"I know you were working really hard on those middle paragraphs in the lab," I replied. "I bet it's a lot better than you think it is, but I'll look at it when I'm reading, and if you want me to, I'll help you revise it next week, okay?"

"Okay," she replied. She shuffled out the door, leaving me to my thoughts. I'd been helping Nicolle with her paper all week. A very conscientious student, she had incredibly high expectations for herself, and I knew she'd been struggling to perfect a key portion of her narrative. I hadn't seen the essay since her last revision after one of our writing conferences the day before, but I knew she couldn't be far off. I also knew she was already going to have an A paper, but that was beside the point.

As promised, I read Nicolle's paper over the weekend. As promised, I responded to it without grading it. I paid particular attention to the middle section that I knew she wasn't sure about, and I tried to leave comments that would address her concerns. On Monday, I passed back the paper and watched as Nicolle studied each of my responses in turn. She jotted down a few notes in her margins, and later that week, when given the opportunity to go back to the lab, she revised. She revised that middle section big time, some of it in response to my comments, and some of it on her own. When she was done, she was much happier with her paper. The dialogue she had added to a key scene helped capture the personality of her cousin, a main character in the story; and the newly added description of the landscape outside their family's cabin was so vivid that I could almost smell the pine trees and hear the fish jumping in the nearby lake. She had also moved a few paragraphs that were once near the end of the story to the beginning, altering the chronology of the story in a way that made me feel compelled to keep reading. As good as the previous draft had been, I had to admit, this one was better.

If I'd have graded Nicolle's paper the first time she turned it in, she would have received an A. It was already a high-quality paper. Unfortunately, if she had received that A, Nicolle's paper would have been done. With the highest grade possible already plugged into the grade book, the only reason she would have had to revise is her own internal desire to end up with the story she wanted to write. Of course, she revised without the grade, for that very reason. I couldn't help but wonder if she'd have thought her paper was good enough, and just let it be, had I passed it back with that letter at the bottom of the last page. At best, an earlier grade would've been irrelevant. At worst, it would have been an impediment to revision. It was Nicolle's classmates who convinced me that the latter was much more likely.

In the stack of papers that I'd taken home that weekend, few had been as polished as Nicolle's. I'd responded to all those other papers the same way I had hers, and given their authors the opportunity to work in the lab as well. What I hadn't done, however, was required them to make any revisions based on the comments I left or otherwise. When the day came for them to turn in their second drafts, the vast majority, including many of the weaker writers, had made major changes. Most of my kids, not just the rare few like before, had gained more writing experience, and they'd done it without receiving any grades. In fact, if my previous semester's class was any indication, they'd been willing to do it *because* they hadn't received any grades.

Putting off the grades had made it possible for them to worry only about telling their stories well, and they had done so. This was promising. It was working. There was one problem, though. The next time they turned in their drafts, I did grade them. Some of the kids would have benefitted from more revision, and I gave them that option, but only a handful chose it. The rest missed out. Waiting to grade later drafts had allowed me to focus on meaningful assessment—meaningful *response*—much longer than I had in the past. Even so, I hadn't been able to meet the needs of all my students. Nobody ever wants to admit they need a plan C, but a classroom full of teenagers has a way of making reality hard to deny. Luckily I had several weeks to develop my plan C before the new marking period would start. In the meantime, I still had several classes to teach.

By the start of the third trimester, all of us, staff and students alike, were exhausted. Still, I practically jumped out of bed and ran to school on that first morning of our last twelve weeks. I couldn't have been more excited, because I would, for the first time ever, be teaching a writing class. Twelve weeks of nothing to worry about except writing. Which is to say, twelve weeks with everything to worry about. Luckily, my experiences with my freshmen had taught me a few things about teaching writing. A very few things, yes, but important ones.

Last marking period, many of my English students had revised only until they received a grade and neglected the opportunity to revise again afterward, even though they needed it. If I didn't want my new junior writing students to miss out on that same opportunity, I needed to rethink my game plan. I needed to do more than create the opportunity for more revision; I needed to set the expectation for more revision. It didn't make sense, though, to require a certain number of revisions from everybody. For some, three drafts might be enough, and for others, it might take six or seven. What I really wanted was for each of them to revise as many times as necessary to make that piece of writing the best it could be. So, that became the new expectation.

My fifth-hour writing students were a bit confused when I first told them about the system. "In this class," I said, "revising papers is a big, big part of how we learn. I'm going to help you find a topic you want to write about for each one, and once you do that, it's your job to keep working on it until we both think it's your best work. Once you're at that point, I'll grade it."

"Wait a minute," Wyatt said. A mischievous grin spread across his face, and I knew right away what he was up to. "What if we write it, but we just want to leave it the way it is and not revise it? Then what?"

Wyatt was looking for loopholes, just as I had expected. "Here's the thing," I began. "I'm guessing, based on what you just asked me, you don't like writing very much."

"I actually hate it," he told me in what I quickly realized was his characteristic excessively blunt style. "I would pretty much rather do anything than write. I'm not even kidding."

"I know you're not kidding. And I'm guessing lots of other people in here probably feel the same way, right?" The other kids nodded and voiced their hearty agreement.

"I wouldn't want to revise either if I hated writing, so I get where you're coming from. But that's the thing. I'm going to do everything I possibly can to help you learn to hate writing less, and find things you actually want to write about. If you meet me half way, I'm pretty confident we can do that, and if we do, I bet revising won't seem so bad."

Wyatt persisted. "I really don't think that's gonna happen," he said, "so if it doesn't, then what?"

"Well, if you didn't revise, you wouldn't get any credit for the paper," I told him. "But," I added with a grin, "you and I don't know each other very well yet, and I don't think you're giving me enough credit. I don't give up very easily." His eyes laughed, and his voice threatened to join them.

"We'll see," he said. "But I'm not making any promises that I'll revise."

"That's fine," I told him. I knew I could find something Wyatt would care about writing, and I knew I could convince him to revise. I wasn't kidding when I told Wyatt I don't give up easily.

A few days later, Wyatt and his classmates dove headfirst into their first major paper, a narrative involving a song that was important to them in some way. Wyatt, true to his nature, swore on his life that there was absolutely no song in the world that had any significance to him at all. And this after doing several quick writes to help him come up with ideas and looking at multiple sample papers. He wasn't even remotely receptive to my suggestion that he look back at those things for inspiration. "I pretty much made up everything I wrote," he told me. "I don't care about any of it." I didn't buy it, but there was no point in arguing.

"Okay, Wyatt, let's start somewhere different then. Did your parents ever sing to you when you were younger?"

"Sometimes, I guess, but nothing specific."

"Did you ever sing things when you were little?"

"Yeah, but I mean, I only remember singing something once." Just like that, I had my in.

"What do you remember singing?"

"It was stupid."

"I doubt it. But even if it was, will you tell me about it?"

"Well this one time, when I was in middle school, my parents and my brother and my sisters and I all went camping, and my sister did something really dumb, and this one song reminds me of it. I sung it over and over again during that whole weekend." With a bit more prodding, Wyatt went on to tell me about his sister Sarah accidentally falling in the water at the campground and soaking her clothes, which forced her to wear their father's much-too-big sweatpants until hers could dry. While she was wearing them, her parents had fixed peanut butter and jelly for lunch and called to their children, who were up a large hill, to come eat. Soon the hungry kids were running as quickly as possible downhill, so much so that Sarah, trying to run while hoisting her father's pants, tripped over her own two feet and rolled head over heels all the way down. "Every time I hear someone sing 'Peanut Butter Jelly Time,' I think about that," Wyatt told me.

"Then that's the story you need to write," I replied. And so he did.

Not only did Wyatt write his story, but, after receiving plenty of written and verbal feedback from me and his classmates, he revised it several times. I don't know if he still remembered our conversation on the first day, but if he didn't, I certainly wasn't going to remind him. By the third week of writing, he had composed a draft that he and I both believed represented his very best work. Despite his ongoing efforts to appear indifferent toward writing, I knew he really did like his piece. As he read the scene in which his sister fell to the class, and listened to their laughter, a smile spread across his face that didn't go away for days.

I couldn't have been more thrilled with Wyatt's progress. Not only had this self-proclaimed nonwriter written a multipage piece that he actually liked, and that had elicited the desired response from an audience, but he had worked through several drafts to do so, and learned more about writing from each and every one. Unfortunately, at the end of the process, I was still disappointed. After all the effort Wyatt had put into his paper, not to mention all the effort I'd put into helping him with his paper, the reality was that, even though it was his best work, Wyatt was still someone who, until three weeks ago, hadn't written or read anything of substance for years and years. His best was a C paper, so I gave him that C, along with much *oohing* and *ahhing* over the great things he had accomplished.

Wyatt wasn't especially bothered by his grade, but I was. Handing him that paper with a C on it, after all his hard work, told him he was a C writer. That was his best. No matter how proud of him I was, at the end of the day, the grade still ruled. I shuddered as I thought of the message that would send to Wyatt, and wondered if, after being labeled a C writer, he would ever willingly invest in any writing he wasn't forced to complete. Of course, I had heard all the arguments about needing to grade kids honestly in order to avoid contributing to grade inflation, and make sure they know where they stand before they get to the next teacher, college, or wherever the next person is going to judge their writing, but those arguments just didn't hold water with me.

I'd also read some research to suggest that grade inflation was a myth. Whether grade inflation was or wasn't a myth, I didn't care. I wasn't the one to create the traditional grading system. I didn't believe it helped me teach better, or my students learn better, and I certainly didn't feel the need to protect its integrity. And as for getting Wyatt ready for his post-Writing 11 life, well, I wasn't teaching the college student Wyatt, or the employee Wyatt, or even the senior English student Wyatt. I was teaching the reluctant junior writer Wyatt, and my only real responsibility was to help him become the best writer he could be and learn to enjoy the process of writing. The grade itself didn't do either one, and I couldn't justify any practice that didn't contribute to those goals. I wanted to do away with grades all together. There was just no way around it.

I spent the summer after my first year of teaching reading every book and article I could find about writing teachers who had found a way to eliminate traditional grades from their writing classes, and especially by those who had studied and analyzed the impact of doing so. Their rationales for eliminating grades matched my own, and their outcomes had been largely positive. It would be a lie to say the prospect of going gradeless in my writing classes didn't make me nervous. How many times had I heard that kids simply wouldn't write if they weren't being forced to in order to avoid receiving a low grade? And how many people had told me that kids would only revise if they needed to raise their grade on a paper? The answer was a lot. Too many to count. By this time, however, I'd spent enough time with kids to know that they do all sorts of things that they're not compelled to do by any external factors. I'd also done enough research to know that kids who worry about how well they're doing don't actually do as well as those who are only concerned with the task at hand.

Ever the idealist I'd so often been accused of being in college, I wanted to create a classroom in which kids wrote because they wanted to write, without worrying about how well they were—or weren't—doing. Fortunately, at my school, where the school improvement process had prevented anyone from putting much stock in grade-related data and the idea that kids should all have a common experience had been displaced by the idea that they should all have a quality experience, I was free to give it a try.

For the first semester of my second year, I decided not to issue grades but rather to help my writing students revise until the paper was their best work. Then I would just give them credit. All the credit. I also knew that the only way to do that was to eliminate firm due dates, so kids would be able to revise as many times as necessary. I went ahead with that plan, but my grand experiment had its pitfalls. I quickly learned that I'd have to work even harder to set up the writing assignments, so that the kids would be more invested in their writing than they had ever been before. Otherwise, they would have no motivation to work on their papers continuously instead of waiting until the last minute and rushing all the necessary revisions. I would also have to be even more diligent about providing in-depth feedback on a daily basis. It was going to be hard, and it was going to be time-consuming, but during the second semester of my second year, when I was teaching a grade-free writing class for the second time, my kids let me know that I was on the right track.

I had long ago learned to expect the unexpected from my kids, but I had never dared to dream I'd hear what I heard as I prepared to leave the building after our last day of classes before Christmas break.

"Ms. Holmes!" I turned around just in time to see Kyla come whipping out into the hallway from the home economics room. She slid a bit on the tile as she struggled to come to a stop and put her arms to the side to regain her balance.

"What's up?" I asked, trying not to chuckle at the sight of her in her ugly Christmas sweater. She, like many of her friends that day, had no doubt dug the most hideous holiday sweater she could find out of the closet of an elderly relative.

"Is there any way Tyvon and I can tear our song paper drafts out of our notebooks? We accidentally left them in there when we turned our notebooks in today."

"There is a way," I said. "I'm headed into my classroom right now. Do you want to come in and dig them out of the bin?"

"Yeah!" she responded as she followed me into the room. She beelined it to the first-hour bin and began foraging through the pile. "There's mine!" she called as she yanked her bright red notebook out from under the stack. "And there's Tyvon's!"

"Got 'em then?" I asked.

"Yup. Thank goodness! We were afraid we weren't going to get to work on them over break!"

A few moments later, Kyla skipped out my door. *She just said, "get to,"* I thought. *Get to.* If the paper was due right after break, or not having it done was going to hurt her grade, I wouldn't think twice about that phrasing. But in my writing class, papers weren't graded, and there were no due dates, and still she said "get to." It was only December 16th, and already I was having a merry Christmas.

Now, at the end of my second year in the classroom, I still struggle every day to be the kind of teacher I want to be. I have to remind myself constantly that Alecia doesn't like her bad mood any more than the rest of us, and Daniel didn't mean to sound the way he did when he made that sarcastic remark to his classmate. I lie awake at night worrying that I'm sometimes far less patient and understanding with my students than I mean to be. I still find myself apologizing to students for not having listened as closely as I should have when they were trying to tell me something, or for reacting to something that bothered me without taking the time to think about why it might have happened in the first place. While I have eliminated traditional grading from my writing-only classes, I still haven't figured out how to do the same under the time constraints and different structure of my combined literature and writing classes. Instead, I come as close as I can, by grading as little and as infrequently as possible and giving my kids all the opportunities I can to do their best without being judged. Because I teach in a school where I am free and encouraged to experiment, to learn, to grow, and to change my practice, a school where I can respond to my students as people, I know that I'll get closer and closer as I go.

Reference

DuFour, R. and Eaker, R. (1998). *Professional learning communities at work: Best practices for enhancing student achievement*. Bloomington, IN: Solution Tree Press.

FOR FURTHER DISCUSSION

1. Sierra pulls her memories of high school front and center and questions them. What did your high school teachers do to cultivate (or to stifle) your love of reading and writing? What did they believe about how students learn?

2. Some secondary schools teachers see more than 100 students each week. Sierra considers "being handed their words, their stories" to be "a tremendous gift." How do you think you will feel as a stack of papers awaiting feedback grows on your desk? Do you find Sierra's approach to giving feedback and grades feasible?

3. After reading Sierra's argument against giving grades to multiple-draft writing assignments, what kinds of data do you think teachers should collect to assess and document students' progress?

Adam Kennedy graduated from Grand Valley State University with a BA in English (Secondary Education) and now teaches English language arts to sixth graders in Maryland. During his four years, Adam has held the roles of department chair, Professional Learning Community facilitator, and teacher mentor. Adam realized he would be a teacher when, during a nightly reading of *The Giving Tree,* he asked his mother, "Why is the tree talking?" Since then he has been hooked.

The Meaning of Success
Adam Kennedy
Elk Park Middle School

In a difficult teaching environment like mine, it can be hard to feel like a success, particularly when success is not clearly defined. Who decides the worth of a teacher? Is it the parents? The administrators? The students? Fellow teachers? My college professors seemed to know what made a successful teacher. They equipped me with the tools that I needed to become one, and they encouraged and inspired me. The problem was that once I began my career, the definition of a good teacher became increasingly nebulous. For many parents, a good teacher is someone who gives their children high grades. Or, if you asked my principal, he might say that "a good teacher works within the curriculum box we design" or "a good teacher shows success on the state tests." These definitions of success were not in keeping with mine, which was based on teachers having autonomy and parents trusting them with the education of their children.

So after the rush of the first few months wore off, I began asking myself, "Is teaching what I expected? Is this what I want?" I don't think I was alone in asking these questions. I think that most new teachers fade toward the end of first year, and by Christmas of the second year, many take stock of their situation and begin to ask, "Do I need to make a change?" Of the fifteen new teachers I knew, four called it quits after the first year and five are contemplating a career change in the near future. How can it be that individuals who were once filled with passion end up leaving the profession before their career ever really gets going?

Yes, some of these people simply could not hack the job. Some of them were not skilled enough or mature enough to be teachers. But for others, like my friend Joyce, it was the constraints of the curriculum that pushed them out the door. Joyce was a talented teacher with degree from a prestigious university. Unlike many struggling young teachers, she did not have a problem with classroom discipline. Joyce simply was used to being excellent at everything, and she was also used to getting positive feedback. And for a period of time during her first year, she got glowing reviews. The administration praised her creativity, her positivity, and her ability to manage the different personalities within a classroom.

Then, county test results started to come back in. Joyce began to resent how much her assessment as a teacher was tied to the results of this single county test. Suddenly, her curricular creativity was not such a good thing if it didn't align specifically with state standards. And where, our supervisors asked, was she getting her resources? Couldn't she just use the assigned texts? Suddenly, exactly what she had been praised for before was being picked apart for flaws. Joyce felt as though she could not escape the weight of bad test scores, and she unfortunately tied her self-worth to her students' performance on these tests. That message was reinforced by the school. Today more than ever, schools are blaming teachers for their students' performances.

No matter how hard Joyce worked, her students performed equally bad every time. It got so bad that some of our teacher peers did not want to be seen socializing with her. She began to question the method of her evaluation and resented that the administration seemed to care only about her test results, not the projects that she designed, not the different clubs she ran, not the positivity she brought to the school and classroom, and not the creativity with which she approached every day. Her superiors became consumed by the data, concluding from the poor test scores that she was an underperforming teacher. What Mark Twain said seems fitting here: "There are lies, damned lies, and statistics." Joyce's superiors ignored the information presented right in front of their faces: her students smiles, enthusiasm, and growing love of reading as they entered and exited her room each day.

Inevitably, Joyce felt disenchanted with teaching. She realized that the classroom was really no place for someone who wanted to be innovative. Worse, the school community that had supported her now treated her as a pariah. She left the profession after her first year, feeling like an outcast at her own school.

Joyce's experience taught me that if you achieve success, people will leave you alone, but if you don't, you may be closely watched and judged. This scrutiny is a bit paradoxical because teaching, more than any other job, feels like its own world. Sure, we work in an organization, but ninety percent of the time, it's just you and the kids. As a result, the classroom begins to reflect your personality. Students enter into it and leave it each day. What happens in that time is entirely dependent on us. We bring not only our knowledge but also our enthusiasm, excitement, emotion, fatigue, and ignorance into the room. We spend hundreds of hours with our students. They learn things about the way we act, our mannerisms, and our personalities. They uncover things we thought we hid or perhaps didn't even know about ourselves. Curriculum includes all of this: it is large and contains multitudes.

Not all of my colleagues suffered the same fate as Joyce. Some retained their personal creativity and power, even in the face of standardized curriculum and tests. Veronica, a veteran of fifteen years, was one such teacher. To describe Veronica: first, she was a little crazy. Second, she was always willing to try new things or to offer help. Her laugh reverberated down the hallway. To call her a large personality would have been an understatement. As the year went on, the pessimism from the veteran teachers bothered me. The only exception seemed to be Veronica.

Why does it seem that some older teachers are cynics? This is a question that began to bother me late in my first year. It worried me. I worried that I might become like them, unwilling, and unable to connect with students or try anything new. It scared me to think that these people once displayed the same type of passion and energy for teaching that I felt, even with the down days. How did this happen to them? Maybe a few had always been cynical, just working the job to collect the paycheck. But I know that most teachers get into the profession because they care. How and why did this transformation take place? How does one go from dedicated educator to burnt-out babysitter? From believing that the kids teach us as much as we teach them to thinking that one has seen everything education has to offer?

For much of the year I steered clear of Veronica, but eventually, I grew to admire the wild lady with the big laugh and the willingness to try new things. I told her that I was impressed with how she was using technology, especially when other veterans were reluctant to use it. She told me that for her, teaching should be constant reevaluation, constant judgment, and constant revision. She said something that stayed with me: "When you let yourself accept that you know everything, you inevitably stop improving and getting better. Continual revision and honest self-assessment help you maintain a willingness to change and try new things."

Great teachers, in other words, realize that change and constant reevaluation are the most important aspects of improvement. They knowingly assess themselves continuously throughout the day, week, month and school year, revising their curriculum and their teaching methods based on what they learn. Teaching makes it easy to repeat the same errors over and over again. Mistakes then become bad habits, ones that we may not even be aware that we have. While it can be painful, we must be willing to honestly appraise our own teaching. Evaluations from principals who only see us sporadically in isolated situations cannot be trusted as the only source of useful feedback. Accepting their evaluation as a complete assessment of our teaching is poor teaching practice. As Veronica said, the best honest assessment is going to come from ourselves.

One self-evaluation technique that I have found very useful is to record myself with a video camera several times per year. This gives me a completely different perspective on my teaching. I look for the little things, small ways that I can improve, and I realize that students watch me do these things every day. Another technique I use is to observe other teachers. The best teachers are also thieves; watching other professionals do their job is a great way to improve how you do your own. It's one thing to find curricular resources in a book or online; it is another to watch it in action. Finally, I ask students to evaluate me. I emphasize that honest criticism helps me improve. In some cases, their evaluations reveal weaknesses that I had never noticed. None of my self-assessment comes from the test scores my students produce, just as none of the curriculum I plan teaches explicitly to the test.

Being a teacher should be a humbling experience. If we can accept that the job will never stop teaching us, then odds are we will maintain our inspiration and dedication throughout our careers.

FOR FURTHER DISCUSSION

1. If you were Veronica, how would you have counseled Joyce to survive her first year and build a successful career as a teacher?
2. Adam mentions several techniques for self-evaluation. What behaviors would you look for on a video of your own teaching to determine whether your curricular plans and your delivery were effective?

5

TEACHER IDENTITY

Introduction
Lindsay Ellis

The week before school started in 1999, I looked in my closet and thought, "I have nothing appropriate to wear." I'd just landed my first teaching job, and I was eager to show my new employers that they could trust me. I, after all, was now a well-trained professional. So what did I do? I went shopping. I bought a blue skirt and matching sweater, dress pants and a white blouse. When I reminisce about my first year of teaching, most of my memories place me in those two outfits. I must have worn them a lot.

Laughably, I'd stood gazing at my limited wardrobe and thought the same thing the year before, when I was an English grad student. I had arrived on campus at the University of Chicago and noticed quickly that I was the only one in blue jeans and a flannel shirt. My classmates—and eventual friends—all wore black and wrapped up against the autumn chill with scarves and leather coats. Compared to them, I looked like I worked at a Colorado group home—which is exactly what I'd been doing until I stepped onto campus. So, what did I do? I bought a new black shirt and a pair of black Dr. Martens (both of which I still own).

In neither of these scenes did I think of myself as conformist. I aimed merely to wear clothes that were appropriate to the setting. Red flannel felt at home among fir trees. Black scarves and black coffee fit in the oak-paneled reading rooms of Chicago. As a teacher in a college-prep high school in Atlanta, Georgia, standing in front of twenty eleventh graders reading *The Canterbury Tales*, I felt I should wear a skirt and matching cardigan.

Clothes may seem a trivial concern when thinking about teacher identity, but the surfaces that they cover run deep. How, in dress, speech, demeanor, and action, do we become comfortable standing in front of the classroom as the teacher? Ideally, we are able to move into this identity by stages: first as assistant, then intern, then full-fledged employee. Because I took a circuitous route into full-time teaching—from counseling, to an MA in humanities, to the classroom, then back for a PhD in English and education—my metamorphosis from graduate student to secondary school teacher was abrupt. No matter our training, however, we all must face our first hour of solo flight. We stand in a room full of students, and they look at us. We are "the teacher." What happens next depends on our understanding of what a teacher does. How students react, in turn, depends on their understandings and expectations, too.

If you were to draw a picture of a "teacher," what would be included? Would the character be located in a classroom with a piece of chalk, a marker, or an electronic device in his or her hand? Would he or she be seated at a laptop computer? If you were to add thought bubbles and speech bubbles to make it clear to a viewer that this was a teacher, what would the character be thinking and saying? In other words, what characteristics do you associate with the identity category *teacher*? Have you ever had a teacher who didn't "act like a teacher"? What type of expectations did that person not fulfill? To read a study of how others responded when asked to draw a teacher, see Weber and Mitchell's (1995) work, "*That's Funny, You Don't Look Like a Teacher.*" Thinking about what your and others' expectations are for teachers is important, because while each person is unique, and each teacher will be unique, many well-trained professionals decide to leave teaching because they never work out the complexities of teacher identity, either in the classroom, among other teachers in a school, or with family and friends (Alsup, 2006).

Before going any further, we should clarify what we mean by an *identity*. The word is pretty vague; it's commonly used to reference both how we see ourselves and how others see us. Scholars define the term both ways, actually. James Gee (2000) suggested that an identity is a kind of category that is recognizable by others. He explains that "when any human being acts and interacts in a given context, others recognize that person as acting and interacting as a certain 'kind of person' or even as several different 'kinds' at once" (p. 99). The kinds of person that a human being is recognized as being is what he calls "identity." Using a more subjective definition in her book on *Teacher Identity Discourses*, Janet Alsup (2006) defined identity as "a general sense of selfhood or understanding of the self; a set of distinguishing characteristics of an individual that emerge from this sense of selfhood" (p. 36). She, too, reminds us that identities are something that develop and change. No one is born a teacher.

The power of this identity category may be the reason why Alsup (2006) thinks that developing "a sense of professional identity that successfully incorporates [your] personal subjectivities into the professional/cultural expectations of what it means to be a 'teacher'" (p. 27) should be a top priority for teacher candidates. She argues that, in the long run, this may be more important to success than the crucial tasks of gaining knowledge of your subject matter, learning classroom management techniques, and understanding the science of adolescent cognitive development. What Alsup's research also suggests is that the identity category of teacher doesn't (and perhaps shouldn't) always fit easily with the other aspects of our identities. This is because we who identify as teachers also identify as other things that may be in conflict. We may also be fiercely partial parents of young children, devoted children to aging parents, vibrantly sexual partners to lovers, and irreverent friends out on a Friday night. As we step into and out of our teacher role, we have to negotiate all of these identities in a society that expects teachers to be exemplary role models to youth: rational, emotionally stable, energetic, attentive, forgiving, impartial, and optimistic.

What are the "subjectivities" that Alsup references that we must reconcile? The word *subjectivity* has even more meanings than the word *identity*. On the one hand, to be a subject is to perceive and to act; it is to be the subject of a sentence rather than its object. (*I* wrote a sentence. *He* chose a shirt. *They* tasted the chocolate. *She* hit the desk.) On the other hand, to be a subject is to be *subjected* to something. For example, to be a subject of a king is to accept the king's laws and the king's authority. In return, the king's subject receives an identity as a member of the kingdom. He becomes a citizen, and citizens have rights and privileges that aliens and exiles don't have. It is this double meaning of subject that makes it worth pondering. To work as a teacher is to accept, to become subject to, a set of norms for speech, dress, demeanor, and action; yet it is through this subjection that we become subjects (i.e., agents) wielding power on the stage of our classrooms (Althusser, 1970; Butler, 1997).

While the norms to which teachers are subject vary according to the values of the school and its surrounding community, they inevitably include the ways of thinking and acting most highly valued by that community, because teachers are mentors for the young. So, developing a nuanced teacher identity is difficult for at least three reasons. First, we each have to work out the inevitable tensions between our multiple identities in the use of our time, our bodies, and our emotional commitments. Sometimes, instead of energetic, optimistic, impartial, and professional our bodies and emotions feel languid, pessimistic, angry, or passionate. How on those days do we get up and go to work, stepping into the role of teacher again and again? Second, developing a nuanced teacher identity is difficult because some norms to which teachers are subject are overly simplistic stereotypes; others are downright harmful. For example, if the stereotype of a teacher is a middle-class, heterosexual, white, self-sacrificing female, it implies norms that are at odds with the prior subjectivities of working-class people, gays, men, and racial minorities. By necessity, some of the ways that a teacher has been defined in the past should be retired. They were not very helpful to students' learning then, and they are not now. Not only do we recognize that students need role models embodying the values of a plurality of subcultures (rather than one white, heterosexual, middle-class construct), but we also know more about learning than we did thirty years ago. We know more about cognitive development (Sweller, Ayres, & Kalyuga, 2011). We know more about students' home languages and funds of knowledge (González, Moll, & Amanti, 2005). We know more about multimodal literacy and sociolinguistics (Cruickshank, 2004). Thus, the actions and interactions that are recognized as good teaching need to change to incorporate this new knowledge.

Opening up and nudging the status quo understanding of a *teacher* to a more diverse and well-researched set of practices is important work. However, teachers new to the profession cannot do it alone. The task is too difficult because it does not require merely pushing back against stereotypes and status quo behaviors with a singular definition of better teaching. Instead, it requires handling conflict and complexity because new knowledge and research is constantly being published by a variety of fields, such as brain science, sociology, cultural anthropology, group psychology, and literary studies. It is hard work to develop new practices that navigate the complexity of these threads, pulling them parallel and aligning them with curriculum and instruction.

As if it weren't difficult enough to develop an understanding of what it means to act like a teacher that doesn't rely on stereotypes or status quo definitions but instead incorporates new knowledge among students, this is only one of the contexts within which teachers work. If the variety of fields that inform good teaching practice are the woof, then the variety of contexts within which teachers work are the warp of the fabric of the teaching life. Teachers interact with parents. They collaborate with colleagues. They report to principals or heads of school. They live in communities. It is a complicated tapestry to weave, and the strain of doing so may remain even when one closes the door and drives home on a Friday afternoon.

The best way to manage the task is for teachers, first, to clarify who we are and what definition of teacher we are trying to enact, and, second, to seek to understand what expectations others have of us in each role. Opening a door for communication and negotiation will pay rich rewards in student learning and professional confidence if we think carefully about each of these contexts in turn.

Being a Teacher Among Students

Students have expectations. Individual students will have unique expectations based upon what they have themselves experienced and been taught about teachers from their family, community, and various cultural media. How will you learn what your students' expectations are? How will you let your students know who you consider yourself to be? How will you let them know in more detail what they should expect of you as their teacher? The best teachers are the ones who both know themselves well and find out what their students' expectations are. This enables clear conversations about what students should expect.

Being a Teacher Among Caregivers

Students' caregivers also have expectations for how teachers should behave. It may be that your understanding of the collaborative roles of teachers and caregivers in the education of each child may align, or it may differ from theirs. It's not fair to have unarticulated expectations on either side, which is the job of letters home and of parent-teacher conferences. How will you learn what the expectations are of your students' caregivers? Are there community norms in the subcultures within which you teach? How can you become clearer about what your role will be in relationship to caregivers so that you can clearly articulate it to them?

Being a Teacher Among Other Teachers

Likewise, your colleagues will have expectations about how a teacher will behave. They may, indeed, have a more complicated view of the variety of types of teachers, but you may feel that they are sizing you up to know what type you are, what category in their mind to put you into. Are you clear about what kind of teacher you want to be, so that you can communicate that to your colleagues? This is all the more complicated because it is a give and take. You are likewise learning what it does mean to be a teacher in this setting. You may be willing, to a large extent, to conform to the norms of what "teachers do" in this school: where to put your coffee mug in the teacher's lounge, how quiet to keep your class in the library, how often it is acceptable to reserve media equipment or computer labs and such. As one of our contributors Lindsay Stoetzel experienced, however, there may be norms about the way that teachers talk (about students, for example) that don't feel comfortable, that are not who you want to be. What then? Or there may be conflicting expectations for what it means to be a teacher in a school—the principal may have one expectation and different groups of teachers may have other expectations. Be alert and prepared to study the culture of your school for the identity categories that are being constructed within it.

Being a Teacher Among Friends and Family

Being a teacher is a full-time job—and then some. Knowing that you are employed as a teacher, your family and friends will expect that to shape your behavior in certain ways. They may be understanding of your need to go to sleep early—or they may not. If you are an English teacher, they may start making jokes about how they need to "watch their grammar" around you. They may comment that it must be nice to have your afternoons and summers free; or they may lament that you are always working and grading papers. Be prepared for comments and conversations about how many hours a week you work as a teacher, the schedule that you will keep, and the politics of schooling. These are an opportunity to discover similarities and differences between the role of teacher as you understand it and as your friends and family do.

Being a Teacher in Society

The work of teachers is important to the future of society, and almost all citizens have attended school, so almost everyone has some ideas about of what kind of person a teacher is, complete with expectations about how a teacher will act and interact. Newspapers and magazines are full of opinion pieces and research articles about schooling—from all angles. By becoming a teacher, you are diving into the heart of public debate about education, an issue that won't ever go away. Some teachers try to ignore the debate, close their doors, and just build caring relationships with kids. Fine. Nurturing students is a big job in and of itself. Ideally, though, we hope that you see that you have something to contribute to the debate about education practice and policy. As a teacher, your firsthand knowledge and expertise will grow. We hope that you will share this knowledge, using your pen and your voice in public, not just behind the closed door of your classroom.

Being a Teacher With Yourself

At the end of the day, teachers reflect on how it went. Personally, a soundtrack of emotion accompanies both my work and my reflection: satisfaction, pride, embarrassment, ambition, shame, anger, and joy. My emotions are complicated, and when I am attentive to them I can learn more about my identity. Reflection allows me to notice what I did instinctually during the day and how what happened made me feel. Reflection helps me to see the influence of my family and community cultures, my own experiences as a student, my study of education, my genetics—all of what shapes my identity.

Becoming more aware of the way my identity shapes my actions helps me to improve. In order to thrive as an effective teacher, I think it's important to assume that not everything that comes naturally to us will be best practice. We have to find the balance between feeling "like ourselves" when we teach and constantly doing better and better for our students. In other words, we need to self-assess and improve our performance without feeling like we are playing a role that is fake. We need to commit to self-assessment, to own it.

In the following narratives, we witness new teachers becoming self-aware through reflection. They tell stories about how they felt when they acted in the role of teacher, about what happened in their classrooms. Storytelling helps these teachers to excavate their identities, to bring them to light, and to better understand what "came naturally." They work to determine whether the identities that feel natural are good for their students.

As you read their stories, be aware of your reactions. Your reactions emanate from your identity. As you read, you might think, "I'm like that" or "I do that in my class, too." Something in the story may feel like looking in a mirror. Alternatively, you may feel admiration for these teachers and think, "I want to learn to do that." Something in the text may align with your aspirations, with who you want to become. At other times, though you might admire another's technique, you may know that you couldn't pull it off. You may think, "I *could* never do that." Your identity is different than the writer's.

All of these thoughts are instructive. It is fine to feel different from these writers. You may struggle to understand their reactions, and this distance, too, testifies to your identity. You can become aware of your identity when you notice yourself thinking critically, particularly the sentiment, "I hope I *would* never do that." Evoking all of these reactions and thoughts is one of the purposes of this book. We hope that your reactions will help you become more aware of your own culture, history, physical characteristics, personality, and knowledge. Reading actively will allow you not only to learn from these new teachers' successes and failures, but also to learn about yourself as you tune in to the feelings, questions, and ideas that come to mind as you interact with this text. You might also consider completing the following activities to help guide your thinking on teacher identity.

- **Picture This**
  Popular films and television give us countless representations of teachers. We see teachers as renegades (*Dead Poets Society*), as bores (*Ferris Bueller's Day Off*), as saviors (*Dangerous Minds* and *Freedom Writers*) and even as criminals (*187* and *Breaking Bad*). Gather images from these depictions or from a Google Image search. Then assemble a visual representation of the images using a tool such as Glogster, PowerPoint, Flickr, or Photostory. What do the images say about the role of the teacher in our society? How do the images support or undermine your understanding of teacher identity?

- **Teaching as Metaphor**
  Borrowing an idea from Janet Alsup's study of *Teacher Identity Discourses* (2006), collect three images that are personal metaphors for either teaching English or being an English teacher. You can either take pictures using a digital camera or find open-source web content. Then spend some time writing to explain the meaning of each metaphorical image. How does it represent your teaching philosophy or your experience of teaching? Feel free to write in whatever mode or genre will best accompany the image.

References

Alsup, J. (2006). *Teacher identity discourses: Negotiating personal and professional spaces*. Mahwah, NJ: Erlbaum.

Althusser, L. (1970). Ideology and ideological state apparatuses. In *Lenin and philosophy and other essays* (B. Brewster, Trans., 1971, pp. 121–176). London: NLB.

Butler, J. (1997). *The psychic life of power: Theories in subjection*. Palo Alto, CA: Stanford University Press.

Cruickshank, K. (2004). Literacy in multilingual contexts: Change in teenagers' reading and writing. *Language and Education, 18*(6) 459–473.

Gee, J. P. (2000). Identity as an analytic lens for research in education. In W. Secada (Ed.), *Review of research in education* (Vol. 25, pp. 99–125). Washington, DC: AERA.

González, N., Moll, L. C., & Amanti, C. (2005). *Funds of knowledge: Theorizing practices in households, communities, and classrooms*. Mahwah, NJ: Erlbaum.

Sweller, J., Ayres, P., & Kalyuga, S. (2011). *Cognitive load theory*. New York: Springer.

Weber, S., & Mitchell, C. (1995). *"That's funny, you don't look like a teacher": Integrating images and identity in popular culture*. London, UK: Falmer.

Bree Gannon graduated with a BA in English (Language and Literature) from Grand Valley State University. She works at a community college as a professional writing tutor while she makes plan to attend graduate school in the coming year. When she does not have her nose in a book, she enjoys being outdoors, running, hiking, and camping with her husband and three children.

Absorbing Fear, Rejecting Fear
Bree Gannon
Harbor Community College

Growing up, my grandmother always told me that she would disown me if I ever married a black man. She would ask me, as if I my eight-year-old self would have an answer: "Where would your children fit in? They wouldn't be really black or white."

I remained silent as I looked at her, a tiny, five-foot-tall woman whom I had heard many call beautiful. All I knew was the clenching in my stomach of fear when she made comments such as this. I was not afraid of her disapproval, or of what she described happening to me. I knew even then that she was wrong in her words. It was the word-spitting anger attached to her comments that caused me to curl my fingers into balls with tension.

As I grew up, comments like these would float around the atmosphere of my life. Though I disagreed, I became concerned that somehow they had absorbed into my skin. I was afraid the odor of them floated around me somehow. The more I learned about cultural distinctions and talked with others about not only the overt offenses but also the subtle ones from well-meaning people, I became more and more anxious that somehow my family's proclivities could be seen in my words and actions.

Morris sat across the room, arms folded, and leaning back in his chair. Alternately, he would stretch out his arms, hold his hands together, and flex his biceps. He inspected each one carefully as he flexed. He had been a basketball star in his high school, and even though the community college classroom was made up of students from all over, the first day he walked into my room (which was really the second day for everyone else) there were several students that enthusiastically greeted him.

"Have any of you heard of spoken word poetry before?" I transitioned the class into a new activity a couple of days later. Morris tilted his chin up, and his long braids fell back off his face. He closed his eyes and stated slowly, "I hate spoken word poetry." He opened his eyes and looked at me still shaking his head. Mentally, I scrambled for a response. Mentally, I felt all of my school lectures and readings throw little ineffective water balloon quips towards the situation and then run for cover.

I landed using the age-old fall back question, "Why?"

"I just do," he replied.

I looked out at the class, not wanting the next forty-five minute unit to begin this way. I made eye contact around the room and decided to speak in third person, a technique I had learned in my professional writing class. In delivering bad news, it is best to speak in third person or to the group as a whole rather than to the one individual you want to target. "It is okay to not like something and even to say that, but try to ask yourself why you don't like it. Giving a strong reason helps to understand your perspective." I finally snuck a glance back at Morris to see how he was responding to my off-target arrow. He was still shaking his head and looking down at his crossed arms.

We began with a video of Sarah Kay and went around the room with each student saying what they noticed and wondered about her performance. Several students gave bland responses, and Morris followed in kind. I played another poet and, fortunately, noticed a lot of the other students connecting with the content and emotion of the piece. Morris, however, sat with arms still folded and eyes rolling for emphasis: "It was too much."

"Too much?" I automatically questioned back.

He replied, "Yes, too much."

The group of young men sitting around him followed his lead and responded with shakes of their heads and similar statements of dislike. Others bravely ventured that they did like it, but said it quietly and staring at their desks or looking at me and not their peers. I felt the safety of expression in the room slowly slipping away, but I did not know how in that moment to get it back under control. How do you address an attitude or a feeling?

"Morris, can you stay in the classroom a moment?" When the class cleared out, I sat down next to him.

"How do you feel like the class is going?" I asked him.

He stayed looking at the table, "Fine."

"I need you to not to talk off-topic in class. It is also okay to not like something, but please be careful that you do not ruin it for other people that may like it."

He sighed and looked away, "Okay."

"Are we good? Is there anything that you want to say to me?"

"I'm good." He stayed looking off towards the wall.

"Okay." We stood up, and he walked out of the classroom, and I felt anything but good.

As the hours and days went on, I would frequently hear him talking to peers during class, but if I would look up or go near him, he would stop. It became this sort of cat and mouse game. When I asked him to move and pointed to a new seat; he sat in the one next to it. When I passed him in the hallway during breaks, he would look away or at the ground and would not greet me or make eye contact. His actions were just shy of overt, but it left me exhausted by the end of the day and dreading another three-and-a-half hours of class with him the next day.

I wandered into the nearby College Success Center. My program had been assigned a group of coaches that met with the students and monitored their progress and issues. I stepped over to the desk of one of the coaches, Taunya. Taunya is a young African-American woman who I later learned grew up in a school that had a forty percent high school dropout rate and a notorious reputation. I told her about the situation and said, "I feel like Morris has some thinly veiled hostility towards me." I expanded and told her at times I even felt intimidated. That word had not been forethought and when it slipped out, I mulled over it. I amended that I did not feel intimidated that he would hurt me, but I felt I had to gather mental courage to walk by his seat.

Her response surprised me: "As a young African-American male, he cannot be doing that. It is unacceptable." This situation had elements I had not consciously considered. Taunya told me she would talk to Morris, which was a relief. Later, as I got into my car, I saw her standing on the edge of the parking lot talking with Morris. He was easily a head and shoulders taller than Taunya. His arms were stilled crossed, but I could see he was looking at her and listening to what she was saying.

The next morning, Morris came into the classroom wearing grey dress slacks, a polo, and stylish black dress shoes. His hair was pulled back out of his face, and even more striking, he sat in the front row, across the room from his friends. That day, we listened to an NPR radio special, talked about how the writer of that piece took a simple question, "Would you rather be invisible or be able to fly?" and took it to a deep level to explore how shame motivates our choices and how often our initial reactions to questions and moments are selfish. Only later, with more careful thought, do we start to think about others. The class offered deep, insightful responses and ideas. They noticed other things that I had never seen, such as the social class of the people being interviewed. Morris offered some insightful comments, but mostly sat quietly and thoughtfully.

Later, during break, he was standing with a group of his peers, all young African-American men. Although I was their teacher, and it was a safe place, my nerves instinctively went on alert as I approached this crowd. I could hear my mother's warnings over the years, "Don't ever approach a group of black men. If they are on one side of the street, you cross to the other." To be honest, I have had a few experiences that seemed to confirm her fear-inducing statements. I have walked past houses in my neighborhood or on my way home from school through clouds of catcalls, looked straight ahead, only to hear "bitch" as I passed. In those cases, I didn't respond and kept staring straight ahead.

My upbringing and experience had given me an instinctual response of fear and awkwardness to large crowds of young African-American men. My rational mind told me, "There is nothing to be afraid of!" I was angry with myself for even having to fight with these thoughts. "These are my students," I counseled myself. I steeled myself to look straight at them and not at the ground. To my surprise, Morris looked up in the middle of the group, looked me in the eye, paused, then smiled at me. I held his gaze and smiled back at him hoping that all of my good intentions and hopes would somehow be conveyed to him in that one, simple act. Others around him stopped talking and followed his gaze and also smiled. As I entered the classroom and sat down at the front, tears of relief fought to fall from the small kindness.

"Taunya, what did you say to him to cause such a drastic change?" I asked as I sat down with her at the end of the day.

She replied, "I told him the things you said, and at first he didn't see it. He didn't think he had done anything wrong." She went on and described how she saw it, even how he was standing with her right then, giving off, "I don't give a fuck." She pointed out his demeanor and asked him if that is what he intended to convey. He said no, and she told him that is what others were seeing, and he needed to adjust his demeanor to his intentions and make sure he was sending off the right signals.

I remembered her comment that had stuck with me: "As a young African-American male, he cannot be doing that. It is unacceptable."

"What did you mean by that?" I asked.

She nodded, "I believe black men are perceived as dominant. They are dominant. When you add to that his demeanor, and that he is an athlete and a basketball player, the odds are stacked against him. He needs to understand his presence and that the light is on you, who you are, and what you represent."

I looked at her. "You realize, Taunya, that I could not very easily have that kind of conversation with him. What do I do if there is no you or someone to reach out to him?"

She surprised me with her candidness. "They are going to try you more because you are white. You will be taken as weak if you cannot control. You assert yourself. You tell them you are not playing those games. They can sense fear. We have a saying, 'If you jump stupid, I'm gonna jump stupid with you.'"

Thoughts and theories were having a dinner party in my head as she talked. We sat for a long while. As she talked, I began to reconcile my own personality with what she was saying. I knew I ultimately would win in the classroom because Morris would have eventually had to leave if it came to that. She agreed. "Feel confident. This is my turf. My boundaries. Push on. Go somewhere else." As she spoke, I remembered a former professor of mine. An African-American woman, she exhibited the behavior that Taunya described towards a group of white students. It came across as so cruel and condescending that less than a dozen finished her class, and those who were left intensely disliked her. I told Taunya about that situation and we mused over some of the cultural differences.

Shifting to a softer tone, Taunya told me something that changed my thinking again. She said, "Because of their cultural background, many young African-American men come in feeling hopeless and lost." She went on to say that most students do not need a personal relationship with their professor, but African-American students really need and want personal attention. They think if you do not pursue a relationship with them that "you are just doing what you are paid to do: teach." The word *hopeless* hit me with a resounding slap in the face. I thought of that smile in the hallway. Why had I not pursued a relationship with Morris or any of the other young African-American men in my class? I told Taunya that I thought they wanted nothing to do with me because of their demeanor. She said that was all defense and hopelessness.

"The opposite is true," she said.

I knew immediately that if my black students had been white, I would have been able to see through that hardness and rough exterior. In fact, reaching out to students and helping them see their potential as writers and students was one of my strengths and chief joys in teaching. So, why had I not done the same with them? I knew right away it was because I was scared and because they were black. This knowledge sunk into my stomach and broke my heart. I suddenly saw Morris and all young black men in my class differently. I saw that word *hopeless* floating above them, and I wanted to help.

At the end of the section, the students retook their placement test. Morris scored the second highest score, and every single person in the class achieved a higher level, a new record for our program.

Ultimately, though I knew our section had been successful, the success came with a wounding. I knew if I wanted to keep teaching, I was going to develop thicker skin, put on my big-girl pants, and step out of my comfort zone. I also knew that I would need cultural guides along the way, and that I needed to continue having these honest conversations.

Once as an adult, I asked my grandmother why she had such a hard time with black people. She told me that once, when she was a little girl, her parents moved to a new area and enrolled her into a school. It turns out that it was an all-black school, and she was the only white kid. She did not give me details, but she said that the cruelty and horror she experienced over the next couple of weeks hurt her so badly that she has hated African-American people ever since. Her parents ended up pulling her out of the school. I thought to myself, "That is probably what black students often experience as the minority in a white school."

How can teachers help bridge these cultural divides? I am convinced that the answer is not to just have more minority teachers teaching minorities and white teachers teaching white students. Even though my grandma's experience was in the distant past, there are still very real gaps between cultures in our classroom. Teachers make myriad split-second decisions in a day, and our cultural backgrounds instinctually play out in our responses to students. Whenever I am tempted to say that I am overthinking it all, I think of Morris and his dress shoes, his smile in the hallway, and his second highest score, and I know that honest conversations offer some very real power for change in addressing these differences.

FOR FURTHER DISCUSSION

1. Bree Gannon is very honest, not only about the racist comments she heard growing up but also about the fear that she felt as she approached a group of young black men. Why is this fear a problem for Bree as she becomes a teacher?
2. How does Bree seek to change this fear?
3. What dispositions and behaviors are parts of your cultural heritage? How well will they serve you as you become a teacher?
4. When Bree and her student misunderstood each other's behavior, a coach helped them. If no intermediary is present, what can teachers do to understand and to be understood by students with different dispositions and behaviors?
5. How would this narrative be different if it were told from Morris' perspective?

 Amanda Brown teaches at a diverse middle school where 80 languages are spoken. She completed her BA in English and Psychology at Grand Valley State University and earned her MA in Educational Technology at Michigan State University. Coming from four generations of educators, she feels that teaching is her passion and true calling in life.

Integrity
Amanda Brown
Hillcrest Middle School

Every new teacher hears horror stories about the first few years of teaching—like how you will always feel like you are in too deep, or barely able to keep your head above water, or overwhelmed with all of the many pressures, changes, responsibilities, and constant scrutiny that a rookie teacher must endure. Nevertheless, I thought I was handling it all with finesse, knocking each dilemma and issue out of the park. Then, the long days leading to spring break came and knocked the wind right out of me.

It was not merely the waning interest of my adolescent students, who desperately needed a break from the monotonous routine of school. No, this was something completely out of left field and had nothing to do with me as a teacher, my degree, my level of preparedness, or my intellectual ability at all. Nevertheless, it had a huge effect on everything that I did, on everything that I had worked so hard to master. It started when my boyfriend of three years broke up with me. I felt like there was nothing strong enough to mend my broken heart. It was then that I felt that I understood the full intent of the Bible scripture, "guard thy heart with all diligence, for from it springs the issues of life" (Proverbs 4:23 KJV). I relinquished my whole heart to my first love and failed to guard it. Now I realized that without heart, nothing in life seemed to matter. Not even my career that I had, thus far, worked my entire life to obtain and maintain with the utmost regard, integrity, morality, and value.

However, just when I thought I was down and out, just when I thought there was nothing—an amazing thing happened. My students came to life. Their love, always seeming to appear wrapped in an exterior layer of adolescent toughness and aloofness, became apparent. From day one, they had been listening. Not just to the curriculum that I was attempting to teach, but also to who I was as a teacher and as a person. They remembered the little idiosyncrasies about me that made me happy, like food. They brought in snacks to pass around while we read stories. They remembered my faith. Many of them suggested churches they wanted me to visit now that I looking to branch out from my parents' home church. They were more well-behaved and cooperative with one another than usual, and they were able to have a great deal more fun. They became fully functional, thoughtful, and contributing members of our class. They actively showed me their love.

But the semester was not finished yet, and there was one difficult challenge remaining. On any given day, an unexpected situation can arise and make you question who you are, what you stand for, and what you are willing to risk. On the heels of my personal heartbreak, the following experience tested my professional integrity and my character.

This particular experience involves a standardized test. Wherever you decide to teach, there will be a standardized test. And if you are not quite sure how you should feel about them, just know that teachers everywhere abhor them. You will likely possess great animosity toward them. You may even hate them as Tybalt hates peace, hell, and all Montagues. And yet, no matter no matter how we loathe and dread them, the tests will come. You must prepare for them. Your students, your school, and your district *must* score well. Your job itself could hang in the balance. On the first day of testing, a student approached me:

"But Miss Brown, I don't understand what I should write about."

"Remember, Rico," I told him, reading the directions from the test booklet, "during this part of the test, I can help you understand the directions, but I cannot give you help on any items. Just try to remember all the practice prompt responses we have been doing over the past month, and I'm sure you will create something wonderful. This prompt is about personal experience—about a time when you were really proud of yourself, or when someone you know made a good decision in a difficult situation. Take a minute to brainstorm, organize your thoughts, and then begin."

As I continued to circulate and monitor the students, out of the corner of my eye I could see Rico fervently at work: brainstorming, diagramming, drafting, erasing, and revising. I was so proud of him. He was a student that tried when he wanted to, but when he really put his mind to it could produce writing that with scaffolding and guidance easily reached the next level of excellence and quality. As I collected the answer sheets, I couldn't help but skim a few, and, of course, Rico's was among them.

I read Rico's response, start to finish. Then I paused, mouth ajar. To be honest, I was not quite sure what to do. Tell him to rewrite it? Was it appropriate? Rico had written about something unexpected. He chose a moment to be proud of, but I did not know if the topic was fitting for the test. Nevertheless, he followed the directions: interesting lead, thesis, supporting information with descriptive detail, and strong conclusive ending.

He opened with a question lead, "Hey guys, what are you looking at? All the kids at the bus stop were gathered around some object. Peering into it. Poking at it. Snickering and trying to decide what to do with it . . ." He later revealed there was an illegal substance in the foil container. Rico took it home to his mom. His mother used it, and then admitted that she had a problem. Thereafter, Rico's mother admitted herself into a rehab clinic. During her time away, Rico stayed with his mother's brother. However, he was so distraught without his mother that he would frequently run away or sleep in his uncle's trunk as he hid out. In the end, Rico writes that he was proud of his mother for making the decision to get help, proud of his uncle for caring for him, and proud of himself for being thankful for the many blessings in his life. It was very heartfelt, and based on the directions in the testing manual, I allowed it to remain as it was.

But in the world of teaching, there are two things that a teacher should never do: (1) have an affair with a student, or (2) mess up the standardized test. And unfortunately, you get an opportunity to achieve number two every year! The rules and regulations regarding standardized tests are strict and warrant extreme consequence if not completed to a "T." The consequences may cost your district thousands of dollars to retake the test or rectify the mistake, may cost you your job or your integrity as a teacher, and may have lasting consequences. So, to prepare, you are required to review the test manual. You must read each itemized procedure and protocol meticulously. After a while, you find yourself going to extremes like refusing to drink water because you, as the proctor, cannot leave the room during testing. During the test, you walk on pins and needles, not just until testing begins, but throughout testing and until the very last test, answer document, and pencil are collected, alphabetized, and handed off to be further processed. And while you wait for the next test to begin, you worry about what to do in a situation like the following, especially if you know you can get away with it if you just remain silent.

"You have about 15 minutes to finish Part 2 of the math test, and then we'll be done testing for today. Please remain silent until the end of the testing period." Many students were already finished and perfectly content zoning out. Out of the corner of my eye, a hand shoots up.

"Yes, Joshua?"

"Are we allowed to use our calculators on this part of the test?"

"Well Joshua, you don't have much time left and I can see that you are almost done. I think you've done quite well thus far without it, so I think it's best if you finish that way." As I walked away, panic set in. There were two math tests administered that day and due to the lack of calculators throughout the building, our students were required to take Part 1 and 2 of the math test in opposite order. One test allowed for calculators and one test did not. My students just finished the portion that prohibited calculators as I scanned my classroom, I saw that their calculators were still accessible, under their desks, sitting idle, some being used to play games on them as their owners waited for other students to finish the test.

My mind was reeling. How many had used them? As I began to collect the materials, I nonchalantly asked how many students felt it necessary to use their calculator on this part due to the difficulty of the test. Only a few students raised their hands, and then I asked how many *did* use their calculator. And again, only a few raised their hands. Then I began to lecture to them about the importance of listening to directions. I told them that I had to report them to the principal and discuss what action he wanted to take.

All of it was a bluff. I knew that I had made the mistake of not recollecting the calculators at the beginning of the administering the directions and testing materials. I knew that I should have been paying closer attention as I, myself, read the directions to the students. Upon realizing the error, I knew that I had to think fast. On the one hand, I could collect the tests as usual, dismiss my students, and forget about the whole ordeal. The students hate the standardized tests almost as much as the teachers, and the chances that a student would even comment to any other adult, teacher, parent, administrator was slim to none.

So, I could definitely have gotten away with it, and no one would be the wiser. On the other hand, there was what most refer to as their conscience. However, I know mine more intimately as the Holy Spirit, reminding me of right and wrong. I had made a mistake and I knew that I would personally and spiritually not have peace if I did not do my best to right my wrong. For, ultimately, integrity is doing what is right even when it is thought that there is no one watching. I would never want to be stuck in a situation in which my principal would have to question my integrity. I have worked hard to represent a Christ-like heart and mind, and to model high values and morals. I also am among the fourth generation of educators in my family. So, for more than just myself, I knew I needed to represent and honor my God, my father, and my family name by stepping up immediately and doing the right thing.

So, I asked our school organizer for the standardized test about what to do. He informed the principal, and when I was called to his office, I saw a fleeting expression on his face that said he would have preferred me to say nothing because he knew rectifying the problem would cost time and money. However, as he shut the door, he exhaled deeply, his shoulders and his body plopped into his chair behind his desk, and he looked me square in the eye. While there are several things that I am sure he wanted to say, he chose, "I'm proud of you. I know you could have chosen to say nothing. I know many people in your position probably would not say anything. And, while I would rather not deal with the paperwork, money, and possible repercussive logistics, I will still rest peacefully knowing that I have a staff that remains honest."

I breathed a deep sigh exiting his office that day. However, the standardized test nightmare was not over quite yet. A second meeting followed the first.

Students are not the only ones who dread hearing their names called over the public address system. My own heart skipped a beat when I heard my name announced. The secretary motioned me in and closed the door behind me. My principal then informed me that we were going to the administration building. We both got into his car and I praised the Lord that our district administration building was only seconds away. In my head I begin to pray, "Thank you God for all of the green lights. Thank you God that my principal knows how to maintain casual conversation as he attempts to ease my obvious anxiety."

When we arrived, we were asked to join the table where my school union representative and two members of our district administration were already seated. Once in my chair, I was so nervous that I barely heard or understood what they discussed at the table. I was just praying that I would not get fired, have to pay for all the test retakes, or have a negative review added to my teacher file. I only remember explaining the situation exactly as it happened. They then discussed what action would be taken next, and how to keep it from leaking into the news.

The meeting was over before I knew it. And while there was less tension in the car on the ride back to school, I was still uneasy. But then, something happened that changed everything. Before dropping me off, my boss gave me a hug. It was like the reassuring hug that a parent gives a child. It was the type of embrace that, even without words, communicated unconditional love, respect, support, and faith in me as a teacher and friend. I do not believe I took a full breath of air until that embrace. At that moment, my anxiety began to drain from my body. I returned to my room, thankful for a small amount of time to expend all the suppressed emotions that were wound tight inside of me. I screamed, used the bathroom, and fixed my face before my next class arrived.

In the end, the students who had admitted to using calculators had to retake that portion of the standardized test. It did cost the district money to follow the necessary and proper protocol. And the meetings with my principal, union representative, and board of administration representatives were the most excruciating experiences of my teaching career by far. I have never questioned the security of my job and relationship quality with administration and leaders more than I had in that single moment.

Within my few initial years of teaching, I have learned that students have a tendency to teach us in areas far beyond our studied major. I always knew that I wanted to teach and that it was my passion and calling. However, experiences like these have shown me that the core of teaching is and always will be love. Love as not only a noun, but as an active verb. Situations and problems that need to be resolved arise, not only in the first years of teaching but throughout one's career. However, when strategizing a solution, remember to keep love at the center and everyone involved and affected is bound to win in the end. Love always wins.

FOR FURTHER DISCUSSION

1. Amanda Brown assumes that being "a teacher" does not mean that she has to hide the fact that she is also a "woman in love." By writing about her personal story, she models how to discover topics for compositions and how to revise to make her meaning clearer. What stories from your life might demonstrate the power of narrative and reflection? Conversely, what stories from your life are still too heavy for adolescents to carry?

2. Amanda Brown is eager to share her joy with her students at the beginning of the year. When her joy turns to grief, however, she wonders how to go on being a "good teacher." How much of one's "I'm in love" feeling is it appropriate to share with one's students? How much of one's grief?

3. Amanda decided that she would tell her principal that she made a mistake and allowed students to keep their calculators at their desks during the second portion of the standardized test. She acted as the kind of person who tells the truth even when it hurts. What kind of person do you tend to be? What would you have done?

 Lindsay Stoetzel is a graduate of Grand Valley State University (BA) and Michigan State University (MA). A former middle school and high school English teacher, she is now a graduate student at the University of Wisconsin–Madison, studying curriculum and instruction, where she works with pre-service education students and teaches literacy courses.

Breaking My Rule
Lindsay Stoetzel
Central Middle School

I beat all the odds to secure a coveted teaching position at a high-achieving district during a period of nationwide cutbacks and layoffs in the education sector. Yet, this miraculous achievement was short lived, as only three years later I walked away from this lifelong dream of teaching high school English and coaching competitive cheer. The reasons I left teaching are actually pretty simple to see, given a little time and reflection to do so. It boiled down to three important factors: the grind, the politics, and the right opportunity. Yet, in the moments leading up to my final decision, I had no clarity; I was stricken with panic and intense anxiety as I grappled to weigh logic against intuition. In the end, my intuition won out, as I felt it impossible to continue teaching under circumstances that left me feeling powerless and perpetually overwhelmed.

My colleagues were shocked and disappointed to see me go. I remember my superintendent sadly stating how surprised he was to lose an "up and coming star." My assistant superintendent referred to my teaching performance in a letter of recommendation as "a master teacher from her first year," so clearly it wasn't the task of teaching that was to blame. A former mentor was confused and concerned, mentioning that I must have been "faking it well." He thought, like many others, that classroom teaching was a natural and seamless fit for me. I was well liked, respected, and doing what I was born to do. I always appeared so happy—what could possibly have gone so wrong?

In the end, it all came down to breaking my own cardinal rule, a rule I had placed upon myself as combination of age-old adage and my own personal mantra. A strong believer in the power of positive thinking, I promised myself that I would not succumb to the black hole of negativity that cropped up in the teacher's lounge. I set a mental light bulb to go off every time a benign conversation began to slip into pessimistic complaints—in the hallway, at a staff meeting, even in the parking lot. I would allow myself only to nod and add a positive note of encouragement without divulging my feelings or misgivings, certainly not adding any personal fuel to the fire. I felt the need to protect my love and passion for going above and beyond for students, agreeing with large-scale administrative changes, and whole heartedly embracing the use of research and technology. I would stand guardian over my optimism and not let anyone else bring me down. And I did.

My first year of teaching was both invigorating and rewarding, so much so that I anxiously waited for spring break to draw to a close so I could return to my classroom and share the exciting work I had been happily grading. The torture of being away from my classroom for the entire summer was only assuaged by the opportunity to begin taking master's degree classes in the evenings after teaching all day so that I could dream up new plans and activities for making learning meaningful. I had made it! I had completed the long, hard journey to become a teacher, and it turned out that I loved it.

The Grind

"Take a deep breath and pause—it's all going to be okay." I said this to myself many times as a teacher of middle and high school students. It helped me to regain clarity and maintain a professional demeanor, especially when faced with some of the harder circumstances (and objects) that were thrown my way. I learned the importance of not taking things personally—something hard to do in a position that is inherently personal. Once an angry student threw a laptop computer at me from across the room because he couldn't get the Internet to work, and with a deep breath, I calmly removed him from the classroom and somehow class continued. I learned how to calmly send or escort disgruntled students to the principal's office, listen to their accounts, and greet them with an understanding smile the next day. I learned to handle being berated by parents through email and telephone, to tactfully allow them to vent, and to solve problems and discredit myths. On my darkest day, I uncovered a laundry list of inappropriate and hurtful tweets and hashtags filled with defamatory remarks about both me and my teaching. I needed a lot of deep breathing to handle the strain of dealing with the emotional outpouring of apologies from students after the administration handed down their suspensions.

In the midst of these dramas, it was emotionally and mentally draining to be "on my game" from the minute I entered the school building until the time I got home. To develop this persona required a strong degree of respect, empathy, and learning to "let go." The rapport I built with my students, nurtured through the tides of unpredictable adolescence, gave me a purpose to come to work every day offering a clean slate and a smile on my face. If I've learned anything in my twenty-nine years, it is the importance of forgiveness and second chances, especially for young people who are just learning "how to be." And while I developed strong and invigorating relationships with some of my brightest students, I found just as much fulfillment and joy from working through tougher times with my at-risk students who needed an ear and a role model more than a lesson on grammar.

Overall, I learned to manage daily difficulties, as they were so greatly outweighed by the positives, which remained the focus in my vision. The genuine happiness to work with my students was the one constant that remained. However, there were other factors related to "the grind" that became less rewarding and more time-consuming as my teaching career sped forward.

Every new professional in any field can expect to put in some of the most exhausting and unrelenting hours in their first few years of work. This should be a surprise to no one. But the key, as argued by so many educational writers, is to find and maintain balance in your life. I wouldn't say that my penchant for saying yes to everything directly resulted in my eventual negativity and early exit, because these were critical learning experiences that helped me to develop and move forward on my career path, but I can say they were taxing times. Without broadening my knowledge and volunteering my time, I wouldn't have been prepared or motivated enough to move on to the next level, but I threw aside another cardinal rule: stay balanced.

How many times have you heard about the importance of not overcommitting? For most of my first year, I was careful to heed the warning. The only real venture I added was joining the District Technology Committee. As an undergraduate, my honor's senior project had been focused on technology in the classroom, and I had already decided to pursue master's work in this area someday. The Technology Committee was a clean fit where I felt my expertise could help to inform discussions while I could also learn from the real-world teaching of those around me. My desire to continue learning about internal school processes and curricular directives beyond technology soon led me into a whole different minefield, however. I found that once I opened my door and proved my mettle, they all came running.

By my second year, I was co-department chair, serving on building leadership, secondary leadership, and school improvement teams. I worked on the differentiated instruction committee, on the secondary Common Core roll-out team, and planned the creation of a new honor's option course. I became the organizer for the seventh-grade field trip, taking 200 students to the Holocaust Museum in Dearborn, and I was attending regular practices as a middle school competitive cheer coach. I helped students to organize a school newspaper and somehow began my master's work at the same time. I planned professional learning community agendas, prepared materials to present at meetings, and led professional development sessions on technology tools for the technology committee. I attended conference after conference on literacy topics and Failure is Not an Option, and I dutifully documented every requirement for Danielson's evaluation system. Of course, this was all on top of what normal new teachers are required to do in their first years: meeting with my mentor regularly, attending state-mandated new teacher professional development sessions, and, oh, yeah—actually teaching in my classroom. If you are looking for a recipe for burnout, look no farther. Add in my weekly ten-hour commute and recurring bouts of laryngitis and my burnout (in retrospect) was virtually guaranteed.

The thing is, I absolutely loved what I was doing and voluntarily chose to do all of these things—mostly without pay—because of my personal thirst for knowledge and my desire to contribute and give back. I wanted to understand what the principal was referring to when he mentioned the school improvement plan. What were our goals? How were they measured? What should I be doing to contribute, and what would we do as a building if we fell short? I wanted to attend conferences myself and learn firsthand about district initiatives, and I wanted to test out these new ideas in my classroom with my students. I wanted to share what I learned along the way and to help to dispel myths and build trust. I wanted to encourage my colleagues to see all of the positive potential in these new initiatives and to help them to jump on board.

Unfortunately, tackling so much so quickly easily became both distracting and dispiriting. Spending too much time organizing and planning can take the joy out of any task, and before you know it, the daily adventures of working with crazy middle schoolers becomes another list of to-do items to accomplish in your overstuffed planner.

I know, I did this to myself. And the ironic thing is that I probably wouldn't change any of those decisions even if I had the chance to. These were critical learning experiences that prepared me to move on, built the confidence and working skill set I needed, and made me one heck of a time manager. But there is no doubt that over-committing contributed to my faster rate of burnout, as well as giving me a firsthand ticket to witness the underhanded and disheartening politics that can often rule the educational atmosphere.

The Politics

When most "new teacher" books and education courses discuss the topic of teacher identity, it is from the perspective of how to transform from Bobby to Mr. White. How do you create an environment of mutual respect with your students, establish yourself as an authority, facilitate from the side, communicate with parents and community members, find your voice and persona for leading a classroom, and build rapport on an individual level? These questions of constructing teacher identity are crucial, especially in the first days, weeks, and years of teaching. Many new teachers struggle to find answers, or they waver between conceptions of who they are and who they are trying to be, lacking authenticity to find just the right balance. For some, this can mean failure to set up appropriate boundaries, and for others it can mean building too many walls. However, these aspects of teacher identity were never a challenge for me—this is the part that came easily. Operating as a compassionate leader, speaking with confidence, reaching out as a role model—these traits are what made teaching a natural fit.

Yet, there is another side to establishing one's teacher identity that I found far more complex, one that I was mostly unprepared to encounter (though I'm not sure what proper preparation would have even entailed). I had a clear conception of who I was to my students, to my parents and community members, and to my administration. But, I had no idea who I was to my colleagues. As the national political debate surrounding education became an even hotter topic on the heels of the recession, I found this question even more pressing.

My educational and professional backgrounds are marked with the success of aligning myself with the right people. Often, this meant with authority figures. When I was a student, my teachers always gushed about my abilities, attributes, and attentiveness in the classroom, and this confidence carried over into sports, jobs, and relationships. I was "that child," the one your parents wanted you to spend time with, the girl you wanted to bring home to mom and dad. Predictable, responsible, probably a little boring . . . that was me. I had great respect for positions of power and for a long time obeyed without questioning. Even when my understanding of "authority" became more nuanced with life experience, I still found myself supporting the structures and rules of institutions as the most natural reaction to any given situation. So, in this vein, I respected, relied on, and sought guidance from my school administrators. After all, these were the people who had seen my potential and hired me to teach in their school. I wanted to make them proud and to learn as much from their experiences as possible. I had no inkling of the degrees of separation that existed between educators and administrators within some school systems. I had never even considered that one group might feel intimidated, undermined, or devalued by the other. I had always thought of the relationship from a team mentality, completely overlooking the implicit underpinnings of power and control.

Having just graduated from an outstanding undergraduate education program, I carried many of the viewpoints of my professors and advisors. I supported open classrooms with constructivist ideals, believed research was central to determining best practice, and sought ways to use technology in creative and thoughtful ways. My excitement for education as well as the potential for reforms made me a strong example and ally for my administrators, but not always for the people I was actually working alongside. Had the political and social context of the teaching field been different, perhaps the mistrust and frustration between educators and administrators might have been different. Unfortunately, the financial burdens of the recession, the cuts to programs, and the layoffs of teachers, intensified by local and state legislation to systematically dismantle the status quo that so many long-time educators had worked so tirelessly to establish (for good and for bad), created a climate of negativity and misrepresentation that put these parties at odds (at least in my specific experience). The polarization of communities, like ours, could be seen on the opinion pages of the newspaper, on the street corners where teachers protested, and across capitol buildings where people gathered to have a voice in the sweeping reforms (mainly centered on union rights, issues surrounding teacher tenure, use of standardized testing, and teacher-evaluation systems linked to performance pay).

These doomsday scenarios left me perplexed and overwhelmed, lacking the confidence and experience to truly form opinions on any of the issues. When you have already aligned yourself with many of the principles and ideas being purported by the "opponents," it becomes harder to see yourself as one with your community of peers. I began to see myself instead as an intruder, an outsider, unsure of what I was supporting and afraid for anyone to find out what I might truly think. Was I just being naive? Did my viewpoints just highlight my inexperience? Was I too optimistic? Had others been hardened through too many years behind the desk and lost perspective of the larger workings and research being conducted around them? Who was I to trust? The unions, who had worked to reinforce seniority over ability? My administrators, who supported me in all of my endeavors and attempted to bring in massive changes to structural and curricular content? National leaders in education, who spoke in terminologies and programs that my colleagues degraded? Or my colleagues themselves, representing shades of "my future" with the retrospective experience of other cycles of political changes? Or should I heed the warning of community members writing op-eds to the newspaper arguing how teachers are just overpaid whiners who deserve to be held to higher standards and blamed for all of society's ills? Was this really what people believed? Was this really a sustainable field in which to build my future?

Navigating political circles can be challenging enough, but trying to forge my own identity within this climate during a time of such upheaval and public dissention only intensified the tensions and insecurities of everyday school life. Every month there was a new meeting devoted to handling the crisis of layoffs, administrative changes, or responses to local and national political initiatives. Writing to senators and representatives, circulating petitions, and trying to understand the impact of future and pending legislative action were not elements of teaching I had ever considered. Of course, I was indoctrinated by the opinions and expectations embedded within my view of teaching through my college education. I had no "real world" experiences to base my conclusions on. I was trapped between an idealized view of the profession based on best practice and solid research and the realities of the world in which my teaching colleagues lived and worked.

It was right about that time that it happened, not all at once in the form of a crushing blow, but piece by piece in the slow progression of the daily calendar—I broke my rule. I lost my focus on maintaining internal optimism; I had let my ambition and drive push me into committees and commitments with zeal and enthusiasm. I had opened myself up to collaboration and leadership, and before I knew it, like a slow growing cancer, the negativity crept in and took over. Once I lost perspective, then I realized that was the end. Somewhere in the midst of meetings and planning for professional development and trying to learn and grow and play an important part in transforming the learning process, I lost track of the reason why I was there. Instead of coming home to gush about my students, I became the complainer, whining about the lack of progress, the endless paperwork, and the fact that we had spent a whole year just trying to align standards to specific grade levels. I must be clear though—neither my colleagues nor my district were to blame. I was lucky to work with some of the most inspiring and tireless teachers and leaders who dedicate their time and energy to make a difference in students' lives, no matter what extrinsic circumstances are placed upon them. No, this negativity stemmed from the much larger politics of education.

As tensions grew, I felt incapable of putting my support behind either side. I saw power grabs and gross oversimplifications of current problems and solutions on both sides. I saw opportunity in revolution and also feared corporatization. I saw accountability and evaluation as necessary and useful structures, and I saw the political side effects of how they might be administered. I became plagued by fear of job loss, confused by the intangibilities of merit pay, choked by the debate surrounding unions, and overwhelmed by the number of curricular initiatives I wholeheartedly worked to support against a tide of growing frustration and complacency. My inability to see clear support for either side of the conflicts left me frozen like a deer in headlights.

When I did finally move, it wasn't to either side of the aisle but instead in a new direction all together—away from the debates, away from the stress and chaos, and even away from the joys with which I used to reach my classroom door every morning. When hushed conversations insidiously joked about early retirements and how to make career changes at forty, I didn't panic. I just began to focus my energy on "getting out" and trying to decide exactly what that would mean for me. I stopped worrying about what either "side" was doing and focused instead on what I needed in order to better understand the many discourses and ideas swirling around my head. I needed time, and I needed knowledge. I needed the opportunity to explore these issues, talk with experts, and come to my own decisions—not influenced by factions with the power to control my fate, but from the outside looking in. What I needed was an opportunity to seize, and I was determined to create one.

The Opportunity

In full disclosure, by the time I completed my teaching degree, I already hoped that my career path would lead beyond the classroom door. I no longer saw myself as a lifelong teacher dedicating twenty or more years to a district and working towards retirement. My goals had shifted towards postsecondary education and a desire to teach new teachers, conduct research, and shape future policies. So, to say I left my teaching career is both inaccurate (as I still teach at a different level) and unfair (as it was only ever a step along a much longer path). The distinction lies in the fact that I had never placed a time limit on how long my secondary teaching career would last. As long as I enjoyed my job and found interesting challenges and opportunities to grow, I could see myself there for five, seven, maybe even ten years on the long end. Who knew, maybe I would build a family and a house and wait to advance my career until I sent my own children off to school. But, instead, it ended abruptly, not marked by a bittersweet parting but by a sweet sigh of relief.

Even though my career ambitions had always been directed towards higher education, I was less certain about how to actually "get there" and what to do once I was "there." As someone who dreamed of being a classroom teacher at the age of five when I first began creating assignments for my younger sister to dutifully complete, I had only ever seen the clear path to teacher certification. Where did the path lead after? How do you pick a graduate school, and more importantly a program that will provide real opportunities? Having only formally taught for three years, I was worried that I might not have enough experience to be considered eligible to begin a program for teaching teachers. I floated helplessly in these questions as my final K-12 teaching year came to a close. And that's when the solution found me.

A former professor contacted me about a potential teaching position at my undergraduate alma mater. It was only for one semester and was based on enrollment, but it would give me experience and insight into teaching at the collegiate level. More specifically, I would be teaching future teachers. I would have just finished my master's coursework in educational technology and would be open for a new challenge, especially one as exciting and useful for guiding my future career decisions. I couldn't believe my luck! The downside was trying to balance my already packed schedule. Between my full-time teaching job, coaching varsity cheer, working on a myriad of committees, and trying to plan my own wedding, I soon realized that in order to move forward I would need to take a deep breath and make the choice to let something go.

The decision-making process was gut-wrenching. Who leaves a teaching position in a strong school district at a time like this? At least that is the question everyone around me seemed to be asking, especially for a short-term, part-time opportunity. Furthermore, where would I turn when the semester ended? Would I pursue positions that put my master's work to use, designing technology-based instructional content? Was that really the path I wanted to take? I even briefly considered leaving education as a whole, maybe looking to use my English degree for positions geared towards communications or writing. Though troubling at times, this soul searching was crucial to my final decision. I needed to feel the insecurities and anxieties of carving a path where a clear one might not exist.

Up until this point, the path for educators had been pretty straightforward. After declaring intent as undergrads, we are siphoned into a program, led through student teaching, directed to district websites, and told how/when to apply. We are saved from the crisis-inducing stress of finding a path within a vague degree program such as "Business." Our end goal is in sight from the start. The experience of living outside that streamlined path can be frightening and invigorating, as I could finally see how many other paths and options actually existed beyond the classroom door. I began to see my career as under my own control once again, a feeling of ownership I had lost to the whims of educational circumstances so far beyond my reach in the K-12 sphere.

The dark side of this freedom, however, was a fear that somehow I had failed—failed my students, my profession, and most importantly, myself.

As I reflected on my choice, I decided that my ambitions and independence would have come to a head in that world eventually, no matter the external circumstances, because my own quest for professional fulfillment would have driven me further. I didn't need to blame anyone or any group, or even myself for leaving the field or falling short of my dream, because the truth was, I wasn't leaving the field at all. I was redefining my position within the field, better matching my attributes with opportunities, and developing my dream into a working reality for who I am and what I believe today—not who I thought I was ten years ago.

With patience and family support, I came to embrace this chance to reinvent myself and my place in education. Eventually, I arrived at the conclusion to pursue a doctoral degree in curriculum and instruction, studying the design, research, and methodology that guide the decision making of district and national leaders. How I will eventually apply this degree remains open—maybe as an education professor, maybe as a district director, maybe as an instructional entrepreneur. The specifics are not yet clear, but the objective remains the same. I was born to teach, and in teaching I find my life's worth. What has changed is merely the context for that teaching and my own reappropriation of the term to include all of the diverse ways in which one can "teach" beyond the four walls of a traditional high school. My bitterness has evolved into understanding, my confusion into a quest for more knowledge. I don't choose to see myself as part of the statistics of teachers who left the profession early, because I realize now that I haven't truly left. I've only repositioned myself along the winding path of my professional career—an act of reflection and evaluation, aligning my expectations with my realities.

Attempting to frame my perspective of my first years in teaching has been a task much harder than I ever anticipated, mostly as a result of trying to uncover what my ever-elusive "perspective" might be—not my gut reactions, or my emotionally charged recollections, but a purposeful and honest depiction of what these years taught me about students, teaching, the educational system, and, most importantly, myself.

I anticipate that this will probably not be the last time I undergo a sense of professional crisis spurred by forces and findings beyond my control. While I will inevitably run into the same issues of balancing the daily grind and navigating political waters in any professional position, I feel better equipped to flexibly handle my relationship to both, with the understanding that there are some things that will remain outside of my control. What I can control, however, is how I choose to respond to, reflect upon, and redefine my relationship with the educational field, a lifelong journey I've only just begun.

FOR FURTHER DISCUSSION

1. Lindsay Stoetzel initially thrives as a new teacher. She enjoys the day-to-day challenge of classroom management and building relationships with her students. She avoids complaining about students and, instead, offers each one a clean slate every day. Something happens, however, to make her break her "cardinal rule." Under what circumstances did Lindsay begin to feel what she calls the "cancer of negativity"?

2. Each person has twenty-four hours in a day, and we allocate those hours to construct our identities. How does the way that Lindsay Stoetzel divided up her time tell us about the multiple identities that she was trying to maintain?

3. By the third year of her teaching career, Lindsay was enacting multiple roles each week. She was a classroom teacher, a cheerleading coach, an education technology graduate student, a committee member, and a curriculum advisor. Beyond the challenge of time management, how did these identities pose conflicts?

4. Education reform movements need the on-the-ground expertise of teachers to guide them in the right direction. How can a person manage the multiple identities, roles, and tasks involved in being both a classroom teacher and an advocate for effective classroom practice in an era of reform?

 Sara VanIttersum teaches sixth-grade Language Arts in southwest Michigan. She earned her Bachelors in Education at University of Michigan and an endorsement to teach English from Grand Valley State University. During the school year she stays busy coaching Girls on the Run, Variety Show, and book clubs. Sara enjoys living by Lake Michigan (especially in summer) and tailgating for Michigan sports with her husband.

First Love
Sara VanIttersum
Jackson Middle School

September 6, 2010. My first day. Years of school and two summers of frustrating job searching were over. I could officially call myself a teacher. My supervising teacher had drilled it into me to arrive early, so being at school by 6:30 was habit. Between the butterflies in my stomach and her voice in my ear, I was at school long before there was another car in the lot. The outside doors had not been unlocked, so I had to use my name badge. I know veteran teachers got sick of wearing them, but that name badge was a point of pride my first year. It validated the six years of college, student loans, work, and internships that landed me my first "real" job. I sometimes left my name badge on in the grocery store. I think, subconsciously (and sometimes blatantly), I wanted others to recognize me as a legitimate teacher.

I have never felt more legitimate than that first day. Over one-hundred sixth graders floated in and out of Room 104. I dealt with all the typical first-day fears and logistics; we spent all day opening lockers, going over syllabi, playing get-to-know-you games, and (if you ask the kids, most importantly) getting them through the lunch line. The principal even threw in a fire drill on that first day, and I felt like I had single-handedly managed it all. I walked out through the doors ten hours later, feeling superhuman.

The road to my first day had not been easy. When I started college, teaching was the last place I thought I would be. I applied for an education program after working in museums. I felt like I had finally discovered what I wanted. Student teaching flew by; I got a long-term sub job at the same school for the next semester, and all seemed to be coming up roses . . . until I graduated into the worst teaching market in decades. All my well-intentioned professors did not tell me that when your only core certification is social studies, it is really hard to find a job. I found that out on my own after several interviews with no real prospects.

I moved out of my college town and back into my parents' house. I began taking classes at another university to get an endorsement in English, and I worked at an afterschool program to make a little cash. That next summer I had significantly more interviews and leads, but by mid-July I still didn't have a job.

I feel like job searching is a bit like dating. You scan the vitals to see if there are any deal breakers, reach out with a phone interview, and hope that they invite you to a longer sitting. If you are desperate, you try speed dating or a job fair. You also feel very vulnerable putting yourself out there over and over and never hearing anything back until you find the right one.

After round and round of rejection, something clicked, and I found myself at an interview for my dream job. For the first time I felt like I was speaking the same language as the twelve people on the interview committee. The interview ended with a question from my future mentor that turned into a long conversation about teaching and learning. I left feeling that they actually got to know me as a teacher and also as a person. I walked away with the same feeling you get after that perfect third date, where you stay up all night sharing the best details of your life and sharing ideas. It was one of those chance meetings in life where you know that even if you never saw the person again, that moment in time would still remain perfect.

When I learned that I got the job, it took a second to register. As soon as I hung up the phone, I cried for a good five minutes as the stress and uncertainty left my body in the form of tears. I had a job. In teaching. In my home state. In middle school. In a great district. At that point in the summer, I would have settled for any two of those. Suddenly I was humming the *Mary Tyler Moore Show* theme song as I prepared to start a new life in a new city. I moved into an apartment only a ten-minute drive from school. For the first time, I felt like a real adult.

Everything seemed too good to be true those weeks before school. I was in and out of school almost every day, excitedly setting up my room. I would peek down the hall every time I heard a voice, anxious to meet some of my new colleagues. Apparently no one but the newbies hangs out at school in August. My first task from my principal was to pick out whatever supplies I wanted to order. School supplies were an addiction for me, and there could have been nothing more exciting that that Staples catalogue. I got excited every time I had a new email from one of my team members or when they left presents in my mailbox. I was anxious to get to know them, to gain any clues about what the team norms were like, and to feel a part of the school.

Everything I was worried about seemed to take care of itself. Our district started curriculum mapping that year, and so in the weeks before school we were given time each week at staff meetings to map out the objectives we wanted to meet and write quarterly assessments together. Because common curriculum was a new thing, the district had carved out time each week to meet as a department and discuss where we were headed. So, suddenly, I had scheduled time to plan with my mentor the type of teacher I hoped to be one day.

My perceived triumph that first day of school did not come from any of my own superpowers. My triumph that day came from the benefit of decades of experience working on my side. I had the type of support most new teachers do not have the luxury of enjoying. I had three weeks to set up a classroom (an eternity to many of my friends who got hired the week before school), a mentor to plan lessons with each week, and a team of teachers that met daily.

In a world of budget cuts and shrinking funds, my school was one of the few schools that still followed the middle school model, which is built on teams. Each grade is split into two teams, almost like two smaller schools. Each team had four core teachers and has a common planning period each day to discuss common policies, plan cross-curricular projects, and keep close tabs on our 100 kids.

Each team had their identity, both in name and in legend among students and parents. I was the newest member of the Thinkers team, and the only newcomer to their team in years. The Thinkers lived up to their name, and after years of teaching together, they had become a powerhouse.

As is true of most things in life, I remember only snippets and scenes from the whirlwind of my first year. If I am being honest, most days were pretty nondescript. I woke up at 5:00, was a human being after a shower and coffee, and got to school by 6:30 to prepare for the day before kids started showing up at 7:00. I would stay until I at least had a settled idea of what I was going to do the rest of the week (usually 5:00 or 6:00). I would put on PJ's the second I got home, as if peeling off the school day, and usually would spend a fair amount of the night creating worksheets or sifting through the endless resources until I had a better idea of what I really liked or didn't like. My boyfriend and I called it the "grandma schedule." We were long distance that year, which was probably the best thing for our relationship. I was a grandma during the week and could focus on school, and then on the weekends I could focus on being more than just Miss Kiel.

Most days I felt like it took me ten times longer than other teachers to do everything. I was at school until 5:00 or 6:00 most nights. As I watched everyone else pull out of the lot each day, I wished I had cabinets full of lesson plans as I imagined all the other teachers did. I had a lot of resources, but it just took me longer to sift through resources and work out lesson plans. Most nights I liked the challenge, but I always wished I was farther ahead and did not feel the pressure of empty plan books. I just hoped it wouldn't be like this all the time.

With my colleagues, I felt both behind and ahead. The same people I looked to for everything didn't know where to find our content expectations and new writing standards, or they didn't know what would be on the standardized tests. Not that data were the most important thing, but I thought that these things would be common knowledge. In department and team meetings, I always felt a hesitancy to be the first with suggestions. I knew where I stood on the totem pole.

Most of the time I enjoyed playing to the newbie stereotype. I found everyone in the building was willing to give me any resources that I asked for. I inherited posters, supplies, books, worksheets, and practical organization tips. I made a point of letting my team and teachers know what I was thinking of for a unit, and inevitably they would suggest a similar project or idea or some advice from activities they had tried. I think teachers genuinely like to help each other, as long as they feel the other person is doing an equal share of the work. I would bring in coffee periodically and volunteer to do some of the grunt work that my team didn't want, in an unspoken exchange for advice.

Still, there was an unspoken hierarchy, and it felt awkward when that hierarchy was breached.

Once, we had a staff meeting reviewing the criteria for teacher evaluation. The principal was looking specifically at the expectations of planning and explaining what he meant about showing student growth on objectives, rather than just covering chapters. When someone asked for an example of what he meant by preassessments, he cited a lesson he had observed as an example. He went on to describe *my* entire lesson that he had sat in on a few days before. I was excited to hear such positive reviews and such validation of what I was doing, but shy about being too excited. The faces around the room looked skeptical.

After my formal evaluations, I was very confident in my job. When budget talks began, however, I soon realized that how much they liked me would have nothing to do with whether I would get to keep my job. As is true of all firsts, my feelings about this experience are exaggerated. The first boyfriend is at the same time your most exciting love and your most crushing breakup.

I was pink-slipped. I thought things like this didn't happen in this district, but with the district needing to cut twelve percent of its budget, there is was. My principal sat me down in a desk designed for eleven-year-olds and just began shaking his head at me. He had as much trouble saying the words as I had hearing them.

That afternoon my mentor and I went for our usual meeting, which was our affectionate term for the collection of teachers that stopped by the local bar at 3:10 every Friday. There all my frustration came out. I was devastated to have invested all of my time and energy and not to have that recognized. In my indignation, all of the imperfections of other teachers in the building changed from funny anecdotes (I can't believe they do that) to infuriating (I can't believe they do that and still have a job and I don't). In a crisis like that, all I could hope for was someone to have a drink with me and help revive the optimism, passion, and sometimes naiveté that drove me as a first year teacher.

"You can't leave teaching yet. You have more to give," my mentor said.

I cried most of that night. In a strange way, it paralleled the moment that I got the call offering me the job. Again, all the stress and frustrations were boiling over. The next day I sucked it up and went in to teach as if nothing had changed. I had to keep reminding myself that it would not be fair to the kids to act differently. Then I got to team meeting, where my ever-efficient team was using this last week of school to make copies for September. I was in shock when they already wanted to edit the back-to-school letters, which included taking my name off of everything. I had expected to return the supplies the school had bought, but I was not prepared to peel my name labels off of everything as if I had never been there.

It was hard to remember that losing my job was not personal. I had to remind myself that this efficiency had benefitted me throughout the year. This was not about me; it was about doing what was best for the school. I know no one meant the planning session for September as a slight to me, but it felt personal. Our product is human, and what we offer is human.

All week, I felt alone in the building. I was detaching and preparing for the possibility of leaving. It did not look like I would be called back, so I wanted to say good-bye to my students.

If I am pink-slipped again, I don't think I want my students to know. My reaction was a bit dramatic, I admit, but isn't that how most firsts go?

I think all of the aspects of my first year are exaggerated. Like most firsts, I remember them as heightened versions of reality. Every minute detail about those first days was exciting, whether filling out tax papers or hearing speeches to kick off the year. Now, a bit later in my teaching career, those speeches that are supposed to be inspirational come off somewhat insincere, after I have heard them more than once. Not knowing exactly what to expect from students heightened the drama of teaching a lesson for the first time. I was constantly amazed by students' creativity and compassion.

Like that first real relationship, I assumed that my first job would be "the One" because it was the first time that I was living out my passion. This made that first breakup much more crushing. Even after I got called back, I felt like that excitement of the first year was lost.

I still love my job. I was still at school by 6:00 on the first day this year. In many ways, I feel more confident in myself as a teacher and more certain of my role in the school. Yet, like a happily coupled person, I still think wistfully on those first days.

Many articles say the key to happy relationships is to not assume you know everything about a person; instead, you should ask questions about him or her. Now that I have settled into a second year of teaching, I have become the teacher with files full of worksheets who no longer feels the pressure of creating units from scratch. While this is a comfort, I miss last year's creative challenge and the opportunity of endless possibilities. Sometimes, I have to channel my inner first-year teacher, setting aside a whole folder of what I did last year to think from scratch about how I can best teach an objective. While I have become the Science Olympiad coach this year, I am trying to cut back on some of the time-consuming routine tasks and give my kids more responsibility in the classroom, freeing me to be more of the teacher I want to be. As I get further from graduate school, I sometimes have to set aside the pile of papers to grade and spend some time reading, just to get excited again about some new books to share with the kids.

In reality, all firsts are a little awkward, with unreasonably high expectations and optimism. Yet, I don't know how you can stay in teaching without a little bit of that. One of the best things about teaching is that it offers a new start each year with an entirely new group. Even every hour is like a mini-first. If it doesn't go well, we have a new start with the next hour. I don't know how else to welcome a group of awkward and needy kids into the room than with some (perhaps) unrealistic optimism of how they will learn and grow. Writing this has forced me to take a more honest look at my first year, with all of its flaws and challenges, but I also miss it. On days when the conversation in the teacher's lounge takes a negative turn, I sometimes just have to leave. I look at that picture of me on my name badge that was taken on my first day of teaching. It reminds me of that teacher who couldn't wait to meet her students, that recent graduate who felt ready to take on the world. While it gets easier to actually teach well, those first-year mementos remind me to be the kind of teacher that I so desperately wanted to become.

FOR FURTHER DISCUSSION

1. How would you feel, wearing your school ID in the grocery store?
2. Sara VanIttersum debates whether she would tell her students the next time if she were pink-slipped. What does she think the proper role of a teacher for her students is in that event?
3. Sara compares her first job to her first love. How does this metaphor help to understand the trials and tribulations of developing a healthy identity as a teacher?

Tracy grew up with her ten siblings in Grandville, Michigan, and graduated from Grand Valley State University with a BA in English (Secondary Education). She currently lives with her husband in Garden City, Kansas, where she teaches English to sophomores and juniors. When she has free time, Tracy dabbles with her writing and reads any dystopian fiction she can get her hands on. She also enjoys making elaborate, crazy meals with her husband, and often she can be found asleep on the couch with a book in her hands.

Holding Their Stories
Tracy Meinzer
Silver Springs Middle and High School

It's a strange thing, evolving from this awkward, unsure teacher assistant nervously standing in front of a room full of students into a confident professional, gliding between and among students, guiding and questioning. I wanted to write about that process, about the incredible changes that take place so subtly and swiftly, but I didn't know where to start. I couldn't pinpoint a specific experience or set of experiences that made me the teacher I am now. I mostly remember the feelings: the anxiety, the nerves, the hope, the pride, the love, the frustration. So I decided to write about the moments when my emotions struck me most powerfully, the moments when I cried.

I am a crier. Pain and sorrow strike me like arrows, their sharp tips sinking deeply. I like to think that because I so embrace the sorrows of life, I also feel joy and peace more powerfully than most. I believe that to appreciate the good, I also need to allow myself to experience the bad. If I want to open my heart to life and light, I also need to open it to shadows and death.

I open up, soaking up all that is life, and often I find myself with tears in my eyes. I am a crier. My students will attest to this.

Mostly when I cry, it is when they are not looking. I cry in my car on the way home or in the empty classroom at the end of the day. I cry at night when their stories keep me awake. I cry in the shower when there is nothing else to distract me, and my tears can mingle seamlessly with the water. I cry about students like my first-hour sleeper. A talk-backer and slacker. Negative, negative, negative. He survived the trimester, passed easily enough in spite of driving me crazy. He completed his English requirements and left my class, yet, day after day, when the final bell rang, he still stopped in to say hi. Day after day, he complained about his exhaustion. "Why are you always so tired?" I teasingly asked him often, gently mocking him about all those mornings when he used the desk for a pillow.

One day he answered honestly. "I don't get much sleep at home. I only got like four hours last night."

"Why? You're not staying up all night playing video games or watching TV are you?" I said, thinking of my seventeen-year-old brother, ready to give a little reprimand about priorities.

"No," he shrugged.

"Then why aren't you going to bed earlier? You really need more sleep than that."

And his story unfolded. He talked and talked. Setting aside the papers I was grading, I listened. Nodded. Prompted. Sympathized. He told his story. Mother. Car accident. Brain damage. She looks like the same person, but she is not. Dad. Can't handle all the work, can't handle all the stress, can't handle the wife who is not the woman he married. Him. Cleaning the house, doing the dishes, making dinner. Driving his drunken older sister from party to party so that she does not drive herself, so she does not end up like Mom or worse. Then, at night, when all is done, pulling out the backpack, the waiting homework, searching for answers in the darkness. Every morning, waking up at the break of dawn, heading to school to work out for baseball, seeking a moment of sanity in the sweat. He told his story.

I felt the injustice of his father's demands and longed to give him freedom. I let him talk, ignoring the "fucks" that sprinkled every sentence, looking beyond his hostile anger and feeling the pain. I let him talk, holding back the threatening tears. They did not fall until he walked out. Then I wept, crying out to the silent white walls.

They fought, my third-hour class. Always trouble, that hour: lower tracked, slower paced, struggling students. They fought. Constantly. Girls. Catty, reaching out with claws determined to cut and tear and shred. They discussed literature and life with cold, bitter tones. They were wrapped up in their wars. *The House on Mango Street* could be sung to them by Lady Gaga, and still they would not listen. We were right in the middle of a discussion when the pointed comments and sharp looks become too frequent for me to ignore. They clearly could care less about our discussion. I pulled the emergency break, screeching us to a sudden halt.

"I can't handle it," I said, frustrated with the harsh emotions vibrating in the air. "I feel like there is so much tension in this room!"

Their response was one of eager nods and of voices agreeing with confident "Yeah"s. Their reactions said, "About time you noticed Mrs. Meinzer." I was about to explore the issue when the bell rang. The room was empty of bodies before my thoughts had even fully formed. I spent the night pondering, struggling, looking for a path to pull my students back.

The next day, I gave them each a paper. The paper contained the outline of two empty footprints. I asked them to fill the prints: one with how you think others see you; the other with things about you that people do not see. "You don't have to put your name on these," I said, "Just be honest."

I collected the footprints. Skimming through them, I pulled out words and phrases, reading them for the class to hear. I read, heart hurting, voice struggling to continue. They needed to know. They needed to know the burdens that their classmates bore. They needed to know the things they do not see:

"What people don't know about me is that I'm not a bad kid and I don't smoke pot or do drugs.

"I'm one of those kids that would like to be your friend and if you have a problem with me I have a problem with you kind of kid. I do all my work I have to get done in school." So says my tough kid, muscles always showing, hat backwards, attitude worn on his shoulder. He is far from being the only one with secrets on his heart.

"People don't know I have a family of just me and my mom."

"My grandpa has had cancer three times."

"I'm really soft-hearted but I don't show it."

"I don't know who I am. I screw up and let people down. I get into fights at home with family and am worried about my career."

"I have family issues and am almost always depressed. I got in very big trouble with the law."

"My life is stressful and I am dealing with friend problems. I feel beautiful inside but not out."

"Drugs. Family problems. Self-confidence. Whisky. Smoke. Drink. Hurt myself. Anger issues. Depression. Stress."

"I don't talk a lot, but I'm crazy and can be very loud. I don't want to be the girl who does not talk a lot."

"Who I really am is . . . a different person . . . I wouldn't consider myself as a normal teenager. I don't get along with my dad, parents divorced, get along great with my mom. Brother hates me. Says I'm not his real sister. Life is just . . . confusing . . . hard . . ."

I read the last one, and one of my girls, with her long black hair, with her sharp wit and high walls, stood up, tears in her eyes. She didn't ask, and I wondered if she inherently knew that it was okay with me. She walked out of the room, carrying her tears with her, unable to share them with the class.

That was the moment when the wavering grasp I had on my emotions, slips. I lost it. Completely. There, in front of them all. I sat sobbing, and I can't stop. Boys shifted uncomfortably in their seats, and I spoke through my tears, trying to gain control.

"You just don't understand. Look at your classmates. Look at what they are dealing with. I don't understand how you can treat each other the way you do. I just don't understand it." I blubbered and apologized for my tears. Mercifully, the bell interrupted me before I could do much more damage to the growing impressions they were forming of me.

It would be easier not to look, to just do this thing called teaching. It would be easier not to feel, but if I do not share their pain, will I ever share their joy, their laughter, or their trust?

My students hold stories. I can't ignore these stories that make up my classroom. I can't change them. I can't erase them. I can, however, listen to them. I can give my students the words to tell these stories. And I can help them write new ones, ones that do not end with tears.

FOR FURTHER DISCUSSION

1. Each of us is a teacher in a body—a body that feels emotions and needs to cry sometimes. In this narrative Tracy Meinzer negotiates the tension between her identity as "a crier" and "a teacher." Do you think that these two identities are mutually exclusive?
2. It is Tracy's empathy for her students' suffering that moves her to tears. How can teachers manage to care for dozens of students year after year without becoming emotionally exhausted?
3. How can teachers handle strong feelings such as sadness during the school day in ways that still contribute to students' growth?
4. What ideas about how a teacher "should act" did this narrative evoke in you?

6
STUDENT BEHAVIOR

Introduction
Robert Rozema

If there is a single issue that most concerns early career English teachers, it is classroom management. Most new teachers are understandably worried about keeping their classes under control. What happens, they might wonder, if my students simply will not stop talking at the beginning of the hour? What should we do if students openly defy us? How can we stop student misbehavior without resorting to detention slips and trips to the office? When students in my methods seminar ask me these kinds of questions—as they often do—I answer with a range of strategies drawn from my experience as a high school English teacher and my observations of many master teachers at work.

In these exchanges, I stress how *deescalating* a conflict is usually the best approach. When a student openly challenges us, it is tempting to up the ante, perhaps by yelling, invading the personal space of the student, or threatening consequences. This is human nature and a physiological response to adrenaline, but it is rarely effective. Instead, I tell students, manage the conflict as discreetly as possible, allowing the student to *save face* in front of his classmates. Then, speak privately with the student after class, using nonconfrontational language whenever possible. In these conversations, questions can help: What can I do to keep you focused during this class? How can we work together to make this class more enjoyable for both of us? As always, it is important to *model* appropriate emotional control during class and in private conversations, though even the most equanimous of us sometimes get rattled.

Even as I make these suggestions, I know that effective classroom management has less to do with strategies and more to do with substance. Simply put, experienced teachers possess *gravitas,* a combination of authority and expertise that preempts many of the classroom conflicts that can derail novices. Gravitas is hard to explain, but easy to recognize: veteran teachers express it through their words, body language, and interactions with students; students can see, hear, and feel it in everything veteran teachers do. Students fall in line intuitively, as the teacher assumes they will. There is no need for a complex set of rules enforcing classroom conduct—*That's three strikes this hour! That means everyone stays three minutes after class!* Instead, students recognize that certain behavior is expected, and while not even a veteran can avoid the occasional run-in with a student, most experienced teachers can go for months, if not years, without kicking a student out of class. One of my recent students, Sarah, remembered how her favorite teacher handled the class:

> I only distinctly remember *one* teacher "owning the room" throughout my entire school career. Mrs. Nelson. She's the reason I wanted to become an English teacher—I always knew I wanted to be a teacher, but she instilled the confidence I needed when it came to English. She always believed in me and told me just that, quite frequently. I don't remember anyone ever talking bad about Mrs. Nelson. I observed her last year, and although she's now teaching at the high school level, *all* of her students still love her. She genuinely cares about the progress of her students and is consistently energetic, no matter the day.

Call it owning the room. Call it gravitas. It's what experienced teachers have and do. But this reality—that it takes time and experience to become a master of classroom management—is hardly comforting to the new teacher who has resorted to flipping the lights on and off to quiet her students. To this teacher and others still struggling to control student conduct, the best way forward may be to focus on the actual learners and not on abstract management strategies. In the English language arts, this begins with knowing more about *adolescent literacy*, an umbrella concept that includes adolescent identity and the variety of literacies that adolescents practice—and still need to practice.

We can begin by looking at the term *adolescent*. As with many of the concepts explored in this book, this one has contested definitions. Traditionally, adolescence has been understood as a period of development, during which time a young person transitions from child to adult. While no two adolescents are alike, this view suggests that all are undergoing development, not only physically but also cognitively, socially, and morally. Grounding the traditional view, the cognitive psychologist Piaget theorized that adolescents are entering the formal operational stage. Beginning at about age eleven and continuing until fifteen or sixteen, adolescents acquire the ability to think in abstractions, a key intellectual skill. Thinking abstractly requires symbolic, hypothetical, and metacognitive maneuvering. Piaget's theory would partly suggest why so many young people struggle to master prescriptive grammar: the ability to think about the rules governing language calls for the cognitive development associated with the formal operational stage—a stage that adolescents are still entering. Socially, the traditional view suggests that adolescents are also in transition, growing into a wide range of new responsibilities. Research conducted in the 1970s characterized adolescents as developing mature relations with peers, discovering proper gender roles, gaining independence from their parents, learning career skills, preparing for marriage, and forming a personal ideology (Havighurst, 1972). This last development, acquiring a personal ideology, has been understood in moral terms. Kohlberg (1976) suggested that adolescents are moving into *postconventional morality*, which is the forming of individualized moral principles and the awareness that these principles may sometimes clash with societal expectations.

More recent examinations of adolescence have complicated the developmental model of adolescence, taking issue with the idea that all young people follow a predictable, linear path as they change from children to adults. Taking a sociocultural perspective, scholars such as Lesko (2012) have argued that young people, like all of us, exist in unique social and culture environments, and are shaped by forces that go beyond psychological and biological growth. These include cultural preferences, economic realities, and changing social understandings of gender, marriage, family, and even adolescence itself. Today, some young people in their early twenties may still live with their parents, work a job rather than a career, and have no future plans for marriage or family. Other youth of the same age may experience nothing of this *extended adolescence*. One-third of all adolescents today live in single-parent homes (Dryfoos & Barkin, 2006). Some spend many hours caring for younger siblings and assume responsibilities helpful to the extended family. Some live on the edge of poverty, work a part-time job to help pay the bills, and may consider independence from extended family financially unfeasible. Some assume that they will attend college and get a job; others don't. Defining adolescence as the stage when one moves to college and to career does not fit the data. According to the U.S. census of the population from 1971 to 2001, less than a third of Americans who started school in kindergarten obtained a bachelor's degree: only thirty-three percent of whites, eighteen percent of blacks, and eleven percent of Hispanics (Dryfoos & Barkin, 2006).

We can say, then, that while all adolescence are undergoing development, their growth varies according to social and cultural conditions. The following examples may further illustrate the complex nature of adolescents. The first comes from Yvonne, a teacher assistant from my recent seminar. When Yvonne's cooperating teacher, Susan, became seriously ill, Yvonne gamely took over teaching her classes, taking charge of advanced placement (AP) English and British literature courses for three weeks. On one tough day, however, a student openly challenged her authority. Yvonne wrote on her blog:

> Susan is still out. In all honesty, it's starting to wear me down. I didn't expect to have so much responsibility so soon. I had an experience in my AP English class today where students were asked to address human vanity in the poem "The Convergence of the Twain" by Thomas Hardy. Ashley bluntly stated,

"I don't get this. This is stupid. I don't understand it. I don't want to do it. Maybe if we had a REAL teacher, I could actually get this." It was rather insulting, to say the least.

In my conversation with Yvonne, I encouraged her not to take the remark personally, though comments like this certainly sting. Her student was frustrated with a daunting text, and she may not have intended her remark to be malicious. She was likely incapable of seeing the situation from Yvonne's point of view—the long hours spent prepping lessons, the exhausting work of grading papers, and the stress of managing a full-time teaching load were lost on Ashley. Without excusing Ashley, her comment may reveal the egocentrism of adolescence that coincides with the formal operational stage of development (Elkind, 1967). At the same time, Ashley's frustration may result from external forces: in a school that values academic achievement, Ashley is enrolled in the most rigorous class, perhaps at the urging of her parents. She expects to perform well on the AP exam, exempting her from one college class and reducing the burden of college tuition on her middle-class parents, albeit slightly. She may see Yvonne as an obstacle to achieving these goals.

A second example again points to the ongoing development of the adolescent mind. A teacher I know has taught *Of Mice and Men* to her ninth graders for many years. A few years ago, she begin using an online forum to encourage her students to discuss the knotty moral dilemmas raised by the book—and especially its ending, in which George kills his mentally impaired companion, Lennie, to prevent him from being lynched. One student was incensed by George's action. He wrote:

> In the Ten Commandments, God doesn't say, "Do not murder unless it's for a friend and you do it painlessly." No. God said do not murder. Period! And I know that shooting a man right in the back of the head is murder. I believe in absolute truth. Murder is murder no matter who you are. Now according to my human instincts, I personally think that George did the right thing. However, don't you think that God might be a little wiser than we are?

This response shows a young person transitioning from a conventional sense of right and wrong to a more individualized and flexible moral system. He still adheres to the rigid "objective truth" that "murder is murder," but he qualifies his answer with a telling admission: according to his "human instincts," George did the right thing. It may be his thinking is flawed or contradictory, owing to his incomplete intellectual development. Here, too, we might consider his background: raised in an evangelical Christian home that stressed the infallibility of the Bible, he is shocked by the violent, abrupt conclusion of the book, which he perceives as an assault on his Christian faith. Whatever the exact cause, it is important to avoid characterizing adolescents as somehow deficient. Instead, we should focus on what adolescents do well, and this is where our conversation turns to adolescent *literacy*.

Over the past two decades, the definition of *literacy* has evolved significantly. Once understood solely as the ability to read, write, and communicate, literacy now entails a wide range of practices that are embedded in unique sociocultural contexts. According to this larger view, the literacy practices of adolescents are rich and varied, best understood as an intersecting set of *multiple literacies*—specialized, sometimes overlapping uses of language that are tied to particular discursive situations (Christenbury, Bomer, & Smagorinsky 2011).

Consider Josephine, a young woman who recently immigrated from Sierra Leone. At home, Josephine speaks Krio, the lingua franca of her native country, to communicate with her family members. When Josephine and her family talk about more formal, important matters, however, they often switch to Mende, the tribal language of southern Sierra Leone. Josephine knows English, too, and needs conversational English to communicate with friends at school, who sometimes poke fun at her formal—and British—spoken expressions. Some African-American students have taken the teasing too far, confronting Josephine for sounding "too white." She also reads and writes academic English, though not as successfully as she would like, due to the interruptions in her formal schooling that resulted from a decade of civil war in her home country. Since her arrival in America, Josephine has gained skill in the digital discourses of Facebook and social media. And like most teenagers, she is fond of texting and has mastered the abbreviations, convenience spelling, and truncated syntax of this medium. To top it off, Josephine is also studying French, hoping that the language will be useful in her future career, which she believes will involve public health care somewhere in Africa. Her literacy practices are indeed multiple: they include forms of cultural literacy, social literacy, digital literacy, and academic literacy. Moreover, she recognizes that different communicative contexts call for different modes of discourse, and she switches fluidly between them.

Not all adolescents are like Josephine, but as a rule, they also make use of multiple literacies in their daily lives. As the racial and ethnic diversity of adolescents has increased (U.S. Census Bureau, 2010), and as digital technologies have become ubiquitous in our society, accompanying concepts of adolescent literacy have expanded to accommodate new practices. A second-generation Hispanic student translates letters from school for his parents; a Japanese middle school student explains the manga *Bleach* to her friend; a high school student writes mods for the multiplayer game *World of Warcraft* and shares them with a fellow player via the web; a young women creates a YouTube video that criticizes the clothing company Hollister for its distorted depiction of teenage sexuality. All of these examples show adolescents using multiple literacies to make meaning.

But what does this expanded—and expanding—definition of literacy have to do with student behavior? How can it help with the class from hell, the one that just refuses to listen? There is no magic solution, but when we recognize and respect the existing literacy practices of adolescents, we can craft curriculum and lessons that engage them. And engagement goes a long way. Simply put, engaged students—those who feel emotionally and psychologically connected to what is happening in the classroom—are much less likely to disrupt class with behavioral problems. On the other hand, disengaged students are more likely to be disciplined, suspended, or expelled (Dupper, 2010). Unfortunately, disengagement is widespread among adolescents, affecting adolescents across racial and socioeconomic lines. But disengaged students are not just disrupting classes—they are also quitting school altogether. In one telling report, Bridgeland, DiIulio Jr., and Morison (2006) found that high school dropouts report disengagement with their classes as the single biggest reason for quitting school. Moreover, disengaged low-income students and students of color are significantly more likely to drop out of school (National Research Council Institute of Medicine, 2004).

If adolescent disengagement is the root cause of many discipline problems, English teachers can reduce classroom strife by adapting their curricula and pedagogies to recognize, respect, and respond to the existing literacy practices of their students. In many cases, this means revisiting the texts that form the foundation of the course. While there are legitimate reasons to teach classic literature such as *The Scarlet Letter*, *Julius Caesar*, and *Great Expectations* (Jago, 2004), many adolescents find these works far removed from the realities of their own lives. A cultural literacy model of education often underlies the inclusion of classic texts: without an introduction to the great works of civilization, the argument goes, students will be culturally illiterate, and by consequence unable to contribute to a democratic society. Overlooked in this argument are the literacies that students already practice, ways of using language that go beyond the reading and writing about classic texts.

In *Reading Don't Fix No Chevys: Literacy in the Lives of Young Men*, for example, Smith and Wilhelm (2002) find that adolescent boys use a range of literacy practices outside of school, but in school, their English classes have traditionally undervalued these practices, widening the literacy gender gap between boys and girls. Drawing on Csikzentmihalyi's flow theory, Wilhelm and Smith argue that boys are most engaged when activities give them a sense of control and competence, an appropriately difficult challenge, clear goals and feedback, and an immediate experience (p. 30). Not surprisingly, nearly all of the boys in the study played videogames, an activity that meets all of the criteria of a flow experience (p. 51). In contrast, the way that reading is taught in schools rarely generates a flow experience. Boys often have little control over what they read, are frustrated by overly difficulty texts, and receive no feedback during the reading process.

Does this mean that we should appease boys by replacing *Macbeth* with *Minecraft*? Of course not. But to keep boys engaged, we might structure our lessons to provide an immediate experience rather than to impart content, as Wilhelm and Smith suggest. We might use the vocabulary of gaming to talk about texts, or to get our students to talk about them: we can discuss *Lord of the Flies* as a real-time simulation game, for example, or debate whether *BioShock Infinite*, an award-winning first-person shooter, meets the conventions of dystopian fiction. We can allow our students to read young adult literature such as *For the Win* by Cory Doctorow, a novel that features expert gamers as its main characters. Or, following the example of a teacher I know, we can allow students to use *Minecraft* to create virtual versions of literary locations. We can let students write reviews of their favorite games and post them on the web. We can ask them to create explanatory screencasts that illustrate how to solve game levels or defeat bosses.

None of this is pandering or dumbing down our curricula. It is meeting students where they are, tapping into their existing literacy practices, and, hopefully, keeping them engaged in our classrooms. No single approach can solve all classroom management issues, but when students are engaged, they will be better behaved, less disruptive, and not as likely to push the boundaries of appropriate conduct. As the narratives included in this chapter illustrate, even new teachers can diminish classroom behavioral problems by making connections between their subject matter and the lives of their adolescent students. Before you read these pieces by Jeremy, Adam, and Amanda, however, consider completing the following exercises. In each of the scenarios below, how would you address the apparent behavioral issues?

- **Scenario 1: The Battles at Hand**
  —From an email written by Jessica, a teacher assistant
  I am teaching *Julius Caesar* in tenth grade. I am trying to use a lot of acting (tableaux, pantomimes, dramatic readings) and group activities, but in one class, there is a huge amount of racial tension and always I feel like they are on the verge of a major blowout, so the lessons usually come crashing down. I was wondering if you knew of any community-building activities I could use to get them to see each other in a more positive light. I have used two of the lessons from Linda Christensen's *Reading, Writing, and Rising Up*, and the writing the students did was wonderful, but they were totally unwilling to read their pieces aloud or share in small groups. My cooperating teacher leaves the room and I am truly worried about a fight breaking out in there, and I would have no way of breaking it up.

- **Scenario 2: Things Falling Apart**
  —From a blog post written by Dan, a teacher assistant
  My CT is on leave of absence after having surgery. So it is up to me to teach *Things Fall Apart*, which my students refuse to read. They're loud, boisterous, have side conversations, and do not want to work. Okonkwo himself would say that he has an easier time than I do trying to engage these students. The text is challenging. There are words that are African in origin and the time frame along with the context is not relatable. But that is still just a cop out. The lack of motivation and apathy has been building up for years in this school system. Even my honors hours have a false belief that they are already good enough. Expectations and procedures have never been established for these students. So, they don't respect mine. To many, college is not a legitimate option, and even those who get the good grades, many will not succeed because they will be unprepared for the reality of accountability and expectation. We will have to try our best to engage these students through critical thought and reasoning. We can try and incorporate it to hopefully raise our best to the top.

References

Bridgeland, J.M., DiIulio, J.J., Jr., & Morison, K.B. (2006). *The silent epidemic: Perspectives of high school dropouts.* Washington, DC: Civic Enterprises. Retrieved from http://files. eric.ed.gov/fulltext/ED513444.pdf

Christenbury, L., Bomer, R., & Smagorinsky, P. (Eds.). (2011). *Handbook of adolescent literacy research.* Guilford Press.

Dryfoos, J.G., Barkin, C. (2006). *Adolescence: Growing up in America today.* New York: Oxford University Press.

Dupper, D.R. (2010). *A new model of school discipline: Engaging students and preventing behavior problems.* Oxford, UK: Oxford University Press.

Elkind, D. (1967). Egocentrism in adolescence. *Child Development, 38,* 1025–1034.

Havighurst, R.J. (1972). *Developmental tasks and education.* New York: D. McKay Co.

Jago, C. (2004). *With rigor for all: Teaching the classics to contemporary students.* Portsmouth, NH: Heinemann.

Kohlberg, L. (1976). Moral stages and moralization: The cognitive-developmental approach. In T. Lickona (Ed.), *Moral Development and Behavior: Theory, Research, and Social Issues* (pp. 31–53). New York, NY: Holt, Rinehart and Winston.

Lesko, N. (2012). *Act your age: A cultural construction of adolescence.* New York: Routledge.

National Research Council Institute of Medicine (2004). *Engaging schools: Fostering high school students' motivation to learn.* Washington, DC: National Academies Press. Retrieved from www.nap.edu/openbook

Smith, M.W., & Wilhelm, J.D. (2002). *"Reading don't fix no Chevys": Literacy in the lives of young men.* Portsmouth, NH: Heinemann.

U.S. Census Bureau. (2010). Population: Estimates and projections by age, sex, race/ethnicity. U.S. Department of Commerce. Retrieved from http://census.gov

Adam Kennedy graduated from GrandValley State University with a BA in English (Secondary Education) and now teaches English language arts to sixth graders in Maryland. During his four years, Adam has held the roles of department chair, Professional Learning Community facilitator, and teacher mentor. Adam realized he would be a teacher when, during a nightly reading of *The Giving Tree*, he asked his mother, "Why is the tree talking?" Since then he has been hooked.

The Exceptions
Adam Kennedy
Elk Park Middle School

Every teacher will deal with students who have unique problems, who deal with difficult situations, and who live lives that we cannot relate to or even imagine. This is inevitable. The decisions you make regarding these students will define who you are as a teacher. One student that made me question myself my entire first year was Terrell. He was a talented but unmotivated C student who displayed a sharp wit and a positive demeanor the first half of the year. He would skip down the halls and smile when entering class. He did just enough to get by, but he was a bright spot in class discussion and added a lot to the general atmosphere.

When Christmas hit, he simply stopped doing work. He stopped smiling. I could see the weight of his problems on his shoulders. He was late to class, and his clothes were uncharacteristically dirty. The reason for his turn-around was no secret: his teachers had been informed that his mother had abandoned him at his grandparents and stopped returning his calls. She had taken his brother with her and left him. His father had recently begun a seven-year jail sentence.

Terrell simply shut down. There was nothing anyone could do to change that. I tried every motivational trick in the book. I got him counseling. I called him at home. I signed him up for sports. I tried bribing him with candy. I tried sitting and talking with him. I tried yelling at him. I tried being his friend. Our entire school mobilized to help get this eleven-year-old through his problems. Nothing worked.

Every teacher will inevitably have his or her own Terrell, the kind of student who keeps you up at night asking, "What can I do?" This problem was clearly bigger than school: Terrell's entire life was falling apart. He was in danger of failing my class—actually, all of his classes. I began to panic. I didn't think it would benefit Terrell to be held back. So instead of giving him zeros, I threw out the curriculum. I asked Terrell to read books with me, and that is what we did for the remainder of the school year. Every book had an assignment with it, but he did absolutely none of it, just as he was not doing his assignments in other classes. I would like to say that he read a bunch of books after Christmas, but the truth is he did not. He read a few books, and we talked about the characters and themes fairly often, but some days he would just sit in the back of the classroom and stare at the page.

Terrell got a D in my class, a passing grade, though he had not completed nearly enough work to warrant the grade. Was it fair to pass him when other kids had to work for their grades in the established curriculum? Probably not, but it was certainly not fair for the life of an eleven-year-old to collapse beneath him. How could Terrell care about poetry when both his parents had left him in a matter of months? When his mother stopped returning his calls? I could not honestly see how anyone, much less an eleven-year-old, could function under those conditions. Because of this, there was no educational philosophy that would allow me to hold him to that standard.

Terrell eventually recovered. He pulled up his grades and graduated with a B average. But more than any other student, Terrell came to represent a dividing point between teachers, splitting them into two groups: those who are willing to bend rules for students like Terrell, and those who are not. Knowing what he was going through, was I wrong to change my expectations in order to pass him? Did I sacrifice some of my educational scruples? Or are we naive to think that school is a vacuum where students should do their work no matter what they face in life?

I decided that holding Terrell back would be another deterrent for a student who was already facing a massive uphill climb to success. The idea that all students should come in quietly, do their work, and return home to a supportive household is a myth. Many students have painful home lives that we must address on an individual and specific basis. For these students to succeed, we must be willing to meet them on their own terms. Being a teacher means ensuring that students learn and grow into successful people; teaching each of them as unique individuals is an important part of ensuring that.

Brandon was another student who taught me about flexibility. The first time I met Brandon's mother, she told me about her childhood Ritalin addiction, a scarring experience that made her absolutely opposed to medicating her own children. While I understood her concerns, her son desperately needed help concentrating in order to be successful in class. Throughout the year, Brandon would simply get up and start running around. He was not an angry child; he was a child who simply could not control his impulses. He would have been an awesome kid to coach, or take to the beach, but in a school setting, he made teaching impossible.

I felt horrible about the situation and tried to do whatever I could to help him. I became extremely lenient with his behavior. Everything that I established for my other students would never work for this student who, despite what I perceived as a disability, was clearly capable of doing good work. I changed my expectations for Brandon and gave him room to move around. He sat in my swivel chair. He was allowed to silently pace in the back of the room.

Did all of this work? Somewhat. Brandon would still disrupt the class to such a large extent that there were periods of time when we accomplished nothing.

I began to realize how much the rest of the class was being neglected while I dealt with Brandon. My permissiveness with him was hurting the overall classroom.

I realized that I couldn't sacrifice my integrity or the progress of the class just to deal with one student. Brandon had a myriad of problems he needed to face, but I couldn't allow his problems to interfere with the success of my other students. They deserved to have a teacher who dealt with their needs and gave them attention as well. When Brandon was only distracting himself, he was the only person suffering, but when he started preventing others from doing their work, we had a problem. So when Brandon did things that drew the attention of the class or forced people away from their work, I quietly removed him from my classroom. I resolved that I wouldn't allow one student to interfere with my class to that extent ever again.

As educators we are hard wired to pay special interest to the "bad" kids. They consume our days because we care, but it's equally important to give attention to all of the students in your class. While they may not so obviously demand your attention, they crave it and deserve it just as much as Brandon and Terrell did. Every teacher must decide how far to go in order to help a student.

Jayquan was another student who tested my limits. He had been tested for every learning and emotional disability out there, but he never quite fit the criteria. He was at the buffet table of disabilities. A little bit here, a little bit there, but never enough to qualify him for supplementary aids and services. This is not really out of the ordinary. Many students with disabilities do not fit into neatly defined boxes.

Jayquan had three erasers. Each one was a little man dressed up for a different job. One was named Kevin (a policeman), another Woody (a cowboy), and the final one George (a cook). These were his best and perhaps only friends. Academically, Jayquan had significant trouble in my class. Socially, he was alienated. Whenever there was group work to do, he would refuse to work with anyone but his three eraser friends. With Jayquan, it became about much more than teaching. It became about giving Jayquan a friend because, boy, did he feel lonely. Due to his communication difficulties, he mostly talked about his one true love: Pixar animated movies. He loved everything Pixar, but *Toy Story* reigned supreme. It seemed as if we were always talking about Buzz and Woody. According to him, my body of knowledge was woefully unacceptable, and when it came to the other Pixar greats, such as *Cars*, it was downright nonexistent.

So what did I do? I watched Pixar movies so we could talk about them. We occasionally did work, but we largely hung out during lunch, before school and after school talking about movies. I could happily go the rest of my life without seeing another talking animal, but it worked to get through to Jayquan. Did he learn much from me that he will remember in five years? Probably not. I am not arrogant enough to believe that. But there a good chance he will remember our many conversations about Buzz Lightyear. He will remember the way he felt when he was around me. A former professor of mine once said that "Students won't remember a thing you teach them, but they will remember how they felt in your class." At the time, I don't think I fully understood the utter truth of his comment, but as my career continues, I recognize the humbling reality that my students will remember me as a feeling more than anything. They will remember the welcome they got as they entered the classroom and the kindness they received even on a bad day.

Finding the individuality in each student and showing that you care is really what teaching is all about. And as a bonus, it will certainly help with classroom management. Jayquan loved Pixar. But all of your students are individuals. Many desperately want to be validated by someone they look up to and care about, even if they don't outwardly show it. The fact that you are willing to sit down, put on some headphones, and discuss the merits of a My Chemical Romance song will get them much more interested than anything you do in class. These students will remember your honest interest in their lives long after the definition of simile and metaphor fade away. Doing this requires no additional planning, just a sincere effort and willingness to engage students one on one.

Sometimes, though, just putting on the headphones will not be enough. Sometimes misbehaving students cluster in a single nightmare class. During my first year, one class seemed summoned from hell solely to torment me. One student in this class, Latasha, told me I was ugly every morning. Sometimes quietly, sometimes loudly, but always, like clockwork. Every morning, "Mr. K, you ugly!" Devon smoked marijuana before school and quickly became well known for "book checking" and "locker checking" students throughout the hallways and classrooms. Kevin would only respond to "Kevin Team Jordan" and had a nice collection of what he lovingly referred to as "sniffing markers." Lamar refused to walk around the room; he preferred dancing. He would pin drop to pick up his pencil. He would pirouette to pass out papers. He would do the Dougie to the front of the classroom. Kelly would write random hate notes about me to her friends and strategically forget to take them with her so I would find them. Many students in my class from hell disappeared for long periods of time, suspended by the school for one offense or another. Many had significant untreated learning and emotional disabilities that made it hard for them to function in the classroom.

I didn't roll over and take all of this abuse. I worked my discipline policy and the school's discipline policy to a tee. I sought out help, though I rarely received it. I felt lost with this class, and because I didn't have the support I needed, they quickly learned that punishments, if they came at all, would be sporadic and temporary. I was at a loss. Things weren't working, and I was intensely frustrated because the kids were not responding to my teaching. I felt the intense and disheartening helplessness of not knowing what to do.

So I decided to change everything. I changed my discipline policy to one focused on immediate punishment through written assignments on the first offense, then cleaning my room during lunch on the second offense. My students balked at these changes but really, it was *my* room and *my* right to change things.

After all, if you teach the same way over and over, you will likely get the same results from students. My classroom was broken. This group of students clearly could not function in the learning environment I had created, and it was up to me to change, not them. I had been inflexible. I realized I needed to tailor my teaching to the kids sitting in front of me. The student autonomy, choice, and group learning that I wholeheartedly believed in slowly disappeared. These students clearly were not ready for that, and I had to be ready to adapt.

This didn't solve all my problems. Students still pin dropped and bookchecked, but I was able to sleep at night because I had a plan to deal with their behaviors in the short term. The worst thing about teaching is feeling the hopelessness of having a problem and not knowing the answer. By accepting responsibility for my students' misbehavior, I admitted to myself that something was wrong and began creating a more effective plan. Many of the minor problems that got in the way of everyday learning disappeared when I adjusted my strategy, and the classroom environment improved noticeably.

If there is one thing I learned during my first year, it's that dealing just with content isn't enough. I don't think there is any way we can grasp the influence that we have on our students on a daily basis. To believe that our words can change how an individual embraces the world is to accept a task that goes far beyond content and into accepting our responsibility as shapers of thoughtful, compassionate people. To believe in this at your core is to go into class every day, working to make a difference.

FOR FURTHER DISCUSSION

1. Do you think Adam did the right thing by passing his student Terrell?
2. In the case of Brandon, Adam decides to remove him from the class when he disrupts other students. In your opinion, is this the correct decision?
3. Examine the case of Jayquan. What existing literacies does Adam use to engage this student?
4. Do you agree with Adam's argument that "students will remember you as a feeling more than anything. . . . They will remember you as the welcome they got as they entered your doorway, and as the kindness you showed them even on their bad days?" If so, what are the implications for your practice?

Jeremy Battaglia teaches high school Engli west. He recently completed an MA in S cation and now leads professional developn planning and formative assessment in his sch daughters, and at the time of this writing, his wife, Melissa, is expecting. In his spare time, Jeremy builds forts in the living room, holds extensive tea parties, and reads a new story every night.

Finding Your Focus
Jeremy Battaglia
Bradley High School

Your basic Teaching 101 prep kit consists of many things: various books containing earmarked pages and highlighted passages, a notebook crammed with scribbled advice from mentors, and copies of handouts and tests from well-meaning colleagues. But no matter how prepared you *think* you are, no matter how much time you spend preparing lessons or reading texts, you can lose it all in the moment when a student ruffles your feathers. Students have a knack knowing when to attack, like predators to prey, and when there's blood in the water, the sharks come swimming.

Of course, I don't mean to imply any malice on their part. It just seems, when something goes wrong, everything snowballs. When you have a serious incident, a real behavioral whopper, suddenly two people need to use the bathroom, one person didn't get their paper printed and needs to use your flash drive, another student has an allergic reaction, an email from an upset parent appears in your inbox, and your principal pops in just to see how things are going. Then the bell rings, signaling for class to begin.

I had more than a few of these days my first year teaching, and I remember one disastrous one near the end of second semester. Like an inmate counting the days until release, I was keeping a mental tally: basic days of successful survival. If 3:00 p.m. rolled around without a catastrophe, I had lived to teach another day. On the day I remember, everything had gone smoothly enough, and in fact a student wandered in after the final bell, wanting to check out a book from my classroom library. I furnished the books myself, many near and dear to me. I relished the opportunity to talk with a student about some of my favorites.

"Ah ha! I'm reaching them!" I thought, congratulating myself. This sudden burst of accomplishment was short lived, however. On the heels of the first student, another burst in, accompanied by a team of his peers for support.

"You made me get SRI!"

I turned.

"Pardon?" I stammered. Surely there was some sort of mix up. I had no memory of giving a student an SRI session—or Student Removed Isolation, the discipline method our school used.

"You marked me tardy, and it was my third one this week, and I have SRI because of YOU!"

It dawned on me that he had been a few minutes late that particular morning, first hour. I hastened to explain this. Surely this fourteen-year-old and I could come to a logical understanding.

Strangely enough, however, he continued his protest, "But I wasn't even in school yet!"

The communicative volley continued. I began to realize that he thought being tardy meant you were messing around in the halls and thus delayed to the next class. He truly felt he was innocent because he was late to school, not even in the building. Suffice it to say his grasp of academic terminology was clearly lacking. Had I not been ruffled, I would have responded better. I would have fallen back on the wisdom I had been given. The problem with training and preparation is that it sounds good on paper, when you are rational and calm. However the minute you are surprised by a comment, you have to think on your feet. Inevitably, all of the training blends together, and you are lucky if you can stammer a few intelligent words.

The good news is that it gets better. Just like public speaking, the more you do it, the better you become. It is the same thing in the teaching world. Don't get down on yourself for flubbing in front of the kids. I promise you, it will not be the last time. But somehow, slowly but surely, you will get better.

You will have plenty of times when a student accosts you and says something stinging, leaving your scrambling for a response. Only after the car ride home and a hot shower are you able to think of the perfect comeback. Like a quip that comes all too late, the words I should have said to the tardy student went something like this: "Oh, I am very sorry. I am with another student right now, so you will just have to wait. Not only that, I would be glad to have this discussion with you when your voice is as calm as mine." Another personal favorite: "Oh, I only argue once a day. You'll have to come back at 7:30 a.m. So sorry."

Instead, I was just taken aback. I did not know how to respond. By the time my senses began to return, the angry mob had moved on. I finished discussing books with my original student who was looking for a good read. By then, I had become incensed. In retrospect, I was probably angry at my reaction and not the tardy student. But at the time, I focused on the student. Here, I had a student inquiring about a book, asking questions we teachers are dying to hear, and yet my whole focus was on the rude young man. Why on earth do we spend so much of our energy on the wrong things?

Well, I couldn't let it go. After the student found a book, I began my search. I stormed the halls, calling outside to other students, asking for the whereabouts of the perpetrator. It became a mission.

"How dare he!" I murmured to myself.

He was not going to get away with this, you can be sure. As I was thundering down the hallways, I nearly walked right over a small, young girl from my class. As I passed, I heard a meek call of my name. I whipped around to find a red apple presented to me. The arm that held it belonged to the petite pupil I had nearly trampled. She simply gave the apple to me. With a wave and slight smile, she turned away.

"Have a good day, Mr. B."

I must have stood there for several minutes. I did not know whether to laugh or cry. Believe me, this was not the last time I would experience these conflicting emotions. In my quest for justice, I almost missed what was right in front of me. I was so determined to get this kid told, I almost missed two positive moments with other students—one asking about books, the other showing her gratitude with a simple, honest gesture.

It is easy to focus on the negative, but early career teachers must remember that many, if not most, of our students want to learn. We are in the classroom because we love teaching; we love helping young people find their way in the world. I teach for those who like to discuss literature, and yet I could not wait to get away from an inquisitive student just moments before. I teach for those who appreciate it, for those whose voice I can help to find, like the shy student I nearly ran over. Yet, somehow, I was focusing ninety-eight percent of my energy on the two percent of students who pushed my buttons. I went home feeling battered and bruised instead of fulfilled.

The series of events that day has shaped my approach to classroom management. For starters, I became more contemplative, trying to review discipline scenarios in my mind ahead of time. But no matter how many rules you make, or situations you read about, there is simply no possible way to prepare for everything. There are bound to be curve balls. I give you permission *not* to have all the answers. You do not need to know what to do in every situation.

Another component of my classroom management is delayed consequences. This is a big tenet of the discipline approach known as Love and Logic. It places ownership on the students:

> Boy, Jim, this is a real bummer. I think we are going to have to have a consequence here. I'm not sure what it should be, but that type of behavior is just not acceptable. I know where you are coming from—I've made mistakes too. It is important for us to learn from them. So here's what we will do. You go home, think about what happened, and come up with a suitable consequence. Try not to worry about it, but give it some real thought. I will do the same. Then, tomorrow, come back and see me. We'll talk about what we both came up with and decide on a consequence.

Love and Logic puts the responsibility on the student. It shows empathy, and it lets the action be the focus, not you. It gives you time to think about it, maybe even consult with another teacher to gets some opinions. And it also gives you and the student a chance to cool off. Many times, when our emotions are charged, we can get caught up in the moment. This is especially true of students. The delayed consequence allows for both parties to calm down and think.

My story signifies something we all do. Many times, we do not pick the right battles. In fact, I could have chosen not to even focus on the fight. I had wonderful students right in front of me, showing interest, curiosity, and decency. Yet, I focused on the wrong thing. I focused on the misbehavior. Certainly, I needed to deal with it. But had I delayed the consequences, I could have found an appropriate reaction, put the ownership on the student, and given us both time to calm down. That would have enabled me to focus on what the other two students needed. Since that day, I have resolved to spend more time with the students who are there for the right reasons.

One tried and true way of spending quality time with students is to become involved in extracurricular activities. During my first years teaching, in fact, I think coaching football was the best thing I did to build relationships with students. Our rapport from the practice field naturally carried over to the classroom, as the lines between teacher and coach, student and athlete blurred.

This was not a surprise to me. My own experiences as a football player taught me that coaches usually demand respect in their classrooms. I went to a Catholic high school, so many of my coaches were also teachers. In fact, I would say about half of the time I raised my hand in class, I was addressing a coach of some sport or another. This had a great effect on the student athletes. It was as though we were always in training. Whether we were on the field or in the classroom, there was always a watchful eye. There was a certain expectation associated with student athletes, and we behaved accordingly.

This was the case with coach DeWaard, my football coach, who even today remains a role model. In Coach DeWaard's classroom, there were zero disciplinary issues. Even athletes from other sports afforded coaches the respect they deserved. Above all, we did not want to disappoint. In fact, about the only time I really cared about my academic performance was when my coach would ask about my grades. I never gave much thought to this. It was just the way it was.

I loved athletics. Sports helped shape who I am today. This is largely due to coach DeWaard and the many coaches I had in my life influencing me in the classroom and on the field. Coach DeWaard had an amazing impact on all those he came into contact with. I remember many times, going to his office in the gym, closing the door, and talking. Sometimes, he just wanted to know what was going on; other times he heard about a party and was concerned with the way I was spending my time. There were times that were far more personal—times I went to him because I did not know where else to go. Regardless of the situation or the choices I made, he was there for me. He was invested in me and my future. I look back on that relationship with great fondness.

So, during my first year of teaching, when an opportunity arose to help out with the football team, I was intrigued. At the time, my wife was pregnant with our first child. My household had not yet been turned upside down. I did have some reservations, however. After all, this was my first year teaching, and there was a great deal on my plate at the time. I was nervous, I wanted to do my best, and I wanted to be as prepared as possible by the time the first day of school began. If only I knew then what I know now: you will never be fully prepared. There is always more to do, more posters to hang in your room, more lessons to prepare, and more materials to read. There is always more to do. So, with great hesitation, I took the part-time coaching position.

One of the nice things about coaching football is that you get to start before the school year actually begins. You get to see your future students in a way the classroom does not afford. By the same token, students get to see you outside the classroom—and this is extremely valuable. Many of my students saw me as coach before they saw me as a teacher. Reflecting back on my own life, one of the reasons I looked up to coach DeWaard so much was that he was far more than a teacher; he was involved with a sport I was involved with and loved dearly.

Student athletes have not changed much since I played football. They love sports more than they love the classroom, though participation in sports often leads to academic success. We could argue about why our culture seems to emphasize sports over schoolwork, but in my experience, it is the truth. Thankfully, the relationships I formed with student athletes allowed me to approach them in a manner other teachers could not. As the year progressed, I had no qualms about blurring these lines. I approached them on the football field as easily as in the classroom. The school community placed such a high value on athletics that many times the parents would want to talk to me about the team, not necessarily the classroom.

Without condoning their preference, I took what I could. I saw *any* conversation as a positive—an invitation into the family. As long as the lines of communication were open, I was happy. My words carried more weight with the parents and students simply because I was also a coach. Rather than bemoan the situation, I tried to use it to my advantage. In fact, I would sometimes discuss events from a previous practice or last weekend's game in the classroom. I have had other teachers ask me about the kind of message this sends—whether I was focusing on the wrong things. To me, it definitely sends the message that I care. It shows students I am there for them on the field or in the classroom. Let's face it: many of our young students, particularly males, lack true role models, men like coach DeWaard.

I was not fully aware of the impact my duel role was having until one day, the head football coach, who happened to be my teaching mentor, dropped in to observe my room. We were doing a choral reading in which students would take turns reading aloud. Certain texts just lend themselves to this method—for example, if a text has several characters, a great deal of dialogue, or dramatic scenes. Any teacher who has ever done a choral reading knows that students sometimes lose their place or stop paying attention. But on this particular day, the entire class was engrossed in the story. Not one single student lost his place; not one single student had to be reminded to follow along. It was amazing.

Later in the day, the head football coach caught up to me in the teacher's lounge. He reflected on the lesson and gave his insight. He went on and on, noting how engaged the students were. It wasn't just that everyone followed along; it was that they were engaged in the story. Students were making connections, telling stories from their own life, and even asking deeper questions. In my naiveté, I was not sure how rare this was. We continued our conversation when another teacher said jokingly: "Of course they were following along. No one wanted to be benched!"

The implication was that because it was my room, because I was an assistant football coach, and most importantly, because the head coach was in the room, the student athletes did not want to risk losing playing time due to their behavior in the classroom. We laughed, and certainly there was truth to the observation, but it made me think back to Coach DeWaard. It was not that I feared losing playing time. It was that I cared so much for football. It was the one thing that truly motivated me. Coach DeWaard was a part of that world, and because of that, everything he was associated with took on great worth in my eyes. I did not want to disappoint him. In a way, I felt I owed him the respect. He was always there for me. In turn, I wanted to be there for him. I saw something similar with my student athletes. The bottom line was, when you are so invested in something, like football, or basketball, or volleyball, you give it your heart and soul. In turn, anyone involved in that arena gets afforded that same kind of reverence.

Many of the kids I coached did not have dads at home. Many of the places they went after practice did not fit my idea of *home* at all. This was a rural community. If, and I say *if*, any of our students went on to college, they were the first of their family to go. This was not familiar to me, but their love of athletics was. I saw students invest in athletics, and all of a sudden, they had a support group, a community that was there for them, even when their families were not. They knew, every day at 3:00 p.m., I would be on that field, sometimes yelling, sometimes encouraging, whatever was called for, but always in a supportive role. These students did not have many things to count on, but they could count on sports, the field, competition, the team, and me, their coach.

There is something sacred about the bond built through competition. So much emotion is wrapped up and left out on the field, and those who are a part of it, who go through it together, are connected forever. I witnessed a great transformation: students who guarded their image so carefully in class were, on the field, surrounded by a support group. Within this group, there was safety. Here was a place they could try, fail, and not feel ridicule but instead adulation. Most importantly, this was done, together, as a team. That is precisely what we need to recreate inside the classroom.

It eluded me for a long time, but essentially, we were successful because I cared. I was there to help them, day in and day out, regardless of what they did, and no matter how bad the error. Out of this, a mutual respect grew. Soon, I actually saw a change in behavior from other students who did not even play football. I can only attribute this to the overall change within the room. Football just worked in my favor. If a nonathlete acted up a bit in the class, a student athlete would be right there, glaring at them, as if to say, "Hey, knock it off, that's coach."

I soon saw changes in other aspects of the classroom as well. I remember one particularly frustrating day, the football season long over. We were approaching Christmas break. I did not know this at the time, but these calendar days can be a source of great stress for many students. Although they do not want to admit it, school is their safe place. Much like the security and repetition of the field, students come to school and find a familiar routine. They know that for seven hours a day, they will be safe. But as Christmas break nears, they know they will have to spend two weeks away from this safe place. Often, they will be forced to spend time with family members they may not like or even feel safe around. This can be a source of immense anxiety.

So, at this time of year, I always noticed increased misbehavior—more students disrupting class, disrespecting classmates, or just goofing off. Fortunately, all three of my football captains were in this class. I went to them privately and basically asked for help. I reminded them of why they were elected captains: others looked up to them, they were leaders, on the field and in the classroom. I relied on them on the field, and now I needed them in the classroom. I asked them to use their leadership skills for good. The students looked to them for cues on how to behave. I reminded them of what I saw in them, qualities that made them good captains. Sure enough, as the weeks before Christmas break came to a close, student behavior improved in my room. I noticed little things; for example, when we were doing a group project, Juan, one of my captains, was hard at work, doing exactly what was asked of his group. As a leader, he was getting his group members to pull their own weight, delegating responsibility to all group members, just as he did on the offensive line.

I pointed this out to Kevin, my second captain, the star of the backfield. A very outgoing, popular young man, Kevin was easily distracted in the classroom. He enjoyed attention, and often sought it out, even if it meant breaking the rules. His behavior was more or less mischievous, never malicious. But his word was law among other students. At one point, when one of his group members began messing around while my back was turned, I overheard Kevin address him. He told the misbehaving student to knock it off, and that was enough. Several others took the cue. By the time I moved to the group in question, they were hard at work.

Jack, the last of the captains, was always putting others first. He floated around and helped those students who needed it. These were the exact qualities that made the captains fantastic leaders on the field. They just needed a little push in the right direction to lead in the classroom as well.

Since my first year teaching, my family has grown. I have put coaching on hold for the time being until my children are a little older. However, I still use a great deal of my coaching techniques in the classroom. I use analogies from the athletic realm. If a person tries to steal second base, slides, and comes up a bit short, or stumbles on his way, the players in the dugout do not laugh. They cheer, they encourage, and they reassure. This is exactly what should happen in the classroom. In fact, the classroom is the ideal place for mistakes to be made. This is exactly how we learn. A coach does not stand silent after a free-thrower shooter misses. He makes small suggestions, corrections, and the athlete tries again. As teachers, when we see errors occur, we make suggestions and have the students try again. It is a recursive process.

The vital ingredient in all of this? Students must know the teacher cares; they must know the teacher is invested. Coach DeWaard was many things to me. But above all, I knew he cared for me. This of course spilled over into my development in the classroom, but it all started on the athletic field. It was where I found my focus as a young man, and where I found it again as a new English teacher.

FOR FURTHER DISCUSSION

1. What are you biggest concerns about disruptive students?
2. Which of Jeremy's strategies for handling upset students do you find the most useful?
3. As a student, did you have teachers who were also coaches? If so, what was your experience?
4. How does Jeremy use his position as a coach inside the classroom?

Amanda Brown teaches at a diverse middle school where 80 languages are spoken. She completed her BA in English and Psychology at Grand Valley State University and earned her MA in Educational Technology at Michigan State University. Coming from four generations of educators, she feels that teaching is her passion and true calling in life.

Innocence and Experience
Amanda Brown
Hillcrest Middle School

One thing to know about middle school students: they will always surprise you. They are a strange mix of maturity and immaturity, wisdom and foolishness, adult and child. Two stories from one of my first years in the classroom show this blend in action. The first story begins with a conversation:

"Miss Brown, do you like cheese?"

"No Alfonso, I do not. Please take your seat."

"Okay, Miss Brown, but I bet you'd love some cheesecake! I'll bring you some cheesecake, okay? Yeah, that's what I'll do."

He sits down, confident in the small discourse that just took place. The students had just finished sharing "good news," a few minutes at the beginning of each class period during which students are invited to share a positive personal experience. As another student corrected the daily oral language exercise on the board, Alfonso made one of his daily proclamations about cheese. Alfonso was a typical eighth-grade boy, a sometimes random, emotional adolescent. He loved personalized praise and attention, and he had no recognizable learning or emotional disabilities. By the end of the year, he had grown and matured, and I said farewell to him, believing he had the skills and resources to succeed in high school. *Farewell Alfonso,* I thought. *You were emotional, affectionate, and possessed an eccentric obsession for cheese, but I still loved you.*

Fast forward to the first day of school of the next school year. I am taking roll during first hour:

"Alfredo."

"Present, Miss Brown."

"Wow! You look familiar."

"Yes, I know, Miss Brown. You had my brother, Alfonso, last year. He told me to tell you 'Hi' and ask, 'Do you have any cheese?'"

"Ha! That's funny. Tell him I said hello. Thank you, Alfredo."

Fast forward a little farther to sixth hour on that same day. I am taking roll again:

"Alberto."

"Yeah, that's me."

"Whoa! I don't understand. Didn't I have you earlier today in first hour?"

"No, that was my brother, Alfredo. We're triplets, Miss Brown." He holds up his hands for emphasis and speaks with a slight lisp. "Alfonso, Alfredo, and I are all triplets."

"So . . ."

"Wait! Hold on, Miss Brown," he says with his hands up in a stop gesture. "I already know what you're going to ask. At birth, Alfonso was the runt of us all, and in order to help him survive, they injected him with a growth steroid to help him put on weight and survive. We think it had an overall effect on his mind and body . . . Yeah!" With that, he sits down with confidence that he has answered every question that my gaping mouth could possibly have uttered.

The first brother, Alfonso, had a unique cheese obsession. Alfredo, his brother, was the calm, cool, and collected triplet of the two that remained with me that year. His academic work was average and he behaved well, at least by himself. He was constantly tired and putting his head down in my class, which always warranted immediate chastising. But, overall, he did as well as his brother Alfonso. On the other hand, Alberto, the third brother, was bolder and stole the show every sixth hour as the comedian, the storyteller, and the news reporter of all events in and outside of my classroom. He kept a notebook of jokes and short stories (typically borderline inappropriate) for any spare moment in class that he may take center stage and perform, which, if time allowed, I'd let him.

All three boys had poor penmanship and anger management issues. Alfredo and Alberto were superb athletes, bickered with each other constantly, and had that bond that could only exist between twins. The two together looked identical, while Alfonso simply looked like an older sibling.

Alfredo and Alberto seemed to be in constant trouble, and whether it was academics or athletics, they always found themselves in the midst of middle school drama. Among their escapades they, of course, attempted to switch places. They picked the perfect day to attempt their plan: the last day before Christmas vacation. I admit I could only tell them apart via the sound of their voices, their mannerisms, and their idiosyncrasies and character traits. On this morning, however, they remained silent and low key. Plan "Switch" was executed almost flawlessly; both boys asked to use the restroom at the same time and switched their clothes before reentering their respective classrooms.

Fortunately, Alfredo's class was next door, and many of my students were doing hallway projects, as were the students in the neighboring class. Purely from instinct, I felt something was amiss as I monitored the hallway. When I asked my neighbor teacher about it, he thought everything was fine. I ended up catching them. I lectured them both and sent them home. But to be honest, they nearly got away with it.

The story of the triplets still makes me laugh when I think about it, but not every memory of student misbehavior is amusing. I remember one student who disrupted class in a way that was completely unexpected. It was a Monday morning during first hour. My eighth-grade English students had just finished writing in and sharing their journals, and I was just getting into a guided reading of Daniel Keyes' *Flowers for Algernon* when one of my students, Jessica, approached the front of the room and asked to speak with me privately. I politely asked her if the matter could wait until the end of class. Jessica hesitantly said it could and returned back to her seat. When the end of class approached, among all the hustle and bustle, Jessica reminded me that she needed to speak with me. Jessica said she would feel more comfortable if she could bring a couple of friends, and if all of us could speak in the hallway.

As the girls and I gathered in the hall, I could tell by their agitated looks and embarrassed body language that something was wrong. I asked them if the problem had to do with me. Was my zipper down, or did I have a booger in my nose? A couple of chuckles lessened the tension but did not eliminate it. I continued to pull teeth in order to get them to spit out the information they needed to tell me. Then, finally, one of the girls blurted out that one of their male classmates, Sebastian, was masturbating in class during the reading demonstration. The girls were frantic and disgusted, and they wanted action. I assured them that the situation would be taken care of, and that they could do their part in this delicate matter by keeping the incident to themselves.

As I thought about the incident after class, I decided it would be best to allow the counselor to handle the situation. After all, I reasoned, this sort of thing is part of his job description: to help, guide, and counsel the troubled adolescents in the building. Furthermore, I doubted that Sebastian would feel even remotely comfortable talking to the youngest female teacher in the building regarding his covert activity. Talk about awkward. I also worried about ending up in the news if my concerns were taken the wrong way. I personally wanted to start my career before ending it.

After I emailed the school counselor with a description of the incident, there was little more that I could do, so I took no further action. It was not until a few days later that I even worked up enough nerve to ask the counselor what action he had taken. The counselor informed me that he had spoken with each of the girls individually, and that he had also talked with Sebastian. I was surprised that was the only action taken. What about notifying his parents? Could his parents be part of the problem? What if the situation happens again?

I could answer none of these questions. Unfortunately, ten days after the first incident, the problem arose again (no pun intended). As other students in the class engaged in a discussion about their homework, Sebastian sat quietly at his desk, doing a miserable job at concealing his behavior. Again, it was one of the girls who witnessed his not-so-secret motions. She quietly raised her hand and, after receiving my attention, pointed toward Sebastian who sat in front of her and whispered, "He's doing it again."

I was flabbergasted. I did not want to draw any additional attention to him by asking him to move seats. However, I had to act quickly because as time progressed more students began to notice what was going on. Finally, I decided to employ the old teacher's trick of proximity. As I continued to ask questions and listen to students respond, I stood next to Sebastian's desk. And, of course, when I stood next to Sebastian he would stop. But as soon as I would move from his desk he would continue. Realizing this, I decided to sit on the top of the empty desk beside him and conduct the remaining few minutes of class from there. He stopped completely and class continued.

All was well until the end of class when the girls who had once again witnessed the behavior Sebastian was performing approached me. This time, one of the girls was infuriated and claimed that I was just idly sitting back allowing it to happen and that such actions were making them uncomfortable. Now, the last thing I needed were the parents of other students voicing their child's outrage (as well as their own) before the situation could be addressed. I knew that what the students said was true. Sebastian was masturbating in class, and while I thought it was taken care of before, it obviously was not.

I decided that if Sebastian repeated his behavior, I would inconspicuously slip him a pass to report the counselor's office. I also notified the counselor that any unexpected visit from Sebastian would be the result of his conduct in class. Fortunately, the situation never happened again. The guidance counselor arranged for Sebastian and the school's social worker to meet. The social worker held individual meetings with Sebastian and additional meetings with both Sebastian and his parents as well. Thanks to the professional expertise of the school guidance counselor and social worker, Sebastian stopped masturbating during class.

FOR FURTHER DISCUSSION

1. What do you think Amanda learned from her encounter with the triplets?
2. Do you think Sebastian should have been disciplined more severely for his conduct?
3. As she considers confronting Sebastian, Amanda writes that she "worried about ending up in the news if my concerns were taken the wrong way." In your state or school, what procedures and laws govern how a teacher can talk to a student about sexual conduct?

Tracy grew up with her ten siblings in Grandville, Michigan, and graduated from Grand Valley State University with a BA in English (Secondary Education). She currently lives with her husband in Garden City, Kansas, where she teaches English to sophomores and juniors. When she has free time, Tracy dabbles with her writing and reads any dystopian fiction she can get her hands on. She also enjoys making elaborate, crazy meals with her husband, and often she can be found asleep on the couch with a book in her hands.

The Heart of Teaching
Tracy Meinzer
Silver Springs Middle and High School

Love, love, love, love, love. It is at the heart of teaching. That is what they tell us, that is what I believe. But there comes a point when my patience, or rather lack of it, interferes with love—a point when I'm not sure I have any love left to give.

There are always some students whom I can't help but love, can't help but take in and shelter. The outcasts, the nerds. The broken ones who are crying out for help. The homosexual girl who feels like a stranger in her own home. The boy who loves reading, writing, and music, but deals with an abusive step-father and drug-addicted mother. Or him, over there, with the dark hair hanging down, the one who tries to hide in his own skin; he wrote of cutting himself late at night. And him, the blonde one. Yes, the skinny one. I worry. He skips lunch almost every day, says he just forgot it or isn't hungry, refuses anything I offer. My instincts, however, tell me that there is no food to be found. I take them in. I am here for them, and together, we make the world a more bearable place.

Then there are those who do not care, who easily slip below the radar. Silently, they sit through the hour, patiently hovering in a place between sleeping and waking. They don't cause a fuss. They don't shout out or share or stomp angrily from the room. For all appearances, they simply have given up. A wall of indifference protects them and isolates them. It is too easy to let them be. At times, it is their mindless cooperation that keeps me from losing my sanity entirely. On the surface, they look just fine, but they are only surviving the day.

My students' names are written across my walls, and I love them all dearly; I want to help them all. Some are just harder to reach than others. Their anger bubbles beneath the surface, ready to erupt and burn any who dare to get close. They swear. They flip me the bird. They stomp out of the room, determined to go to the library, even though you told them no. They talk and talk and talk and talk. They never stop talking. They sigh and groan. They poke their classmates, snatch their phones off desktops. They challenge every single move you make, and make you feel as though you are fighting a war. If you let your guard down for even a moment, it will all be over.

My eighth-hour class enters the room with their usual end-of-the-day energy. The bell work is displayed on the board, but their eyes don't even bother to look at it. These Trade Academy students have no interest in learning how to punctuate dialogue; most of them have no interest in school at all. They don't need a high school diploma to get a job at the Tyson plant or work at a feedlot. Two of my repeater students carry their high confidence and low grades into the classroom and immediately set about their ritual teasing of the three girls in the class. Meanwhile, the others listen to music and show each other the hottest new YouTube hits.

One student sits in the back row, slouched comfortably, ignoring them all. His chair is pushed back all the way against the wall, and he leans it on two legs so he can rest his head. On his lap, his hands busily play games on his phone, but when I speak, I know he is listening. Quick as a whip, every statement I make is received by him and returned with a cocky comment. Every assignment that he turns in pushes the boundaries that have been set. Just once, for just one class period, I would like eighty minutes to pass without a single smart-ass comment leaving his mouth. Shoot, I'd even settle for five minutes of peace.

"Miss M," he says, "why do we have to read books?" Inside, I heave a sigh. I can't remember how many times in the last few weeks I have discussed the importance of reading. On the outside, I force my lips into a smile.

"Because it's good for you, Manuel."

"Seriously. Reading is so pointless." *Breathe. Just breathe, Tracy.*

"Really, pointless huh? So you would never have to read for your job?"

Soon we are going back and forth, tossing our reasoning like punches in a boxing match. Quickly, I have forgotten about today's lesson. The rest of the class has slipped into the edge of my awareness. Although they are out of focus, I know they are listening with curiosity, waiting to see who will win.

I throw every reason I have at him. As I speak, confidence and arrogance lace my words; I am sure he will see how right I am. It's so obvious; I cannot possibly lose. Reading is closely connected to higher test scores. Reading is important for every single job out there. Even if you think you know of a job that doesn't require reading, it's important if you want to be a good citizen. If you want to know what is going on in your country, if you want to make informed decisions about life, you need to be able to read.

But he's sure he doesn't need to improve his reading skills. Doing this reading stuff for class is pointless. The bell rings with him sitting back in his chair, arms crossed, stating coolly, "There's nothing you can say that will convince me reading is important." And I leave school frustrated and angry, my heated temper boiling just below the surface. My hands long to reach out and shake him until some sense sinks into his brain.

Thank goodness I have two days to cool off before seeing him again because I realize I had forgotten to mention one key argument. I forgot to talk to him about how amazing it is to read a book, forgot to mention that reading saved my soul. I took the time to argue, but I didn't take the time to describe the feeling of being transported into another world by the words on a page. I forgot that reading isn't really something you can be convinced to do; at the end of the day, it needs to be experienced. Manuel is right. There is nothing I could *say* to convince him, but I know there are things I can do.

The next day I go to the school library and scour the shelves. Manuel blatantly refuses to check out books there because he "will not support that place." So I go. I search dirt bikes and motorcycles in the catalog, write down titles and numbers, and start pulling books off the shelves. After searching for a while, my hands pull out a blue book from the biography section. It's a little thicker, a little more color-ful than the others. It is the story of an extreme dirt biker, complete with colored pictures, and I know that this is the right book. My fingers close around it, and I carry it up to the desk. Suddenly I can't wait to see Manuel tomorrow.

During reading time, he sits, not reading, as usual. I walk over with a smile, and set the book on his desk. "Try this," I say. He looks up at me and then looks down at the book. He picks it up, flips through the pages, shrugs, and settles back in his chair. Only this time, the book is in his hands. This time, he settles back to read.

Manuel still will gladly tell everyone and anyone how stupid reading is, but he finished that book, read it cover to cover.

We try to reason with our kids. We try to make them understand, attempt to force them to see the light. They are used to this. They are used to parents trying to shove broccoli down their throats. They are used to being hounded with the things they are supposed to do. When they are two percent away from passing, we try to pound into their heads how important the final is, but they decide not to turn it in anyway. We review the instructions over and over, but no one follows them. We justify the in-class activities, explaining why these skills are important, yet the activities go uncompleted. We offer them pizza or ice cream for reading outside of class, yet the books sit sadly on the shelves, their pages untouched.

At the end of the day, they don't want our arguments or rationale. They are emotional creatures. They want to be loved and persuaded, want to be shown the way instead of just told about it. They don't want to know broccoli is good for them. Instead, they want airplanes flying toward their mouths. They want the green vegetable ground up and hidden in a cheesy casserole. They need to watch others down it greedily before they will believe. And eventually, when they are ready, they need to take a bite because they *want* to, not because it is being forced through their lips, causing them to gag and choke on something that is supposed to be so good for them.

If you chose to fight, you will win some, but you will lose more. The important thing is to do your best not to make it a battle. I know. I know. That is so much easier said than done, especially when all they want is a good, bloody fight. I'll be honest with you; very few of my stories end as nicely as this one does. There is no one, easy, perfect solution for dealing with students, and my "solutions" are often experiences in failure more than anything else. Frequently things end with a student storming out of the classroom or end with my voice saying things I later regret. They often end with pain and anger and mistake after mistake after mistake. I rarely do the right thing, but I'm trying, and I'm learning as I go. My experience with Manuel offered me a valuable reminder, an important lesson. Every experience does, if I'm willing to see it.

FOR FURTHER DISCUSSION

1. What strategies did Tracy use to engage Manuel?
2. Tracy writes, "At the end of the day, they don't want our arguments or rationale. They are emotional creatures. They want to be loved and persuaded, want to be shown the way instead of just told about it." Do you agree or disagree with her depiction of adolescents?

CONTRIBUTORS

Jeremy Battaglia

Jeremy Battaglia teaches high school English in the Midwest. He recently completed an MA in Secondary Education and now leads professional development for lesson planning and formative assessment in his school. He has two daughters, and at the time of this writing, his wife, Melissa, is expecting. In his spare time, Jeremy builds forts in the living room, holds extensive tea parties, and reads a new story every night.

Amanda Brown

Amanda Brown teaches at a diverse middle school where 80 languages are spoken. She completed her BA in English and Psychology at Grand Valley State University and earned her MA in Educational Technology at Michigan State University. Coming from four generations of educators, she feels that teaching is her passion and true calling in life.

Lindsay Ellis

Lindsay Ellis is Associate Professor of English, Grand Valley State University, USA. She directs the Lake Michigan Writing Project.

Bree Gannon

Bree Gannon graduated with a BA in English (Language and Literature) from Grand Valley State University. She works at a community college as a professional writing tutor while she makes plans to attend graduate school in the coming year. When she does not have her nose in a book, she enjoys being outdoors, running, hiking, and camping with her husband and three children.

Sierra Holmes

Sierra Holmes lives and teaches in her hometown in West Michigan. She has a BA in English (Secondary Education) from Grand Valley State University. She is currently earning her MA in English and enjoys participating in the Lake Michigan Writing Project summer institutes. When she is not at school, Sierra spends her free time with her family, friends, and very spoiled pets. She can often be found scouring the shelves of local bookstores for new additions to her classroom library.

David Jagusch

David Jagusch teaches high school English at an alternative high school in Detroit, Michigan. He earned his BA from Grand Valley State University and his MA from the University of Michigan. When he's not teaching and coaching his school's boys' varsity basketball team, David spends his free time writing poetry and playing guitar.

Adam Kennedy

Adam Kennedy graduated from Grand Valley State University with a BA in English (Secondary Education) and now teaches English language arts to sixth graders in Maryland. During his four years, Adam has held the roles of department chair, Professional Learning Community facilitator, and teacher mentor. Adam realized he would be a teacher when, during a nightly reading of *The Giving Tree*, he asked his mother, "Why is the tree talking?" Since then he has been hooked.

Kristyn Konal

Kristyn Konal graduated with honors from Grand Valley State University with a BA in English (Secondary Education). Since then, she has worked with several school districts around her hometown in Michigan as a substitute teacher, summer school instructor, and interventionist for at-risk youth. When she isn't teaching or exploring graduate opportunities, Kristyn enjoys experimenting with new recipes in the kitchen, traveling with friends, and spending time outdoors with her two rescue dogs, Abbey and Cooper.

Tracy Meinzer

Tracy grew up with her ten siblings in Grandville, Michigan, and graduated from Grand Valley State University with a BA in English (Secondary Education). She currently lives with her husband in Garden City, Kansas, where she teaches English to sophomores and juniors. When she has free time, Tracy dabbles with her writing and reads any dystopian fiction she can get her hands on. She also enjoys making elaborate, crazy meals with her husband, and often she can be found asleep on the couch with a book in her hands.

Robert Rozema

Robert Rozema is Associate Professor of English (Secondary Education), Grand Valley State University, USA. Before coming to Grand Valley, he taught high school English for eight years.

Lindsay Stoetzel

Lindsay Stoetzel is a graduate of Grand Valley State University (BA) and Michigan State University (MA). A former middle school and high school English teacher, she is now a graduate student at the University of Wisconsin–Madison, studying curriculum and instruction, where she works with pre-service education students and teaches literacy courses.

Blaine Sullivan

After a 20 year career in the corporate world, Blaine earned his BA and teaching credentials at Grand Valley State University. He most recently taught at a school for underprivileged youth in western Michigan. When not teaching, Blaine enjoys reading, cooking, traveling, writing, and following his beloved St. Louis Cardinals. He and his son Connor live north of Grand Rapids.

Tami Teshima

Tami Teshima graduated with a BA in English (Secondary Education) from Grand Valley State University. Since then, she has taught high school English and middle school language arts. Her teaching experiences have taken her to various places, from Northern Michigan to Cape Town, South Africa, to the gulf side of Florida. She now resides in San Jose, California, where she spends her leisure time hiking along oceanfront trails, eating good *pho*, reading great books, and obsessing over crafts on Pinterest that she will likely never attempt.

Sara VanIttersum

Sara VanIttersum teaches sixth-grade Language Arts in southwest Michigan. She earned her Bachelors in Education at University of Michigan and an endorsement to teach English from Grand Valley State University. During the school year she stays busy coaching Girls on the Run, Variety Show, and book clubs. Sara enjoys living by Lake Michigan (especially in summer) and tailgating for Michigan sports with her husband.

INDEX